MASTERING

CATERING SCIENCE

MACMILLAN MASTER SERIES

Banking
Basic English Law
Basic Management
Biology
British Politics
Business Communication
Business Microcomputing
Catering Science
Chemistry
COBOL Programming
Commerce
Computer Programming
Computers
Data Processing
Economic and Social History
Economics
Electrical Engineering
Electronics
English Grammar
English Language
English Literature
Financial Accounting
French
French 2
German

Hairdressing
Italian
Japanese
Keyboarding
Marketing
Mathematics
Modern British History
Modern European History
Modern World History
Nutrition
Office Practice
Pascal Programming
Physics
Practical Writing
Principles of Accounts
Social Welfare
Sociology
Spanish
Spanish 2
Statistics
Statistics with your Microcomputer
Study Skills
Typewriting Skills
Word Processing

MASTERING
CATERING
SCIENCE

S. R. DUDLEY

MACMILLAN
EDUCATION

First published 1988

Published by
MACMILLAN EDUCATION LTD
Houndmills, Basingstoke, Hampshire RG21 2XS
and London
Companies and representatives
throughout the world

Typeset by TecSet Ltd, Wallington, Surrey

Printed in Hong Kong

British Library Cataloguing in Publication Data
Dudley, S. R.
Mastering catering science.—(Macmillan
master series)
1. Food   2. Caterers and catering
I. Title
641.1′024642   TX353
ISBN 0–333–42133–7
ISBN 0–333–42134–5 Pbk
ISBN 0–333–42135–3 Pbk export

To my parents, Jean and Stan

CONTENTS

I   NUTRIENTS IN FOOD

CONTENTS

CONTENTS

CONTENTS

LIST OF TABLES

LIST OF TABLES

LIST OF FIGURES

LIST OF FIGURES

LIST OF PLATES

ACKNOWLEDGEMENTS

I should like to express my sincere thanks to the many friends and colleagues who have given help and offered encouragement during the preparation of this manuscript. In particular I should like to thank Konrad Holleis, Pat Main, Mike Bairds, Harry Cracknell and John Howie for their time and helpful suggestions: Richard Gilbert, Director of the Public Health Laboratory Service, 61 Colindale Avenue, London, M. Humphrey of the Medical Statistics Unit, Office of Population Censuses and Surveys, K. Lewis, Food Additives Branch, Ministry of Agriculture, Fisheries and Food, for the provision of statistics and factual information; Peter Bateman, Director of Rentokil, for his kind help with the photographs and technical details in Chapter 11 concerning pests; Kathyrn Asscher, Public Relations and Advertising Manager, Zanussi CLV Systems, for the photographs of kitchen equipment; R. B. Jackson for his excellent cartoons; the Collens and Farishes for the use of their homes, and Peter Oates, Macmillan editor, for his patience and advice.

However, this book would not have been possible without the generous help of Chris, my wife, who typed the manuscript, was two parents at once, and still had the kindness and strength to offer encouragement.

The author and publishers would like to thank the following for permission to include copyright material: Thorsons Publishing Group for data from Maurice Hanssen, *E for Additives*, in Table 13.1 and Figure 13.1; William Heinemann for data from G. V. Robins, *Food Science in Catering*, in the summarised Table 7.6; Churchill Livingstone Medical Publishers for Figure 4.1, taken from J. S. Garrow, *Treat Obesity Seriously*; The Royal Institute of Public Health and Hygiene for notes on the care of a refrigerator; the Controller of Her Majesty's Stationery Office for Crown copyright nutritional data from the *Composition of Foods* and the *Manual of Nutrition* in Tables 5.3, 5.4, 5.5 and 5.6 and Appendix 2b; the Office of Population Censuses and Surveys, London, the Public Health Laboratory, London, and the Communicable Disease Surveillance Centre, London, for Crown copyright material; the Department of

Health and Social Security for material in Table 4.1 and Appendix 2a.

In addition, the author and publishers wish to acknowledge with thanks the following photographic sources: Rentokil Ltd for the photographs of pests in Chapter 11; Biophoto Associates; Alan Thomas; C. J. Webb; WHO. The publishers have made every effort to trace the copyright-holders, but if they have inadvertently overlooked any they will be pleased to make the necessary arrangements at the first opportunity.

S. R. DUDLEY

INTRODUCTION

This book covers all the important areas of Catering Science that are
included in the syllabuses of the City and Guilds Craft Catering
courses and Business and Technician Education Council (BTEC)
Hotel, Catering and Institutional Management Operations. The aim
has been to deal with the science in a basic, simple-to-understand and
practical way that would be particularly appreciated by Craft-level
students. However, it is my belief that the more detailed BTEC-level
courses also benefit greatly if the science is presented in a
straightforward, practical and applicable manner, which leads to a
better understanding by the student.

The book should also be useful to students of Home Economics
and Domestic Science, to members of the Catering Industry (chefs,
waiters, barmen, kitchen assistants) and to anyone who works in a
kitchen who is interested in nutrition and health, food, cooking, or
hygiene. The content of the book is up to date in its coverage of
current trends in catering and the information has been presented in
accordance with the most recent syllabus changes in City and Guilds
and BTEC courses.

The book contains exercises at the end of each chapter to test the
student's knowledge of the material he/she has just completed, the
answers to which are to be found in the preceding text. It also
contains multiple-choice questions at the end of the book, which,
although not meant to simulate the questions set in external examin-
ations, do serve as a 'quick' testing mechanism for each chapter.
Answers to these are given. The book also uses in-text tasks to enable
the student to continue a theme discussed in the text, to relate theory
to catering practice, and to test points made in a particular section.
Some of the tasks are of a practical nature and some practical
experiments have been suggested, although I do not consider it to be
within the scope of a basic text of this sort to include an extensive
scientific programme of experiments. A comprehensive glossary
gives the student a concise and simple definition of most of the terms
used.

The study of Catering Science should not be a separate subject, but
should be integrated with the catering theory and practical work. In
the same way this text should be used in conjunction with good
catering theory and catering practical book(s).

S.R.D.

PART I

NUTRIENTS IN FOOD

FOOD

AND

DIGESTION

The word food refers to the chemical substances taken into the body at the mouth to keep the body in a healthy, active condition.

1.1 WHY DOES THE BODY NEED FOOD?

The body needs food for the growth, repair and replacement of its tissues and to provide energy for these and other processes.

Food therefore needs to provide.

1 Raw materials

The cells and tissues of the body are made up of a wide variety of chemicals which are assembled to form the complex structures shown in Figure 1.1. These chemicals must be present in the food we eat, in order that the body can function correctly.

2 Energy

Energy is required to assemble the raw materials as indicated and for body processes such as muscle contractions, nerve activity, digestion and cell respiration.

3 Regulating substances

Chemical reactions within the body must take place at a controlled rate. Vitamins and minerals are examples of substances which are involved in this regulation and control, and must therefore be present in food.

> **Task 1.1** List of some of the activities that you undertook yesterday that involved the use of energy. Which activities used up most energy?

Figure 1.1 *Drawing of a generalised animal cell*

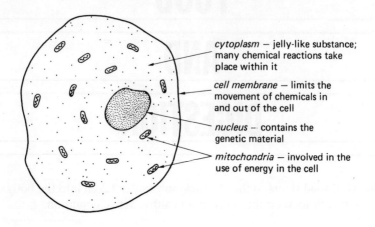

1.2 THE COMPONENTS OF FOOD

Most foods contain a variety of chemicals or nutrients which can be divided into groups depending on their structure and/or main use in the body.

These groups are:

1. Carbohydrates
2. Lipids (including fats and oils)
3. Proteins
4. Vitamins
5. Mineral elements
6. Water

Each of these groups will be dealt with in the following chapters. However, it is possible to show their main functions in diagrammatic form, as in Figure 1.2.

> **Task 1.2** Make a list of the foods, including snacks, that you ate yesterday, and use the tables in Appendix 2 to indicate the main nutrient(s) in each.

Other chemicals, which are not nutrients, nor rich in energy, may be present in the food we eat. These include additives to food (for the purpose of colouring, flavouring or preserving food), dietary fibre (carbohydrates which are not digested by the body – see Chapter 4,

Figure 1.2 *Main functions of the food components*

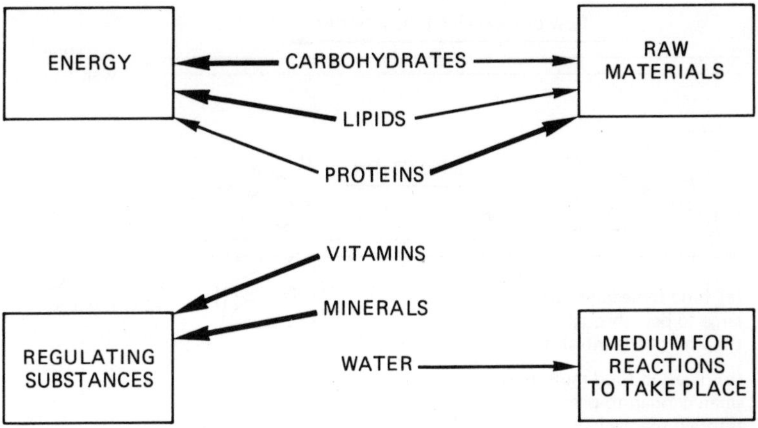

section 4.9), and contaminants that find their way into the food accidentally (such as pesticides or trace elements).

Task 1.3 Select a particular group of foods, such as breakfast cereals or convenience snacks and make a list of the additives and dietary fibre contents, shown on the packet.

1.3 THE DIGESTION AND ABSORPTION OF FOOD

In order that the body can use the chemicals in food, they must be in a form that can be absorbed into the blood system and transported around the body.

When food is eaten most of the chemicals are too large to be absorbed *through* the lining of the intestine into the blood system. The function of the digestive system is to reduce the size of the food molecules to enable them to pass through the intestinal lining into the blood vessels that are present. They are then transported in the blood to the liver (see Figure 1.3).

The breakdown of food takes place in two ways:

1 Physical breakdown
In the human mouth there are, if all are present, 32 teeth which are able to tear, chop, grind and crush food into smaller fragments, enabling it to be swallowed more easily. The teeth are set in the upper and lower jaws which are brought together by strong muscular action (see Figure 1.4).

6

Figure 1.3 *Breakdown of food molecules*

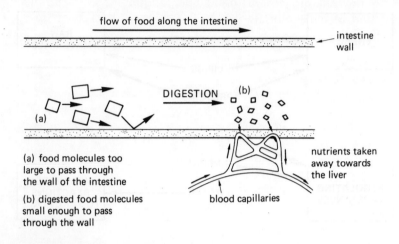

flow of food along the intestine

intestine wall

DIGESTION

(a)

(b)

nutrients taken away towards the liver

blood capillaries

(a) food molecules too large to pass through the wall of the intestine

(b) digested food molecules small enough to pass through the wall

Task 1.4 By using a pair of mirrors or your fingers, count the number of teeth in your mouth. Can you tell by their shape which teeth do what?

Figure 1.4a *Diagram to show the jaws and teeth of a human*

Figure 1.4b *Diagram to show the incisor tooth in section*

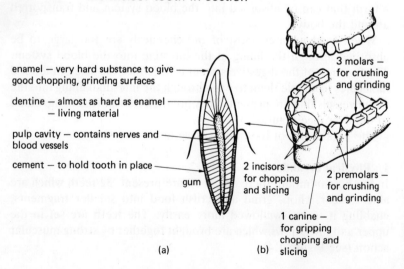

enamel — very hard substance to give good chopping, grinding surfaces

dentine — almost as hard as enamel — living material

pulp cavity — contains nerves and blood vessels

cement — to hold tooth in place

gum

3 molars — for crushing and grinding

2 premolars — for crushing and grinding

1 canine — for gripping chopping and slicing

2 incisors — for chopping and slicing

(a)

(b)

> **Task 1.5** Imagine you are about to eat a stick of celery. Work out how the movements of the lips, tongue and jaws and the action of the teeth change, as the celery is broken off and chewed.

2 Chemical breakdown

This is achieved by *enzymes* produced by the digestive system. As food passes down the alimentary tract it is acted upon by a variety of enzymes, each one of which breaks down specific components of the food. Protein molecules, for example, may be broken down into smaller units in the stomach and further broken down, by different enzymes, in the small intestine (see Figure 1.5).

Figure 1.5 *Diagrammatic representation of enzyme action*

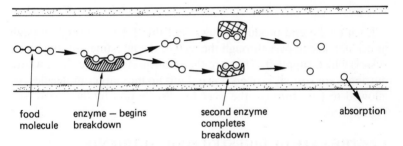

food molecule | enzyme — begins breakdown | second enzyme completes breakdown | absorption

Enzymes are proteins produced by the body that alter the rates of chemical reactions (usually accelerating them). They are affected by temperature and pH (see glossary) and are very specific in their action. In digestion the main chemical process is *hydrolysis* which involves a chemical reaction with water (H_2O) and enables large molecules such as carbohydrates and proteins to be broken down into much smaller ones such as glucose and amino acids, respectively. The smaller molecules can then be absorbed through the wall of the intestine

The human digestive system

The digestive system includes the alimentary tract and associated glands and organs as shown in Figure 1.7. The alimentary tract is tubular and possesses muscles for pushing the food along in waves, a process called *peristalsis* (Figure 1.6).

As the food is pushed along it is mixed with the various secretions of the digestive system. The useful materials from digestion are absorbed, while undigested material continues into the large intestine, is stored temporarily in the rectum, and is passed out through the anus (see Figure 1.7).

8

Figure 1.6 *Movement of food along the alimentary tract*

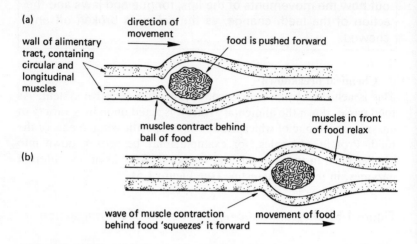

(a)

wall of alimentary tract, containing circular and longitudinal muscles

direction of movement

food is pushed forward

muscles contract behind ball of food

muscles in front of food relax

(b)

wave of muscle contraction behind food 'squeezes' it forward

movement of food

Each of the end products shown in Table 1.1 has a small enough molecular size to pass through the wall of the intestine into the blood vessels which supply it. They are then transported to the liver, where nutrients are stored, broken down, built up into larger molecules, or allowed to pass through the liver for distribution by the blood (see Figure 1.8).

1.4 THE FATE OF DIGESTED FOOD NUTRIENTS

Figure 1.8 outlines the possible fates of some of the nutrients after they have been absorbed from the small intestine.

With the exception of some of the fatty acids which are absorbed through the lacteals into the lymphatic system, all other nutrients travel via the hepatic portal vein to the liver.

The nutrients, once absorbed from the alimentary tract are dealt with in different ways:

(a) Glucose
Glucose and other monosaccharides (see Chapter 2, section 2.2) may be stored as glucose, may travel through into the general circulation or may be converted to glycogen or fat in the liver. The balance of glucose to glycogen is controlled by several hormones (one of which is insulin, produced by the pancreas) to ensure the level of *blood sugar* is correct. It should be approximately 0.1% of the blood. For example, after a meal containing a large amount of carbohydrate, the

Table 1.1 Summary of the main stages of digestion

Region of alimentary canal	Carbohydrates	Fat	Proteins	Enzymes
Mouth	starch → ①→ starch, maltose	fat → fat	protein → protein	① salivary amylase
Stomach	starch, maltose	fat	protein → ②→ protein, polypeptides	② pepsin, rennin
Duodenum	starch, maltose → ③→ starch, maltose, glucose	fat → ④→ fat, fatty acids & glycerol	protein → ⑤→ polypeptides, amino acids → ⑦→	Pancreatic juice: ③ amylase ④ lipase ⑤ trypsin ⑥ maltase ⑦ peptidases
Ileum	starch, maltose, glucose → ⑧→ maltose, glucose, glucose; ⑥, ⑨→ glucose	⑩→ fatty acids & glycerol; fatty acids & glycerol	polypeptides, amino acids → ⑪→ amino acids, amino acids	Intestinal juice: ⑧ amylase ⑨ maltase ⑩ lipase ⑪ peptidases

Figure 1.7 *Diagrammatic representation of the human digestive system*

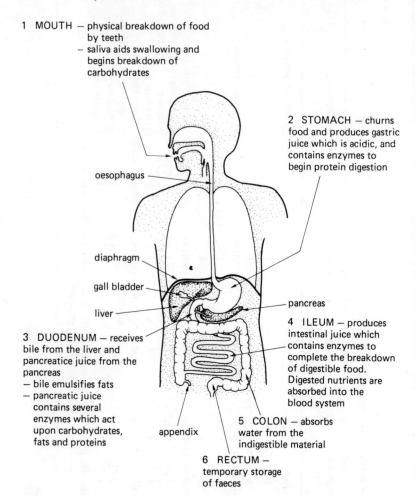

1 MOUTH – physical breakdown of food by teeth
– saliva aids swallowing and begins breakdown of carbohydrates

oesophagus

2 STOMACH – churns food and produces gastric juice which is acidic, and contains enzymes to begin protein digestion

diaphragm

gall bladder

liver

pancreas

3 DUODENUM – receives bile from the liver and pancreatice juice from the pancreas
– bile emulsifies fats
– pancreatic juice contains several enzymes which act upon carbohydrates, fats and proteins

4 ILEUM – produces intestinal juice which contains enzymes to complete the breakdown of digestible food. Digested nutrients are absorbed into the blood system

appendix

5 COLON – absorbs water from the indigestible material

6 RECTUM – temporary storage of faeces

glucose absorbed will be converted to glycogen in the liver to prevent the blood sugar level rising excessively. There is then a controlled production of glucose from glycogen in the liver, which enters the blood to balance the fall in blood sugar that occurs as glucose is used up by the tissues of the body (see Figure 1.9).

(b) Fatty acids and glycerol
Glycerol and the shorter-chain fatty acids are absorbed into the blood and travel directly to the liver. Here they may undergo several

Figure 1.8 Absorption of and fate of nutrients

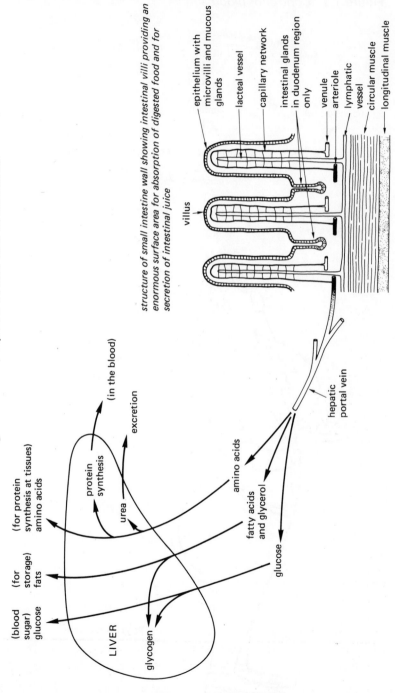

structure of small intestine wall showing intestinal villi providing an enormous surface area for absorption of digested food and for secretion of intestinal juice

Figure 1.9 *Control of blood sugar*

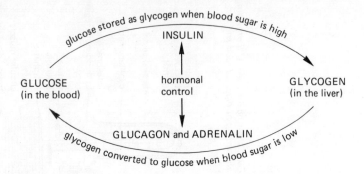

'*Excess glucose may be changed into fat to be stored . . . in the lower layers . . .*'

changes to produce energy, or to be converted into other chemicals, or to be stored as glycogen. The useful chemicals produced are released into the bloodstream, as is glucose when it is produced from glycogen. Excess glucose may be changed into fat to be stored in the body, for example, in the lower layers of the skin.

The longer-chain fatty acids are first absorbed into the lymphatic system and then enter the bloodstream which takes them eventually to the liver. Here they are dealt with in the same way as the shorter-chain fatty acids.

(c) Amino acids

Amino acids arrive at the liver where they are stored as amino acids, or are converted into proteins. Amino acids and proteins are then released into the blood as necessary, being transported to the various tissues of the body. Here they are converted into tissue proteins or other compounds such as hormones. Amino acids that are surplus to requirements are broken down in the liver to produce useful compounds for the body's metabolism (see glossary) but poisonous compounds are also formed which are then converted into urea. Urea is excreted (that is, eliminated from the body) by the kidneys.

EXERCISES

1. Why does the body need food?
2. What is food made up of?
3. List four structures that would be found in a human cell and describe their function.
4. Why does the food we eat need to be broken down?
5. List the final breakdown products for each of the following:
   (a) carbohydrates,
   (b) fats,
   (c) proteins.
6. How does food move along the alimentary tract?
7. Imagine you have eaten a sandwich made with wholemeal bread, butter and cheddar cheese. Refer to the food tables in Appendix 2, and note the main nutrients in each item, and then describe how the sandwich would be digested and absorbed in your body.
8. Through which organ of the body do most of the digested nutrients travel after being absorbed?
9. What role do *enzymes* play in the digestion of food?
10. State two conditions necessary for the correct functioning of enzymes.

CHAPTER 2

CARBOHYDRATES, LIPIDS

AND PROTEINS

It is useful to consider these groups of food chemicals together since they are the major components of our food (excluding water). They are all organic compounds, that is, they contain the element carbon. Carbohydrates and lipids both contain carbon (C), hydrogen (H), and oxygen (O); proteins contain these three elements plus one or more from nitrogen (N), sulphur (S) and phosphorous (P).

CARBOHYDRATES

2.1 FOOD SOURCES OF CARBOHYDRATES

Foods which contain significant amounts of carbohydrates include sugar, rice, cereal products (such as bread, pasta and breakfast cereals), vegetables (such as potato), fruit and milk (see Figure 2.1).

> **Task 2.1** Make a list of the foods you have eaten in the last two days that contain significant quantities of carbohydrates. Use Appendix 2 if necessary.

Table 2.1 shows the carbohydrate content of some foods.

2.2 THE STRUCTURE OF CARBOHYDRATES

Carbohydrates can be divided into two main categories:

(a) Simple sugars – containing one or two sugar units (*mono*saccharides and *di*saccharides).
(b) Compound sugars – consisting of long chains of sugar units (*poly*saccharides).

Figure 2.1   *Carbohydrate foods*

Table 2.1   *Carbohydrate content per 100g of various foods*

Food	Amount of carbohydrate (g)
White sugar	100.0
Rice	87.0
Cornflakes	85.0
Spaghetti	84.0
White bread	50.0
Potatoes	21.0
Banana	19.0
Milk	4.7

A single sugar unit or *monosaccharide* such as *glucose* consists of the three elements C, H and O arranged in a ring structure with side branches (see Figure 2.2).

The energy is released when the ring structure is broken and the molecule is reduced to smaller units.

Task 2.2   Using the information in Chapter 1, give examples of how the body uses this energy.

Disaccharides consist of two monosaccharides (that is glucose, fructose or galactose) joined together chemically. *Maltose*, for example, contains two glucose molecules (see Figure 2.3).

Figure 2.2 *Glucose (a monosaccharide)*

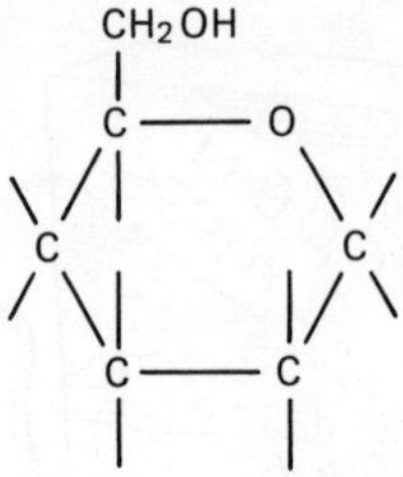

CH2OH
C
O
C
C
C
C

Figure 2.3 *Maltose (a disaccharide)*

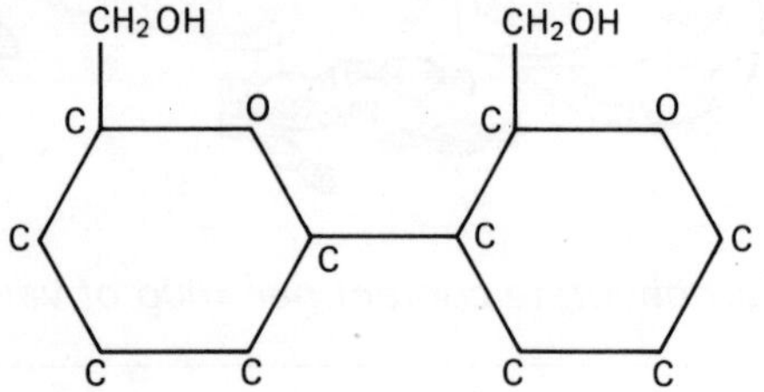

CH2OH
CH2OH
C
O
C
O
C
C
C
C
C
C
C
C
C
C

Other disaccharides are *sucrose* (table sugar) and *lactose* (milk sugar).

Polysaccharides are made up of many sugar units linked together in a chain which may be straight or branched. Starch, for example, is a mixture of two polysaccharides: amylose (long straight chains of glucose units) and amylopectin (highly-branched chains of glucose units) (see Figure 2.4).

Figure 2.4 *Starch: amylose and amylopectin*

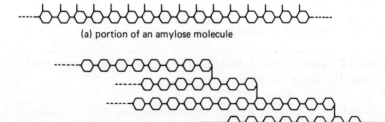

(a) portion of an amylose molecule
(b) portion of an amylopectin molecule

2.3   THE FUNCTION OF CARBOHYDRATE IN THE BODY

The main function of carbohydrate is to provide *energy*. Energy is obtained from carbohydrate foods by first breaking down the foods into units that can be absorbed (see Chapter 1) and then by chemically breaking down the carbohydrate molecules, which releases energy. Oxygen is required in the latter process which is called *oxidation*.

The amount of energy provided by carbohydrate is 16 kilojoules (3.8 kilocalories) per gram, or 16kJ/g (3.8 kcal). If more carbohydrate is consumed than is being used up in energy by the body, then the excess is converted to fat, by the liver, and *stored* in the adipose tissue of the body, most of which is found in the lower layer of the skin.

Task 2.3   State one advantage and one disadvantage of storing excess energy, in the form of fat, in the body.

One function of carbohydrate in the body is to provide enough energy for the individual (in combination with the lipids present) and thus prevent proteins being used for energy. This is referred to as 'protein sparing'.

Certain carbohydrates such as cellulose cannot be broken down in the digestive system and have the important function of giving 'bulk' to the material passing through. These indigestible components of food are referred to as 'dietary fibre' (see Chapter 4, section 4.9).

2.4   DIETARY REQUIREMENT OF CARBOHYDRATE

Since carbohydrates are only one source of energy for the body, there is no accurate guideline for carbohydrate consumption. However, the average male adult requires daily between 10 500 kJ (2500 kcal) and 14 000 kJ (3333 kcal) of energy. Recent evidence suggests that it is best to obtain a large proportion of this energy in the form of carbohydrate rather than fat (see Chapter 4).

2.5   THE EFFECT OF PREPARATION AND COOKING ON CARBOHYDRATES

To describe the main effects of cooking on carbohydrates it is useful to divide them into sugars and starches, since their properties are quite different.

(a) Sugars

The most common sugar used in catering is sucrose. Like all the other sugars, sucrose is sweet to taste, is a white crystalline solid, and dissolves in water. Some of the functions of sugar are given in Table 2.2.

Table 2.2 *Some of the functions of sugar in catering*

Function	Examples
As a sweetener	Drinks, cakes, pastries
To provide colour	Browning in cakes, pastries, caramels
As the main ingredient	Sugar is the main component of crystalline confectionery, e.g., boiled sweets, toffee, fondant
As an important structural ingredient	The structure of foods containing eggs, starch, gelatin and pectin is affected by the amount of sugar present, e.g., egg-white foams are stabilised with the help of sugar
As a substrate	Sugar is the material used by yeast for fermentation, e.g., in bread dough

The cooking of sugar can be looked at in two ways:

(i) *Dry heat* If sugar is heated in little or no liquid, caramelisation occurs. In this process the sugar molecules, on heating, begin to break down, and the smaller molecules produced join together in a complex set of reactions to form a chain or polymer. The polymers are brown and give the characteristic aroma and texture to caramel.

> **Task 2.4** Make a list of some of the cooking processes in which caramelisation takes place, using catering theory textbooks if necessary.

(ii) *Moist heat* If a solution of sugar in water is heated a variety of products can be made, depending on the proportion of water to sugar and on the temperature to which the solution is heated. Boiled sweets, fondant, toffee and other confectionery are produced in this way.

> **Task 2.5** Referring to catering theory textbooks, extend the above list of products made from sugar in water and note the different temperatures required in their manufacture.

(b) Starch

Starch is a white powdery solid which, unlike the sugars, is not soluble in cold water and is not sweet. It is found in plants as a storage compound and appears in granules. The granules differ from plant to plant.

Starch has many important functions in cooking such as the thickening of sauces, soups, gravies and some puddings, all of which rely on its ability to *gelatinise* or form a *gel* (two different processes). As with the sugars, starch reacts differently to dry and moist heat.

(i) *Dry heat*   The main examples of starch being cooked under dry conditions are in baking. In bread-making, for example, the outer layer of dough, which contains starch, undergoes a series of reactions, resulting in the characteristic brown colour, aroma and taste. It should be pointed out, however, that although polymerisation reactions (the joining together of many small molecules to form a larger one) occur, the process is quite different from caramelisation as described in sugars.

Task 2.6   Make a list of *products* in which the above reactions take place.

(ii) *Moist heat*   If starch granules are heated in liquid, they absorb moisture, swell and eventually break open, this is an example of a *sol*. Some of the molecules are released into the liquid and with the broken granules cause the mixture to become more viscous, that is, it becomes thicker and less easy to pour. This process is called *gelatinisation*. In some cases, if the proportion of starch molecules to liquid is high enough, a *gel* may form after cooking. In a starch gel the molecules form a meshwork trapping the liquid which leads to a much more rigid structure. Starch gels can be seen in custard, which contains cornflour, semolina pudding thickened by semolina, and blancmange where arrowroot has been used. Many sauces and stews are thickened with gelatinised starch and may form gels when cool (see Figure 2.5).

LIPIDS (FATS AND OILS)

Lipids include several types of related chemicals. This section concentrates on one group of lipids in particular, the *triglycerides*, that is, fats and oils. Fats are solid at room temperature, around 20°C, whereas oils are liquid. Other examples of lipids of relevance to

Figure 2.5 *Diagrammatic representation of gel formation*

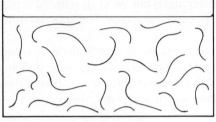

(a) sol — starch molecules in water

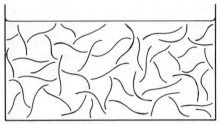

(b) gel — starch molecules form a meshwork
which 'holds' the water

nutrition and catering are cholesterol, an important body lipid, and lecithin, an emulsifying agent.

2.6 FOOD SOURCES OF FATS AND OILS

Foods that contain a large proportion of fat are cooking oils, lard, margarine, butter and other dairy products, meats and nuts (see Figure 2.6).

Table 2.3 shows the approximate fat content of some foods.

> **Task 2.7** From the above section write down the foods which are common in your diet. If you wanted to reduce the amount of fat in your diet for health reasons, which foods would it be easiest for you to eat less of or cut out?

2.7 THE STRUCTURE OF FATS AND OILS

Fats and oils are made up of molecules which contain *four* parts: three fatty acids and glycerol. The molecule can be shown diagrammatically as in Figure 2.7.

Figure 2.6   *Foods containing fat*

Table 2.3   *Fat content per 100g of various foods*

Food	Amount of fat (g)
Cooking oil	100.0
Butter	82.0
Margarine	81.0
Double cream	48.0
Bacon (raw)	41.0
Cheese (Cheddar type)	34.0
Herring (raw)	19.0
Beef (raw)	14.0
Chicken (raw)	4.3
Milk (fresh)	3.8

The glycerol part of the molecule is the same, irrespective of the fat or oil, but the fatty acids vary. Some fats contain three identical fatty acids but, more often, mixtures of fatty acids are present. Fatty acids can be saturated or unsaturated.

(a)   Saturated fatty acids

Fatty acids consist of a long chain of carbon (C) atoms with hydrogen (H) atoms branching from it and an acid group (COOH) at the end. If

Figure 2.7 *Triglyceride structure*

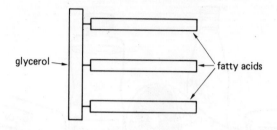

glycerol — fatty acids

the carbon atoms are linked with single bonds, the fatty acid is *saturated* (see Figure 2.8).

Animal fats have a large proportion of saturated fatty acids and it is thought that these have the effect of increasing the deposition of lipids within the blood vessels, leading to circulatory problems and possibly heart disease (see Chapter 4). Recent nutritional reports advise a decrease in the amount of fat eaten, particularly the saturated fats.

Figure 2.8 *A saturated fatty acid*

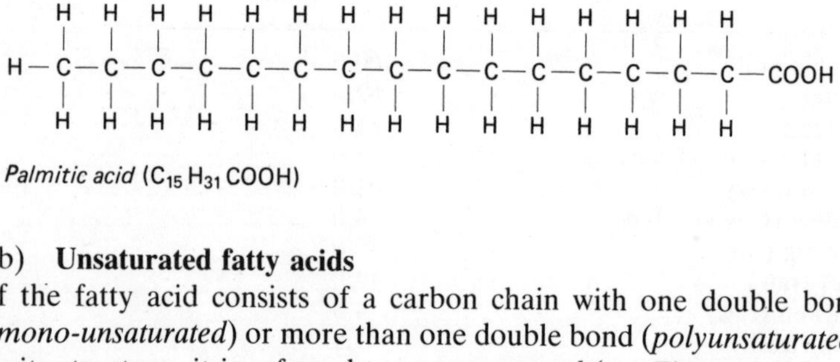

$$H-\overset{\overset{H}{|}}{\underset{\underset{H}{|}}{C}}-\overset{\overset{H}{|}}{\underset{\underset{H}{|}}{C}}-\overset{\overset{H}{|}}{\underset{\underset{H}{|}}{C}}-\overset{\overset{H}{|}}{\underset{\underset{H}{|}}{C}}-\overset{\overset{H}{|}}{\underset{\underset{H}{|}}{C}}-\overset{\overset{H}{|}}{\underset{\underset{H}{|}}{C}}-\overset{\overset{H}{|}}{\underset{\underset{H}{|}}{C}}-\overset{\overset{H}{|}}{\underset{\underset{H}{|}}{C}}-\overset{\overset{H}{|}}{\underset{\underset{H}{|}}{C}}-\overset{\overset{H}{|}}{\underset{\underset{H}{|}}{C}}-\overset{\overset{H}{|}}{\underset{\underset{H}{|}}{C}}-\overset{\overset{H}{|}}{\underset{\underset{H}{|}}{C}}-\overset{\overset{H}{|}}{\underset{\underset{H}{|}}{C}}-\overset{\overset{H}{|}}{\underset{\underset{H}{|}}{C}}-\overset{\overset{H}{|}}{\underset{\underset{H}{|}}{C}}-COOH$$

Palmitic acid ($C_{15}H_{31}COOH$)

(b) **Unsaturated fatty acids**

If the fatty acid consists of a carbon chain with one double bond (*mono-unsaturated*) or more than one double bond (*polyunsaturated*) in its structure, it is referred to as *unsaturated* (see Figure 2.9).

Figure 2.9 *An unsaturated fatty acid*

$$H-\overset{\overset{H}{|}}{\underset{\underset{H}{|}}{C}}-\overset{\overset{H}{|}}{\underset{\underset{H}{|}}{C}}-\overset{\overset{H}{|}}{\underset{\underset{H}{|}}{C}}-\overset{\overset{H}{|}}{\underset{\underset{H}{|}}{C}}-\overset{\overset{H}{|}}{\underset{\underset{H}{|}}{C}}-\overset{\overset{H}{|}}{\underset{\underset{H}{|}}{C}}-\overset{\overset{H}{|}}{\underset{\underset{H}{|}}{C}}-\overset{\overset{H}{|}}{\underset{\underset{H}{|}}{C}}-\overset{\overset{H}{|}}{C}=\overset{\overset{H}{|}}{\underset{\underset{H}{|}}{C}}-\overset{\overset{H}{|}}{\underset{\underset{H}{|}}{C}}-\overset{\overset{H}{|}}{C}=\overset{}{C}-\overset{\overset{H}{|}}{\underset{\underset{H}{|}}{C}}-\overset{\overset{H}{|}}{\underset{\underset{H}{|}}{C}}-\overset{\overset{H}{|}}{\underset{\underset{H}{|}}{C}}-\overset{\overset{H}{|}}{\underset{\underset{H}{|}}{C}}-COOH$$

'double bonds' = unsaturated

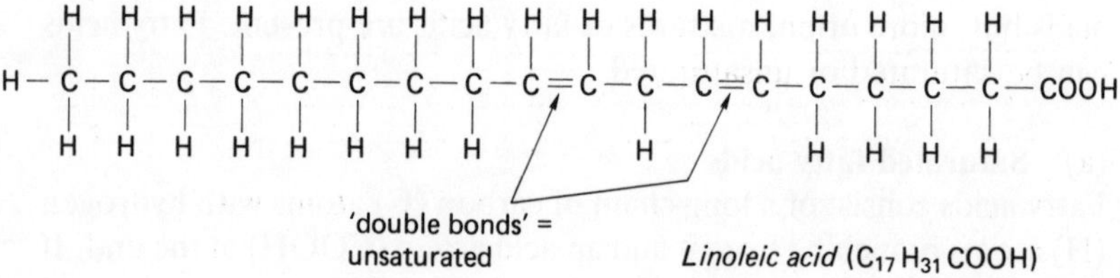

Linoleic acid ($C_{17}H_{31}COOH$)

'A Saturated Fat... An Unsaturated Fat'

Plant oils have a large proportion of unsaturated fatty acids which it is thought do not have the same effect on the blood vessels as saturated fatty acids. Use of plant oils instead of animal fats is therefore considered to be beneficial to health.

The type of fatty acids present in a triglyceride determines the melting point. The degree of saturation is one factor, with unsaturated fats having lower melting points than saturated ones (that is, plant oils melt at lower temperatures than animal fats). The length of the carbon chain is another factor. Longer chains give rise to higher melting points.

Task 2.8   Draw up a table of the common fats and oils used in cooking, indicating next to each one whether it has a low or high melting point and give examples of the uses to which they are therefore suited in catering.

2.8   THE FUNCTION OF FATS AND OILS IN THE BODY

Fats, like carbohydrates, are an excellent source of *energy*. In fact, 1g of fat provides 38kJ (9 kcal) of energy, which is more than twice that provided by carbohydrate. Once again the energy is released from the molecules by oxidation. An important point is that fat provides a very rich source of energy, and it is easy to consume more energy than the body needs. This results in *storage* of the excess energy in the adipose tissues of the body. Adipose tissue is important as an energy store and for insulation of the body against heat loss, but excess storage of fat can occur (overweight and obesity) and may lead to other health problems such as circulatory diseases and diabetes.

As well as providing energy, fats are required in the diet for the *essential fatty acids* that they provide and for the absorption of *fat soluble vitamins*: A, D, E and K (see Chapter 3).

2.9   DIETARY REQUIREMENTS OF FATS AND OILS

While a small amount of fat is required daily to provide essential fatty acids, there are no real guidelines as to how much fat is required in the diet. As indicated in section 2.4, it is recommended that a large proportion of the energy requirement of an individual is provided by carbohydrates, which have much less energy than the same amount of fat (that is carbohydrates have a lower 'energy density' than fats).

2.10 THE EFFECTS OF PREPARATION AND COOKING ON FATS AND OILS

Fats and oils are insoluble in water and are stable at high temperatures; frying temperatures, for example, are usually between 175° and 195°C. They are used, not only as a component of food, but also as a means of heating other foods, as in frying. They have many other properties which enable them to be used in foods to increase tenderness, aeration and palatability.

(i) Effect of heat

As the temperature of a fat is raised it undergoes a series of changes in its state, as shown in Figure 2.10. The temperatures of these changes are different in each fat and the 'oils' have already melted when the temperature is as high as 20°C (room temperature) (see Figure 2.10).

Figure 2.10 *Changes with temperature of butter and corn oil*

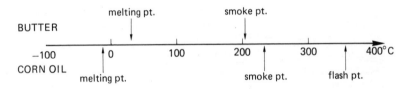

If the fat is heated further (above the melting point), the temperature increases and may reach the *smoke point*. This is usually above 200°C and is caused by the fat breaking down or decomposing and giving off a blue haze. One of the products formed during decomposition is *acrolein*, which gives the characteristic aroma of smoking fat. The smoke point is lowered steadily as the fat is used regularly.

If the fat is heated above the smoke point it may ignite, causing a fire. This is called the *flash point* and is usually well above 300°C.

(ii) Other properties of fats

Many of the properties of fats are related to their *plasticity*, which is, in simple terms, the ability to change shape or be moulded. Some fats have a wider range of plasticity than others because their triglycerides melt over a wider temperature range. These fats are more suitable for spreading or 'creaming' than fats with a narrow range of plasticity.

Creaming is the process by which small bubbles of air are incorporated into food structures, such as cakes, during mixing. This process makes a 'lighter' product and fat is therefore an important component of the structure.

Shortening Another important function of fats in preparation is their ability to 'shorten' products such as baked goods. The fat is rubbed into the flour of pastries and biscuits and coats a large proportion of the flour granules. There is therefore less starch and gluten available to form a network and less water can be absorbed, giving a lighter product. The temperatures at which fats are used in this way is important since it is easy to produce a 'greasy' product if the fat melts. Therefore the more fat in a recipe, the higher the baking temperature should be. Puff pastry, with 50 per cent fat, for example, should be baked at between 200°C and 220°C to prevent the fat melting before the product structure is formed.

Figure 2.11 *Diagram to illustrate shortening in pastry*

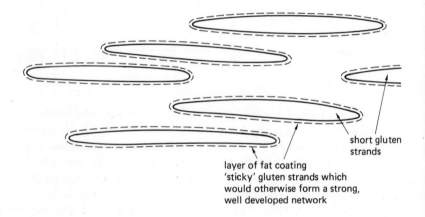

short gluten strands

layer of fat coating 'sticky' gluten strands which would otherwise form a strong, well developed network

Emulsions Food emulsions are a particular example of how fats are involved in the structure of a product. Naturally occurring emulsions, such as milk, and synthetic emulsions, such as mayonnaise, are made up of at least two components which normally do not mix, stabilised by a third component which is called an *emulsifying agent*.

In the preparation of mayonnaise an oil is 'dispersed' throughout a liquid, which is vinegar, and is prevented from separating out or 'splitting' by the lecithin in egg yolk, which is the emulsifying agent (see Figure 2.12).

Figure 2.12   *The emulsion structure of mayonnaise*

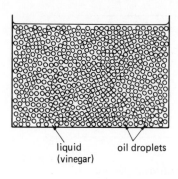

liquid   oil droplets
(vinegar)

(a) Mayonnaise – oil 'dispersed'
through a liquid

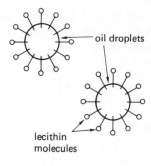

oil droplets

lecithin
molecules

(b) Two oil droplets – emulsified
by lecithin – the droplets cannot
get close enough to join up and
separate from the liquid

Other examples of emulsions include hollandaise sauce, French dressing, butter, and margarine.

Task 2.9   Construct a table using examples of cooking processes not explained in the previous paragraphs that involve the use of fats, stating the main role of fat in the process, that is, creaming, shortening or emulsification.

PROTEINS

2.11   FOOD SOURCES OF PROTEINS

Many fats which contain proteins also have a high proportion of water and fat and often protein is not the main component. Foods which provide significant amounts of protein are meat, fish, poultry, cheese, milk, pulses and some vegetables. It must be stressed that some high protein foods, meat and cheese, for example, also contain large amounts of saturated fats (see Table 2.4 and Figure 2.13).

2.12   THE STRUCTURE OF PROTEINS

Proteins are long chains of smaller units called *amino acids*. There are over 20 different types of amino acid and each protein has a particular

28

Table 2.4   *Protein content per 100g of various foods*

Food	Amount of protein (g)
Cheese (Cheddar)	26
Beef (stewing, raw)	20
Chicken	18
Cod	17
Pork (average, raw)	14
Bread (white)	8
Peas	6
Potatoes	2

Figure 2.13   *Foods containing protein*

sequence, many amino acids being repeated. The length of the chain is from around 50 amino acids to several hundreds (see Figure 2.14).

Protein structure is very complex, but in simple terms the amino acid chain forms a spiral structure which is then held in a 'globular shape' (egg albumen, for example) or is 'fibrous' (muscle proteins, for example). The final structure is held together by cross linkages

Figure 2.14   *The sequence of amino acids in a protein*

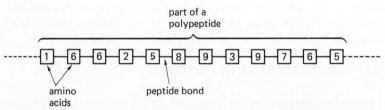

Each of the numbers represents an amino acid. Any protein consists of a set sequence of amino acids

(hydrogen bonding) between amino acids from different parts of the chain (see Figure 2.15).

Figure 2.15 *Protein structure*

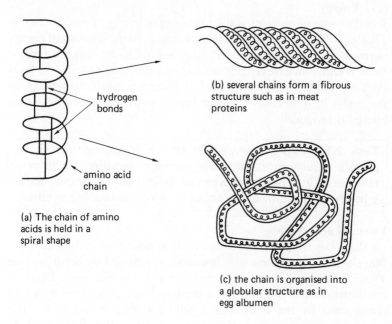

hydrogen bonds

amino acid chain

(a) The chain of amino acids is held in a spiral shape

(b) several chains form a fibrous structure such as in meat proteins

(c) the chain is organised into a globular structure as in egg albumen

2.13 THE FUNCTION OF PROTEIN IN THE BODY

Protein is essential to the body since it is a major constituent of body cells. The proteins taken into the body in food are broken down into amino acids which may be built up into cell structures or used to make enzymes, antibodies and some hormones. The amount of protein required by an individual depends on how much growth, maintenance and repair of tissues is occurring in the body at any one time.

(a) Growth

In order for any part of the body tissues to increase in size, new cells must be produced, which means that amino acids, amongst other things, are needed. During the most important growth stages, such as childhood and adolescence, there is a high requirement for protein.

(b) Maintenance and repair

Proteins are required to provide the necessary amino acids for the repair of damaged or worn-out cells, as well as replacing those broken down in 'routine maintenance'.

(c) Energy

Another role of proteins is the provision of *energy*. Proteins contain 17kJ/g (4.0 kcal) of energy, which is similar to the amount of energy derived from carbohydrates. Protein is used as an energy source if there is either an excess of amino acids for the body's needs (the body does not store excess amino acids), or if there is *insufficient energy* for the body. In both cases the liver breaks down the amino acids and energy is produced.

> **Task 2.10** Explain why each of the following groups of people require more than the 'average' requirement of protein per day: a pregnant woman, an athlete, a person recovering from a motor-cycle accident, a breast-feeding mother.

Essential amino acids

Of the 20 or so amino acids, the body is unable to make nine from other amino acids (the ninth, histidine, is required by children) (see Table 2.5). This means that these *essential amino acids* must be consumed in food, otherwise some important proteins will not be constructed by the body and it will not function correctly. The remaining amino acids are 'non-essential', since they can be made in the liver from other amino acids.

The quality of protein in food is measured according to how well it provides the particular amino acids needed by the body. Animal foods provide a better blend of amino acids for man than plant foods do, and are said to have a *high biological value*. However, it is important

Table 2.5 *Essential amino acids*

1. Isoleucine
2. Leucine
3. Lysine
4. Methionine
5. Phenylalanine
6. Threonine
7. Tryptophan
8. Valine
9. Histidine – required for growth in children

that a variety of proteins are present in the diet and that they have a *supplementary* effect on each other; that is, bread may be low in one amino acid, but can be eaten with cheese which is high in the same amino acid. It is possible to have a diet of only plant foods (such as the diet of a *vegan*, who is a person who does not eat foods derived from animals) which, by supplementation, provides all the amino acids required for body growth, repair and maintenance.

2.14 DIETARY REQUIREMENTS OF PROTEIN

Table 2.6 shows the dietary requirements of protein in the body.

Table 2.6 *Recommended daily amounts of protein for different age groups*

Age group		Male	Female
Children	1 year old	30g	27g
	7–8 years	49g	48g
Adolescents	15–17 years	72g	53g
Adults	18–34 years	72g	54g

It can be seen from the table that protein requirements are slightly higher for males. This is because of their slightly greater average body size.

2.15 THE EFFECTS OF PREPARATION AND COOKING ON PROTEIN

The structure of protein molecules is affected by heat, mechanical action, pH (see glossary), and salt. In each case the shape of the molecule is affected when the cross linkages are altered, leading to a change in the properties of the molecule. This process is called *denaturation* (see Table 2.7). As denaturation proceeds the nutritive value is not altered, but the structure is changed irreversibly and the protein becomes insoluble and more viscous. This is called *coagulation*. Several examples of coagulation are shown in Table 2.7 and indicate how the properties of proteins are important in the preparation of food and in cooking. The setting properties, caused by a rise in temperature, are important in egg dishes, for example; the addition of acid or salt speeds up setting in milk dishes, cheese, yoghurt and egg dishes. The production of foams as indicated in the table is a

Table 2.7 *Types of denaturation*

Cause of denaturation	Examples
Heat	Egg proteins become more solid when heated; gluten in bread sets during baking.
Mechanical action	Whisking causes partial denaturation of proteins in egg whites (meringue), cream (whipped cream).
pH	A decrease in pH causes coagulation of milk proteins in yoghurt and cheese manufacture.
Salt	Addition of salt aids coagulation in poached eggs and several dishes which rely on the properties of eggs.

complicated process in which air is beaten into the food and some of the protein molecules present are partially coagulated by the mechanical action. The protein molecules form a layer around the air bubbles, trapping them in the product to give a very light texture. In addition to the examples in the table, this process takes place in soufflés, sponge cakes and baked meringues, where the cooking process 'sets' the proteins around the air bubbles.

EXERCISES

1. List the three elements that are present in carbohydrates, lipids and proteins.
2. Make a list of foods (referring to Appendix 2 if necessary) that contain:
    (a) carbohydrates,
    (b) fats,
    (c) proteins.
3. Describe the changes that occur to sugar when it is heated
    (a) in a small amount of liquid,
    (b) in a larger amount of liquid.
4. Describe how gelatinisation takes place using a named catering example.
5. What is meant by saturated and unsaturated fats? Briefly describe why unsaturated fats are considered to be less harmful to the body.
6. What is the main function of fat in the body? What is likely to happen if an individual consumes far too much fat for the body's needs?

7. Explain each of the following terms:
   (a) smoke point,
   (b) flash point,
   (c) plasticity,
   (d) shortening.
8. What is the function of amino acids in the body?
9. (a) What is an essential amino acid?
   (b) Explain the term 'biological value' and give a list of foods which have high biological value.
10. When proteins are heated they are *denatured* and may *coagulate*. Explain what this means and how it relates to the cooking of a boiled egg, fillet steak and baked egg custard.

CHAPTER 3

VITAMINS, MINERALS

AND WATER

3.1 INTRODUCTION TO VITAMINS

Vitamins are organic compounds required in small amounts (μg or mg, see Appendix 1) for the correct functioning of the body. They vary greatly in chemical structure and are not usually made in the body. They were discovered early in the twentieth century, when they were found to be responsible for various *deficiency diseases*, if they were not present in the diet. In recent times it has been possible to reduce the occurrence of deficiency diseases by more careful consideration of the diet. Vitamins can be divided into two main groups:

(i) **Fat soluble** – these include the vitamins A, D, E and K, which can, because they dissolve in fat, be easily stored in the body. In extreme cases fat soluble vitamins can be stored to toxic levels, resulting in illness or even death.

(ii) **Water soluble** – these include all the vitamins of the B group and vitamin C, which are less easily stored in the body, since excesses are excreted in the urine.
  Only the more important vitamins–A, B, C and D–are discussed in this chapter.

3.2 VITAMIN A (RETINOL)

Food sources
Retinol can be obtained in two ways – from animal foods as retinol, or from plant foods as carotene which is then converted into retinol. Foods rich in retinol include: fish-liver oils, liver, carrots, margarine, butter, cheese, green vegetables and milk.

Function and deficiency diseases
Retinol is important for correct growth and maintenance of body cells, particularly those involved in surface tissues such as the skin, respiratory tract and cornea of the eye. It is essential for the formation of one of the pigments responsive to light in the eye (rhodopsin) and a lack of retinol can lead to *night blindness* (difficulty in adjusting to dim light conditions). Other effects of retinol shortage include lack of growth in children, disorders of the skin and lowered resistance to infection. *Xerophthalmia* is a condition in which the cornea dries out and blindness can occur. This is an extreme effect of retinol shortage.

Dietary requirement of retinol
An average male adult needs to obtain 750 μg of retinol per day. Since retinol is widely available in food, is not easily destroyed by normal cooking, and can be stored in the body, the deficiency diseases described above are not a major problem in the UK.

Task 3.1 Make a list of the foods in your diet that contain useful amounts of vitamin A.

3.3 VITAMIN D (CALCIFEROLS)

Food sources
Oily fish, margarine, butter, eggs, liver, milk and cream are the main foods providing vitamin D in the UK diet.

Functions and deficiency diseases
Vitamin D is needed for the correct absorption of *calcium* from the intestine and its utilisation in the body. Since calcium is important for the formation of bones and teeth, a lack of vitamin D in the diet results in malformation of these structures. In children a softening of the bones may occur which may lead to 'bow legs' or 'knock knees' which are characteristic of the disease *rickets* (see Plate 3.1). In adults a similar disease called *osteomalacia* occurs. *Dental caries* (tooth decay) can occur if the amount of vitamin D is low in the diet, since tooth formation is dependent on the absorption and utilisation of calcium.

Dietary requirements of vitamin D
The amount of vitamin D needed by an individual from food varies since the proportion synthesised in the skin differs, depending on the amount of sunlight received and other factors (such as skin colour).

Plate 3.1　A child suffering from rickets (*World Health Organisation – WHO*)

However, during periods of important bone and teeth development it is recommended that 10 μg of vitamin D is taken in daily. Vitamin D is not easily destroyed in normal cooking.

Task 3.3 Outline the most suitable cooking methods for vitamin D for someone who receives only a small amount of sunlight on the skin, which can happen, for example, with Asian immigrant families in the UK.

3.4 THE B VITAMINS

There are several important vitamins in the B group and these are shown in Table 3.1 (see also Plate 3.2). They are water soluble and are involved in enzyme reactions in the body. They are not usually stored in the body. As well as being water soluble the B vitamins may also be destroyed by heat, and therefore most cooking methods result in significant losses of these vitamins, particularly thiamin (vitamin B_1). Riboflavin (vitamin B_2), while being the least affected by cooking, is unstable in direct sunlight and large amounts can be lost from milk which is exposed to sunlight for long periods of time.

Task 3.2 Outline the most suitable cooking methods for a variety of cuts of beef in order to retain the maximum quantities of B vitamins, bearing in mind that these are lost most easily when food is cooked for a long time and at high temperatures. Describe how the use of gravies and stocks can reduce these losses.

3.5 VITAMIN C (ASCORBIC ACID)

Food sources
Citrus fruits, blackcurrants, strawberries, tomatoes and green vegetables are good sources of vitamin C. In the UK, potatoes, which are not a particularly rich source of vitamin C, provide the greatest amount in the diet, since they are consumed in large amounts.

Function and deficiency diseases
Vitamin C is important in the formation of connective tissue which is a 'packing' and 'binding' tissue for the cells of the body and also in the absorption of iron. If there is a shortage of vitamin C, the deficiency disease *scurvy* may result, in which there may be haemorrhaging under the skin, swollen and spongy gums (and the teeth may become loose) and the inability to recover quickly from illness (see Plate 3.3).

Table 3.1 *The main B vitamins*

Name	Food sources	Function and deficiency disease	Intake
B$_1$ (thiamin)	yeast, cereals, meat (particularly pork and bacon), bread and milk	Involved in the release of energy from food. If this process does not occur correctly, there may be a chemical build-up resulting in a weakening of the muscles, and problems with nervous and circulatory systems. This deficiency disease is called *beri-beri*.	An adult male requires approx. 1.2 mg thiamin per day.
B$_2$ (riboflavin)	yeast, liver, kidney, cereals, cheese, eggs, meat, milk and potatoes	Also involved in the release of energy from food. There is no specific deficiency disease associated with riboflavin, although it may be involved in preventing a soreness and cracking of the skin around the lips and a reddening of the tongue.	An adult male requires approx. 1.6 mg riboflavin per day.
Nicotinic acid (or niacin)	yeast, liver, meat, cheese, bread, fish, eggs, potatoes and milk	Also involved in the release of energy from food. A prolonged shortage of nicotinic acid may lead to *pellagra*, the symptoms of which include diarrhoea, dermatitis of the skin and mental disorders. (See Plate 3.2.)	An adult male requires approx. 18 mg nicotinic acid per day
B$_{12}$ (cyanocobalamin)	liver, milk, meat, fish and eggs	Involved in the formation of red blood cells (along with another B vitamin – folic acid). If insufficient vitamin B$_{12}$ is absorbed (this is more likely to be because of a faulty absorption mechanism than dietary shortage) then too few red blood cells are made and a serious condition, *pernicious anaemia*, results.	No recommendation

Plate 3.2 A man suffering from pellagra (*World health Organisation — WHO*)

Plate 3.3 Deficiency of vitamin C – swollen and bleeding gums, loose and decaying teeth (*C.J. Webb*)

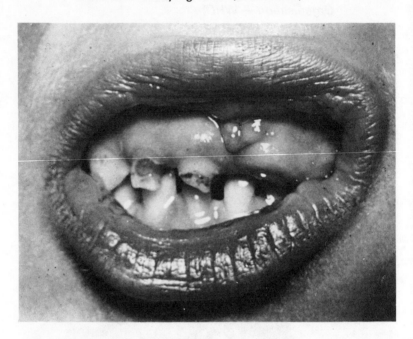

Anaemia also accompanies these symptoms, since there is a lack of iron for haemoglobin formation (see section 3.7).

Dietary requirements
For prevention and cure of scurvy the average male adult requires 10 mg of vitamin C per day. However, in the UK the DHSS recommends an intake of 30 mg and other researchers have suggested that much larger amounts have a protective effect against such conditions as the common cold. Vitamin C is easily lost during cooking.

> **Task 3.4** Many diets today are lacking in fresh fruit and vegetables. Explain why this may mean that more people are likely to suffer from the milder symptoms of scurvy.

3.6 INTRODUCTION TO MINERALS

There are about 15 important mineral elements required by the body which must be taken in as part of the diet. They are present in food as inorganic salts or as parts of larger organic compounds and are taken into the body in amounts ranging from parts of a milligram up to several grams daily. They can be divided into two groups depending on how much they contribute to the over-all body weight.

(a) **Major elements** – iron, calcium, phosphorus, potassium, sodium, chlorine, sulphur and magnesium.

(b) **Trace elements** – iodine, fluorine, zinc, copper, manganese, chromium, and cobalt.

3.7 IRON

Food sources of iron
The following foods contain good to moderate quantities of iron – liver, kidney, meat, wholemeal bread, eggs, some green vegetables and potatoes.

Function and deficiency disease
Iron is required mainly as part of the blood pigment *haemoglobin*, which is responsible for the transport of *oxygen* around the body (from the lungs to the body's tissues). Although most of this iron can be recycled when red blood cells are broken down, the body still requires a steady supply from the diet. If there is a lack of iron, then insufficient haemoglobin is made and the efficiency of the oxygen transport system is reduced. This results in tiredness, lassitude and other symptoms such as dizziness and headache, which are characteristic of *anaemia*.

Dietary requirements
An average daily requirement for iron is 10 mg per day, but this figure is slightly higher in most girls and women, since blood is lost during menstruation. However, greater amounts of iron than 10 mg per day must be taken into the body since the absorption rate of iron from the gut is only about 10 per cent.

Task 3.5 Investigate a range of commerical breakfast cereals (and other foods) and note which contain iron as an added ingredient. What do you conclude from your investigations?

3.8 CALCIUM AND PHOSPHORUS

Dietary sources
Phosphorus, since it is a component of most living cells, is found in most foods. Good sources are cheese, eggs, meat, poultry, fish and

milk. Calcium is added to white flour by law and is also found in milk, cheese, bread, and other cereals. Both minerals are therefore easily obtained in a typical UK diet and deficiencies are rare.

Function and deficiency disease
Calcium and phosphorus are both involved (mainly in the form of calcium phosphate) in the formation of bones and teeth. Calcium is also involved in the clotting of the blood, contraction of muscle fibres, and the correct functioning of nerves. Phosphorus is important in the release of energy in the body's cells.

As with vitamin D deficiency (see section 3.3), if there is a lack of calcium (there is unlikely to be a lack of phosphorus), the diseases *rickets* (in children) and *osteomalacia* (in adults) may occur.

Dietary requirements
The normal adult requirement for calcium is 500 mg per day, but this should be increased for pregnant and breastfeeding women, and is also' higher in children, since growth is still occurring in teeth and bones. An important point is that calcium is found in hard water and this can form a useful addition to the calcium intake.

3.9 POTASSIUM, SODIUM AND CHLORINE

Although each of these minerals performs several individual functions in the body, they are all concerned with the precise 'balance' required in the fluids inside and outside the cells of the body and in the blood. They are particularly important in the correct functioning of the cell, nervous system and muscle action. Potassium is found in a variety of foods, while sodium and chlorine occur together as salt, either in the pure form, or as an ingredient of other foods such as bacon, dairy products, bread and most vegetables.

Task 3.6 Make a list of a variety of foods in which salt is an added ingredient.

3.10 IODINE

Whilst iodine is required in only small amounts (probably less than 0.2 mg per day), it is an important mineral since it is essential for the formation of the hormone *thyroxin*, which is made in the thyroid gland in the neck. This hormone has an effect on the *rate* at which the body functions (basal metabolic rate – see Chapter 4 section 4.3) and a lack of iodine results in a swelling of the thyroid gland called *goitre* (see Plate 3.4).

Plate 3.4   This mother and child are suffering from goitre and
marasmus respectively (*World Health Organisation
– WHO*)

3.11 OTHER IMPORTANT MINERAL ELEMENTS

Magnesium is a major mineral required for bone structure, as a cell component and for the functioning of some enzymes; it is rarely in short supply.

Fluorine, in very small amounts, increases the acid resistance of tooth enamel, therefore decreasing the incidence of tooth decay (dental caries); it is often added to water supplies.

Copper, zinc and **manganese** are trace mineral elements required in enzyme reactions.

3.12 WATER

Water is taken into the body in drinks such as tea, coffee, fruit juices, milk, carbonated drinks and water itself; also as a component of solid foods of plant and animal origin. Table 3.2 shows the approximate water content of some foods.

The human body is made up of more than 70 per cent water and the balance of water gain and water loss has to be critically controlled to prevent disruption of cell activities. The chemical reactions taking place in the cells are sensitive to changes in the concentration of the cell contents (that is the ratio of water to cell solutes), and therefore the water content of the body has to be monitored.

Table 3.2   *Water content of some foods (percentage)*

Food	%
Cucumber	96
Tomato	93
Carrot	90
Cabbage (raw)	88
Milk (whole)	88
Orange	86
White fish	82
Potato	79
Beef (stewing steak, raw)	69
Sausage (pork)	45
Bread (white)	38
Cheese (Cheddar)	37
Butter	15
Almonds	5

Figure 3.1 shows the main water gains and water losses from the human body.

Figure 3.1 *Water gains and losses from the human body, per day*

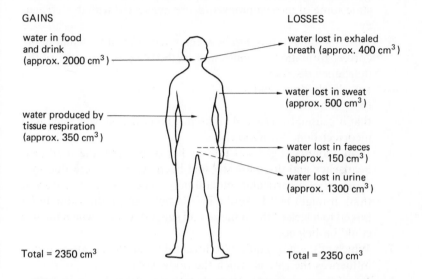

GAINS

water in food and drink (approx. 2000 cm³)

water produced by tissue respiration (approx. 350 cm³)

Total = 2350 cm³

LOSSES

water lost in exhaled breath (approx. 400 cm³)

water lost in sweat (approx. 500 cm³)

water lost in faeces (approx. 150 cm³)

water lost in urine (approx. 1300 cm³)

Total = 2350 cm³

Task 3.7 Investigate over a 24-hour period your water intake and output by:
(a) measuring the quantities of liquids consumed. Note that this does not include the water present in food.
(b) collecting and quickly disposing of the urine produced in that day. If you assume that water intake equals output for that day and that the amount of water in food is negligible (which it is not!), how much water is lost from the body in other ways? How will the temperature of that day affect these figures?

EXERCISES

1. Divide the most important vitamins into two groups depending on their solubility in water.
2. Which vitamin is required for the formation of rhodopsin (one of the pigments responsive to light in the eye)? How might a lack of this vitamin affect an individual? Make a list of foods that could be supplied to such a person to replace their deficiency.

3. If a person was in the habit of boiling most of his/her food in large quantities of liquid, which vitamins would be easily lost from the food?

4. In a diet lacking fresh fruits and vegetables one vitamin in particular is likely to be in short supply. Name the vitamin and state some of the symptoms that are associated with its deficiency.

5. Describe the relationship between vitamin D and calcium in the correct formation of bones and teeth. What is the name of the deficiency disease:
   (a) in children, and
   (b) in adults,
   that is caused by a lack of vitamin D and calcium, which leads to incorrect bone formation?

6. If an adolescent girl was told by her doctor that the tiredness, headaches and dizziness she had been suffering were due to a shortage of a particular mineral in her body, which one do you think it might be? Describe briefly how the tiredness might be linked to a lack of this mineral and suggest ways in which the girl could be helped.

7. Which mineral is required to form thyroxin–the hormone which influences the rate at which the body works?

8. Name three elements, other than those referred to in questions 5, 6 and 7, that are required in the body.

9. Make a list of foods that you could eat in a day that would provide useful quantities of each of the vitamins and minerals discussed in this chapter. Next to each food indicate which vitamins and minerals it is rich in.

10. State the ways in which water is lost and gained in the human body.

THE HUMAN DIET

The previous chapters have shown what food consists of and why each nutrient group is important. It is now necessary to look at how these nutrients make up a 'healthy diet'.

4.1 A HEALTHY DIET

A healthy diet is one which provides all the necessary nutrients in the correct amounts, that is, with no deficiencies and no important excesses. The particular requirements of an individual vary according to several factors such as age, sex, occupation and general health, and this leads to a wide variety of suitable diets for individuals in the population.

National guidelines are set out in the UK by the Department of Health and Social Security (DHSS) for the minimum amounts of nutrients and energy required by groups of the population. Table 4.1 shows a comparison of the minimum requirements for an active adult male and a young female. There are several obvious differences between the two columns, for example, the increased requirements of energy and protein in the adult. Most of the differences are related to body size, directly or indirectly, and are not surprising. However, the table shows that even though the young female has a smaller body-weight, she has a greater requirement for calcium and vitamin D. This is because more bone and tooth development is occurring in the child compared to the adult.

Task 4.1 List other differences between the two tables.

The food eaten by an individual over a period of time should therefore provide *at least* the quantities of nutrients indicated in the

Table 4.1 *Recommended daily amounts of nutrients for a 4-year-old female child and an active 25-year-old male*

	4-year-old female	Active 25-year-old male
Energy	6250 kJ (1488 kcal)	12000 kJ (2857 kcal)
Protein	37 g	72 g
Calcium	600 g	500 mg
Iron	8 g	10 mg
Vitamin A	300 μg	750 μg
Thiamin	0.6 mg	1.2 mg
Riboflavin	0.8 mg	1.6 mg
Nicotinic acid	9 mg	18 mg
Vitamin C	20 mg	30 mg
Vitamin D	10 μg	-

Source: DHSS (1979).

relevant group of the 'recommended daily intake of nutrients' tables (see Appendix 2).

Since the choices of foods for one person differ greatly from those of another person (food choice is affected by many factors such as cost, availability, tradition, preparation time, results of advertising, and so on), it is impractical to describe a normal or correct diet. However, by referring to the 'composition of foods' tables, it is possible to calculate whether a given set of foods, satisfies, approximately, the requirements of a given individual (see questions at the end of the chapter).

> **Task 4.2** Construct a simple questionnaire to investigate some of the factors affecting food choice in your group/ college/family/other group of people.

4.2 ENERGY IN THE DIET

One of the most important aspects of any diet is its total energy value, measured in joules/kilojoules or calories/kilocalories (see Appendix 1). This value should be approximately equal to the amount of energy being used up by an individual if the body is to remain stable. If *more* energy is taken in than is used up, then the excess is converted to *fat*, which is stored in the body causing the individual to become overweight or obese. If energy intake is *lower* than energy usage, then fat stored in the body is broken down to make up the shortage and therefore body weight decreases. This latter process occurs until the fat stored in the body has gone and then important 'structural' proteins are broken down and used for energy. This has a serious affect on the body and is one of the effects of starvation.

> **Task 4.3** Using the food tables in Appendix 2 and Table 4.4 add up the approximate energy value of the foods you ate yesterday and compare it with your approximate energy usage for that day. Explain what might happen to your health if there was a permanent difference between these two sets of figures.

The *regulation* of body-weight is not, however, as straight forward as the previous paragraph might indicate. This is because the rate at which the body uses energy (the *metabolic rate*) varies from person to person and is influenced by several factors.

4.3 BASAL METABOLIC RATE (BMR)

Basal metabolism is the amount of energy required to keep the body alive when 'resting', that is, for breathing, the circulation of the blood and other essential processes. (The definition of basal metabolism has been simplified here. Under experimental conditions basal metabolism actually means 'the energy required by an individual when rested, after fasting, and in warm, comfortable conditions'.) The rate at which this energy is used is referred to as 'the basal metabolic rate' (BMR).

BMR is influenced by:

(a) Body size
In simple terms, more energy is required for a larger body to function than a smaller body; for example, in a large body, circulation of the blood will require more energy. However, it is not just body size that is important; the ratio of lean tissue to fatty tissue is important since more energy is used up if there is a high proportion of lean tissue. One reason for this is the insulating effect of fat causing a reduction in the amount of energy required to maintain body temperature (see Table 4.2).

(b) Age
The BMR tends to fall as age increases. This is because the amount of energy used up by an individual in his occupation and leisure

Table 4.2 *Recommended resting energy requirements, per kg
of body weight, with age*

	Weight (kg)	Resting energy requirement in thousands of kJ/day (kcal/day)	kJ/kg/day (kcal/kg/day)
Infant (1 year old)	10	2.1 (0.5)	0.21 (0.05)
Child (8 years old)	25	4.2 (1.0)	0.17 (0.04)
Adult woman	55	5.4 (1.3)	0.1 (0.02)
Adult man	65	6.7 (1.6)	0.1 (0.02)

activities decreases with age; also the ratio of lean tissue to fatty
tissue falls (see Table 4.2).

(c) **Sex**
Women tend to have a lower BMR than men, since even if they have
an identical body-weight, the ratio of fatty tissue to lean tissue is
higher. For example; an average 60kg male requires 4.5 kJ/min
(1 kcal/min) or 6480 kJ/day (1542 kcal/day) for basal metabolism, an
average 60kg female requires 4.1 kJ/min (1 kcal/min) or 5900 kJ/day
(1404 kcal/day) for basal metabolism (see Table 4.2).

(d) **Growth**
During periods of rapid growth such as childhood, adolescence and
pregnancy, more energy is required for the formation of new body
tissue. Lactation, the production of breast milk, is a process which
also increases BMR.

(e) **General health**
The condition of the body at any one time affects its metabolism. The
most obvious example of this is the condition of the thyroid gland
which produces the hormone *thyroxin*. Thyroxin controls the metabolic rate of the body and can be produced in greater or lesser
amounts than normal if the thyroid gland becomes over- or underactive. In *hyperthyroidism* (overactive thyroid gland) a person tends to be
overactive, underweight, excitable, and has protruding eyeballs. The
opposite is true in *hypothyroidism* (underactive thyroid gland), where
underactivity and weight gain are likely.

Convalescence from illness, which involves an increase in repair
and growth of body tissue is another general condition of the body
which affects basal metabolism. Energy requirements in convalescence are often complicated by a decrease in physical activity.

(f) **Climate/environmental conditions**

Since one of the essential processes included in the 'basal metabolism' of the body is the maintenance of body temperature, it follows that more energy is required to keep the body at 37°C in cold conditions than in a warmer climate.

One other factor influencing basal metabolism is the *thermic effect* of food. This is the increase in energy usage which occurs when food has been absorbed. The absorbed materials are metabolised which produces heat and stimulates BMR.

4.4 PHYSICAL ACTIVITY

In addition to the basal metabolism, the physical activities undertaken by a person affect his/her *total energy requirement*. Included in this category are the activities involved in a person's occupation, domestic life and leisure time. Table 4.3 shows a range of occupations and their approximate energy requirements. Similar occupations for women have a slightly lower energy requirement in each case for the reasons indicated in section 4.3c.

Table 4.3 *Average energy requirements, per day, for various male occupations*

Occupation	Average energy usage (kJ/day (kcal/day))
Office worker	10500 (2500)
Technician	11900 (2833)
Student	12300 (2928)
Builder	12600 (3000)
Farmer	14400 (3428)
Coal-miner	15400 (3666)

The energy required for various specific activities is shown in Table 4.4; figures are given in kJ/minute (kcal/min) and kJ/hour (kcal/hour) for ease of calculation. Task 4.3 in section 4.2 involves the use of these tables to calculate the approximate energy usage for an individual over a 24-hour period.

4.5 OVERWEIGHT AND OBESITY

If energy intake is greater than energy usage then, as we have seen, the excess is stored as fat. The individual is said to be overweight (see

Table 4.4   *Energy requirements for various activities*

	Energy per minute (kJ (kcal))		Energy per hour (kJ (kcal))	
Sleeping	5.3	(1.3)	318	(76)
Sitting	6.3	(1.5)	378	(90)
Writing	6.7	(1.6)	402	(96)
Washing dishes	7.1	(1.7)	426	(101)
Ironing	7.1	(1.7)	426	(101)
Typing	7.5	(1.8)	450	(107)
Walking	17.6	(4.2)	1056	(251)
Gardening	20.9	(5.0)	1254	(299)
Metal working	11.3	(2.7)	678	(161)
Standing	10.5	(2.4)	630	(150)
Sawing wood	31.4	(7.5)	1884	(449)
Cycling	38.0	(9.0)	2280	(542)
Playing football	36.7	(8.7)	2202	(524)
Swimming	33.4	(8.0)	2004	(477)
Polishing	29.3	(7.0)	1758	(418)
Running	62.7	(15.0)	3762	(896)
Walking upstairs	69.8	(16.6)	4188	(997)
Running very quickly	86.5	(20.6)	5190	(1236)

Figure 4.1). If the storage of fat reaches 10 per cent of the body-weight then the condition is referred to as *obesity*. Obesity is in fact the most common form of *malnutrition* (any condition caused by a bad diet) in the western world and is associated with a shortened life expectancy. Some of the disorders with which obesity is linked are coronary heart disease, varicose veins, high blood pressure and diabetes (in middle age). It can also lead to problems during pregnancy and after surgery.

Body-weight can be reduced by:

(a) **Reducing the energy intake**
This can be done by changing the foods eaten to foods with lower energy values, as well as decreasing the amount of food consumed.

(b) **Increasing the energy usage**
This can be done by increasing the physical exercise undertaken in occupation and/or leisure activities.

In practice, a combination of (a) and (b) is most suitable. However, if body-weight is to be reduced, it is first necessary to identify the reason(s) for overeating or underexercising. The reasons

Figure 4.1 *Height and weight*

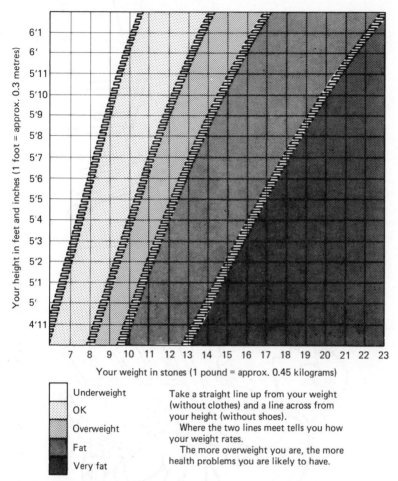

Your height in feet and inches (1 foot = approx. 0.3 metres)

Your weight in stones (1 pound = approx. 0.45 kilograms)

Underweight	Take a straight line up from your weight (without clothes) and a line across from your height (without shoes).
OK	
Overweight	Where the two lines meet tells you how your weight rates.
Fat	The more overweight you are, the more health problems you are likely to have.
Very fat	

Source: J. S. Garrow, *Treat Obesity Seriously* (Churchill Livingstone, 1981).

are many and varied and include social and economic factors, as well as psychological, hormonal and hereditary reasons.

4.6 CURRENT NUTRITIONAL TRENDS

There has been a great deal of interest in nutritional research in recent decades and our knowledge of food and its relationship with health is still growing as a result of scientific work. It is not possible to discuss all of the relevant research here, but the work of one committee, the National Advisory Committee on Nutrition Educa-

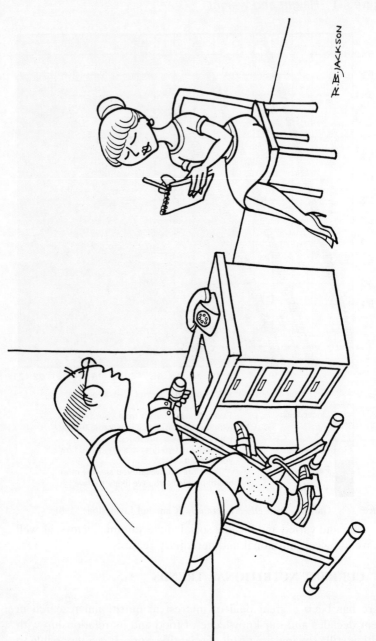

'... increasing the physical exercise undertaken in occupation ...'

tion (NACNE), is of particular interest. NACNE was set up in 1979 to investigate the state of the UK diet and to make recommendations as to how it could be improved to reduce nutritionally-related diseases. Much controversy ensued over the conclusions of the committee because of the far-reaching implications of its findings. (For example, objections were raised by some of the food industries for economic reasons.) In fact, publication of the report was delayed by two and a half years. However, the Medical and Nutritional Professions are overwhelmingly in support of the following recommendations which are set out in the report:

(a) **Fat** intake should be *reduced* (by about a quarter)

(b) **Sugar** intake should be *reduced* (by about a half)

(c) **Alcohol** intake should be *reduced* (by about a third)

(d) **Salt** intake should be *reduced* (by about a half)

(e) **Dietary fibre** should be *increased* (by about a half)

(f) **Starch** intake should be *increased* (by about a half)

It is recommended that protein levels remain unaltered.

Task 4.4 Either (a) write down what you ate for dinner last evening, or, (b) obtain a restaurant menu and assess whether any of the above points (a) to (f), should be applied. Make suggestions as to how the menus could have been improved.

4.7 FAT, SUGAR AND SALT

One reason for considering these nutrients together is that they have all been linked with heart disease and stroke. However, it must be stressed that they are only three factors amongst many other 'risk factors' associated with these diseases (see Figure 4.2).

(a) **Fat**
Recent research recommends that:
(i) The *amount* of fat in the diet should be reduced, enabling the energy intake to be more easily controlled (see section 4.2).

Figure 4.2 'Risk factors' in heart disease and stroke

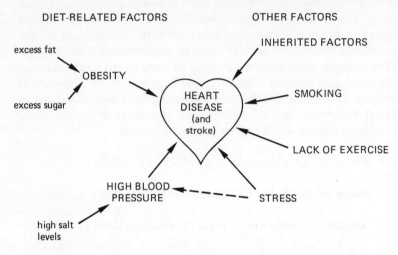

(ii) The *type* of fat should be altered (of the fat consumed there should be a greater proportion of unsaturated fat), leading to a reduction in the cholesterol level of the blood (see section 2.7).

It is thought that high levels of cholesterol in the blood are linked with an increase in the amount of fatty material deposited in the lining of the arteries (*atherosclerosis*) (see Figure 4.3). This has the

Figure 4.3 *Atherosclerosis*

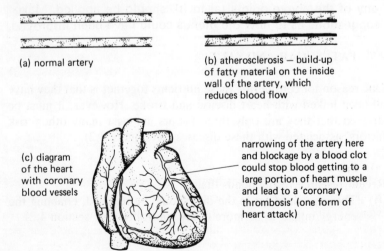

effect of narrowing the arteries (causing a restriction in blood flow, such as in the condition *angina pectoris*, which is characterised by severe chest pain), and increasing the chance of blood clots forming which can block a small artery. If an artery is blocked in this way (called a *thrombosis*), then blood flow to important tissues cannot occur, for example to heart muscle (coronary thrombosis – a type of heart attack) or brain tissue (a stroke).

(b) Sugar

Sugar is a substance which is very rich in energy but has no other nutritive value. The fact that it has such a high 'energy density' means that it is easy for an individual that has a high content of sugar in his/her diet to exceed their daily energy requirement and become overweight. We have already seen that overweight and obesity are factors considered to increase the risk of heart and circulatory diseases.

Sugar is also a major factor in *tooth decay* since it is converted, by bacteria in the mouth, into acid, which causes the erosion of tooth enamel.

Task 4.5 Make a list of any alternatives to sugar that you know of that are used for sweetening food or drink.

(c) Salt

Although the evidence is not totally conclusive, links have been made between high salt levels and high blood pressure. What can be shown is that high blood pressure is an important factor in heart disease and strokes, since it increases the amount of 'wear and tear' on the heart and arteries.

Task 4.6 Ask a chef how much salt he would normally add to a dish such as Scotch Broth, Irish Stew and Carbonnade of Beef, and ask the reason for his doing so. Do you think that people could adapt to having *less* salt in their food?

4.8 ALCOHOL

Alcohol is absorbed very readily from the stomach, unlike most other foods, and is rapidly and efficiently absorbed. It has a high energy value, 29kJ/g (6.9 kcal/g), although the amount of pure alcohol in equivalent amounts of alcoholic drinks varies (for example 3–5 per cent in beer, 30–40 per cent in whisky and other spirits). This can lead to excess energy intake and the problems associated with it (see section 4.5). If the amount of alcohol in the diet increases significantly, then it has the effect of 'displacing' other important nutrients; a common deficiency in alcoholism is that of thiamin (vitamin B_1). Thiamin is actually required in greater amounts than normal to metabolise the alcohol, so shortages are common. In serious cases beri-beri can occur (see Chapter 3, section 3.4). Other harmful effects due to excessive consumption of alcohol occur to the liver (the risk of *cirrhosis* is much greater), digestive system, heart and circulatory system, lungs, muscles and nervous system (see Figure 4.4).

Figure 4.4   *The amount of alcohol in common drinks*

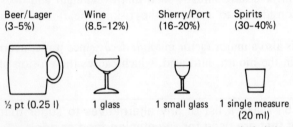

Beer/Lager (3–5%)	Wine (8.5–12%)	Sherry/Port (16–20%)	Spirits (30–40%)
½ pt (0.25 l)	1 glass	1 small glass	1 single measure (20 ml)

Each of the above measures provides a similar amount of pure alcohol. Approximately five of the above drinks is equivalent to the legal limit for driving in the UK, for an average-sized male.

4.9   DIETARY FIBRE

This is the plant material found in food that is indigestible to man, that is, man does not possess the enzymes necessary for its breakdown. Dietary fibre, or roughage, includes *cellulose* and other compounds such as *lignin*, which are found in cereals, breakfast cereals, vegetables and fruit (see Table 4.5).

Dietary fibre is important to the body because it gives 'bulk' to the material passing through the intestine and it also reduces the amount of energy in a given meal. For example, a breakfast cereal containing bran such as 'All Bran' has six times as much fibre and a quarter less energy as a cereal without bran, such as 'Rice Krispies'. Meals rich in fibre are therefore said to have *low energy density*.

Movement of food in the intestine is stimulated by bulky foods and if there is a lack of fibre in the diet, movement slows down, the faeces become dry and more concentrated and *constipation* may occur. Associated with constipation and a lack of fibre are haemorrhoids (piles), diverticular disease (see Figure 4.5) and cancer of the bowel (large intestine). It is recommended that a diet should contain about 30g of fibre per day or more.

Table 4.5   *Foods containing dietary fibre per 100g*

Food	Amount of dietary fibre (g)
All Bran	27
Almonds	14
Wholemeal bread	9
Blackcurrants	7
Peas	5
White bread	3
Potatoes	2
Lettuce	2
Apple	2
Cornflakes	2

Figure 4.5   *Diverticular disease*

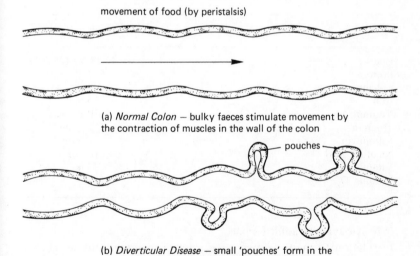

movement of food (by peristalsis)

(a) *Normal Colon* — bulky faeces stimulate movement by the contraction of muscles in the wall of the colon

pouches

(b) *Diverticular Disease* — small 'pouches' form in the wall of the colon, probably caused by the increase in pressure as a result of little 'bulk'

Task 4.7   Make a list of foods that you eat which are high in fibre. If you wanted to increase your fibre intake, you might decide to choose a breakfast ceral rich in fibre; apart from 'All Bran', which ones could you choose?

4.10 DIET AND MENU PLANNING

The previous sections of this chapter outline the general principles of a healthy diet. It is now necessary to discuss the variations in diet of specific groups within the population. (Questions at the end of the chapter require the use of this information and the food tables in Appendix 2 to translate general dietary principles into actual food choices.)

(a) An average adult male

The dietary requirements of an average adult male (18–34 years old) are given in Table 4.6. A diet to provide all the nutrients outlined in Table 4.6 could be constructed from an infinite combination of foods which in a typical UK diet would be eaten in three separate meals of breakfast, lunch and dinner. It is not essential that each meal is 'balanced' in its provision of the daily requirements, as long as the *average* content is balanced and consists of a *variety* of foods.

Table 4.6 *Recommended daily dietary requirements for an average adult male 18–34 years old*

	Daily requirement
Energy	12000 kJ (2857 kcal)
Protein	72 g
Calcium	500 mg
Iron	10 mg
Vitamin A	750 μg
Thiamin	1.2 mg
Riboflavin	1.6 mg
Nicotinic acid	18 mg
Vitamin C	30 mg
Vitamin D	--

(b) An average adult female

In relation to men, women have a lower average body-weight and therefore require a lower energy (and hence B vitamins) and protein intake. The requirement for iron is slightly higher to replace iron lost in the blood during the menstrual period.

During *pregnancy* and *lactation* the requirement of most nutrients is increased, since new tissue growth or milk production is taking place. Particular importance should be attached to the vitamins B, C and D as well as the minerals, iron and calcium, at this time.

(c) Children
With the exception of calcium and vitamin D, children and infants require smaller quantities of each nutrient than an adult. However, in relation to their body size they actually require more of each nutrient (that is they require more grams of nutrient per kilogram of body-weight – see Table 4.2). This is because they are growing quickly and are usually very active.

(d) The elderly
Elderly people require a lower energy intake and fewer grams of protein per day as they tend to be less active and are not growing. Their diet may also vary because of influences such as cost, ease of preparation and difficulties in chewing or digesting food.

(e) Lactovegetarians and vegans
Some vegetarians eat no meat, but may eat milk, cheese and eggs, while vegans (strict vegetarians) eat no food of animal origin. In both cases the nutrients which are normally provided by animal foods such as protein, B vitamins and iron must be obtained by a variety of plant foods. A vegetarian diet usually contains larger quantities of cereals, pulses, nuts, soya bean products and green vegetables than a non-vegetarian diet.

(f) Slimmers
Males and females who are overweight need to reduce energy intake as part of their programme to lose weight. A reduced energy diet must be constructed carefully from foods that provide all the other nutrients, while still having a lower energy value. The most energy-rich foods, such as those containing large amounts of fat, should be avoided, while those high in fibre and starch can be encouraged.

Task 4.8 Construct a table with two columns and list foods that could be included and foods that should be excluded in a slimming diet.

(g) Convalescents
People who are recovering from illness or surgery need, in addition to their normal requirements, more protein (for replacement of damaged tissue), more energy (for repair) and more vitamin C (which is involved in the repair mechanism). Other nutrients may be needed in greater amounts in specific conditions.

(h) Immigrants

Immigrants to the UK, particularly children, often require an increase in the amount of vitamin D in their diet, particularly if they retain a traditional diet. Customs may prevent them from obtaining sufficient vitamin D by synthesis of the vitamin in the skin after exposure to sunlight.

4.11 THE ROLE OF THE CATERER IN NUTRITIONAL POLICY

This particular role is often underestimated. Caterers have a great responsibility regarding the type of food they produce. If meals or menus are constructed with healthy eating as a major objective, improvements can often be made.

Improvements might range from small changes which involve putting less salt in food, reducing the amount of sugar added to dishes, using less fat in preparation and cooking, or changing to unsaturated fats; to major menu changes where wholemeal bread is offered, jacket potatoes replace potato chips, and a wider variety of healthier foods is made available.

Many of these changes are already taking place, particularly in institutional catering such as hospitals and schools. In private businesses it may be more difficult because of increased costs and the uncertainty of consumer preferences. However, as more and more people become aware of the importance of good nutrition, more selection of healthier food will take place, particularly if the caterer adopts a *positive* attitude towards changing consumer preferences.

4.12 WORLD NUTRITION

This chapter so far has dealt with the recommendations that have been made for typical UK and other western diets and has highlighted many of the problems of overnutrition. However, in many parts of the world there is *under*nutrition, where people are not able to obtain a satisfactory food supply. Their problems range from temporary specific vitamin or mineral deficiencies to much more serious long-term protein and energy shortages. Examples of diseases which are prevalent in Asia, Africa and Latin America, due to undernutrition, are pellagra (particularly in areas where the diet is largely maize), beri-beri (where polished rice is the main food), anaemia, blindness, kwashiorkor (caused by a diet low in protein – see Plate 4.1) and marasmus (this involves a shortage of protein and energy in the diet). The last two diseases are particularly common in children and are often seen if early *weaning* occurs; this is

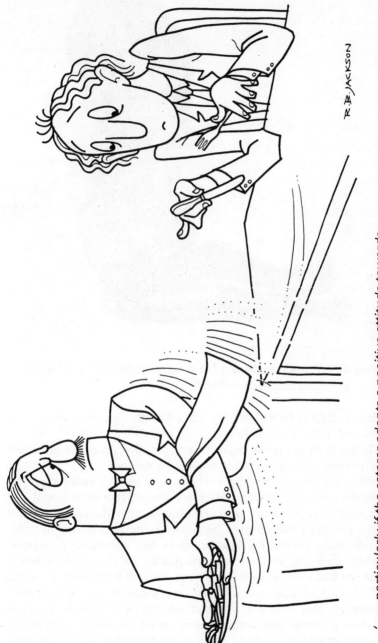

'. . . particularly if the caterer adopts a positive attitude towards changing consumer preferences.'

Plate 4.1   A child suffering from kwashiorkor (*World Health Organisation – WHO*)

when a child is taken abruptly off the mother's milk, which is not replaced with an adequate diet.

It has been estimated that about 500 million people in the world suffer from undernutrition of one sort or another.

The reasons for world food shortages in the underdeveloped countries are complex and involve political, economic, social and administrative problems. A food shortage occurs when the amount of food produced (which may be reduced unexpectedly in drought, flood and/or disaster) is insufficient to feed the whole population (which itself may be increasing too quickly for the available food). The obvious solution to this is to transfer food from one area of the world where it is in excess to the area where it is in short supply. However, this is a very difficult process and involves political, economic, social and administrative problems. Often one of the greatest problems (once the political and economic factors have been overcome) is the transport and distribution of food over large distances. Any permanent solution must therefore involve financial aid to underdeveloped countries, which enables them to increase their own food production.

Task 4.9 By researching the current national newspapers, find out where in the world the most serious food shortages are at present, or have been recently. If possible, briefly discuss which of the factors described in this section were the cause of the food shortage and what help or solutions are being offered to solve the problems.

EXERCISES

1. List some of the factors which affect food choice in humans.
2. Explain why the energy value of the food eaten by an individual is an important aspect of his/her diet.
3. List some of the factors which influence basal metabolism in humans.
4. Why do women tend to have a lower BMR than men of the same body-weight?
5. Describe some of the health risks that are associated with obesity.
6. What is the current nutritional advice regarding the following substances in an individual's diet: fat, sugar, alcohol, salt, dietary fibre and starch? For each substance briefly describe the suggested effects they have on the health of an individual.
7. Briefly describe *modifications* that should be made to an average adult diet for the following groups of people:
   (a) pregnant women,
   (b) a 70-year-old male, and
   (c) a lactovegetarian.
8. For the menu set out below calculate the amount of each nutrient provided, using the tables in Appendix 2. Discuss how well these foods would provide the recommended daily amounts of nutrients for an average adult male, 20 years old.

   Comment on how 'healthy' you consider the meals to be and point out any shortfalls. Make suggestions as to how you think they should be improved. (If time is short, this question can be attempted without detailed calculations, but with general comments.)

Menu *Breakfast*: Cornflakes 30g
Toast (white bread) 60g
Butter 25g
Jam/marmalade 30g
2 cups of tea
Sugar 30g

Lunch: Steak and kidney pie 150g
Potato chips 150g
(old potatoes)
Baked beans 100g
Beer 500ml

Dinner: Grilled pork chop 175g
Boiled potatoes 150g
(old)
Canned peas 100g
Bread (white) 60g
Butter 40g
Apple pie 100g
Custard 100g
Beer 1000ml

9. Plan a day's menu for a specified group of the population, to include three meals that provide healthy foods and satisfy the recommended daily amounts for that group of people. (Refer to Appendix 2.)

10. Design a questionnaire to be used with a group of people to determine the awareness of the general public of the current advice regarding 'healthy eating'.

PART II

TYPES OF FOOD

FOODS FROM ANIMALS

5.1 INTRODUCTION

This chapter includes the foods obtained from animal flesh. Animal products such as eggs and milk are dealt with in Chapter 6.

Many types of animal are eaten by humans. Some are reared commercially on a large scale, others are hunted in small numbers. They provide protein of high biological value (see Chapter 2, section 2.13) and other nutrients.

5.2 MEAT

The term 'meat' refers to the flesh taken from the carcase of an animal. Butcher's meat usually refers to the meat from cattle (beef and veal), sheep (lamb and mutton) and pigs (pork and bacon).

The meat of an animal changes considerably with its age and it is referred to by different names which are explained in Table 5.1.

Table 5.1 *Classification of common types of meat*

Meat	Animal	Age
Beef	Cattle	18–36 months (best at about 18 months)
Veal	Cattle	up to 6 months (best at about 3 months)
Lamb	Sheep	up to 12 months
Mutton	Sheep	up to 36 months
Pork	Pig	up to 7 months

Structure and quality

The eating quality of a piece of meat is determined by the components of its structure and how they react to cooking. The structure varies from one cut of meat to another, but the following tissues are present in varying proportions (see also Figure 5.1).

(a) Muscle tissue
(b) Connective tissue
(c) Fat (adipose tissue)
(d) Blood

Figure 5.1 *Structure of meat*

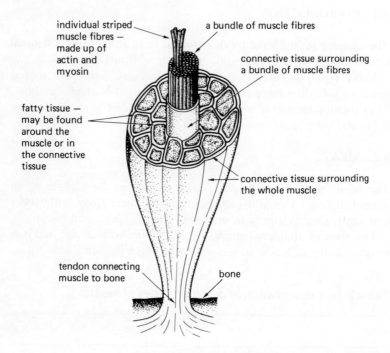

The muscle tissue is usually skeletal muscle (hearts are an exception) and is composed of elongated fibres which appear striped when viewed under a microscope. The fibres are made up of the proteins *actin* and *myosin* which overlap with each other during muscle contraction, enabling movement in the animal. As the animal ages and more work is done by the muscles, the thickness of the fibres increases and the meat becomes tougher. The muscle fibres are bound together with *connective tissue* which varies in its composition.

Task 5.1 Take a small piece of stewing beef and investigate its structure with a magnifying glass. The fibres should be easily identifiable, as should the connective tissue which is present in sheets. If you have a microscope, tease a fibre from the meat and observe it under low and high power – the stripes should be visible.

Most of the connective tissue in meat is white and contains a higher proportion of *collagen* than *elastin* (these are the two main proteins in connective tissue). The amount of connective tissue, and its degree of development, increases with age and work done by the muscle, and leads to a tougher piece of meat. Therefore meat taken from the rump of a young animal has much less connective tissue and is much more tender than meat taken from the shin or neck of an older animal (see Figure 5.2).

During cooking the two proteins are affected differently – collagen can be converted to a soluble protein – *gelatin* – if sufficient water is present, whereas elastin becomes tougher during cooking.

The amount of *fatty tissue* in meat varies from 10 per cent to 50 per cent. It may be present around the muscle (in which case it can be removed if necessary) or as particles of fat in the connective tissue of the meat (invisible fat). In some cases the fat is visible as thin strips running along the muscle fibres, which is referred to as 'marbling'. Fat melts during cooking and helps to maintain tenderness in the meat; therefore marbling is often considered to be a good quality in meat. The colour of the fat may be an indication of the age and quality of the meat, since the pigment carotene, derived from foodstuffs such as grass, is deposited with age, turning the fat yellow (see Figure 5.2).

Task 5.2 Visit a large, good quality, butcher's shop and make a list of all the types of beef you can find. Using a catering textbook determine where on the animal each cut of meat originates and make notes on its fat content, amount of bone and so on. Does the price per pound reflect the quality you would expect from the different types of beef?

A significant amount of *blood* remains in the meat after the hanging and butchery processes, the main effect of which is to give colour to the meat.

Figure 5.2 *Meat from different parts of the animal*

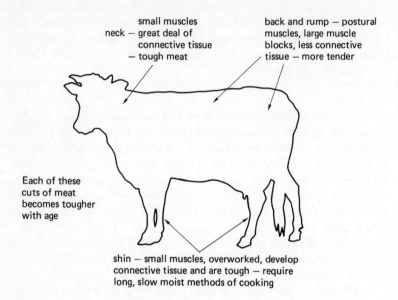

small muscles
neck — great deal of
connective tissue
— tough meat

back and rump — postural
muscles, large muscle
blocks, less connective
tissue — more tender

Each of these
cuts of meat
becomes tougher
with age

shin — small muscles, overworked, develop
connective tissue and are tough — require
long, slow moist methods of cooking

Colour

The colour of meat, which is often used in assessment of age and quality, depends on the two pigments present: *myoglobin* (in muscle) and *haemoglobin* (in blood). The most important effects concern myoglobin, which changes colour in several ways. It is normally a reddish purple colour but is affected by cooking, reaction with oxygen in the air, and salting or curing. Some of the changes in myoglobin are shown in Figure 5.3.

Figure 5.3 *Changes in myoglobin*

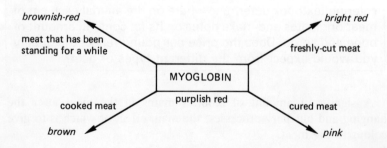

brownish-red

meat that has been
standing for a while

bright red

freshly-cut meat

MYOGLOBIN
purplish red

cooked meat

cured meat

brown

pink

Slaughter and storage

Careful treatment of the animal carcase during and after slaughter is important for the production of good quality meat. The animal should be killed quickly and with the minimum of stress, as stress brings about chemical changes that lead to a reduction in the quality of the meat. Several factors affecting quality are important during the period between slaughter and preparation of the meat for cooking:

(i) *Temperature control* Meat should be kept below 5°C to restrict microbial deterioration during storage (see Chapter 10). The possibility of rancidity in the fat of meat is also reduced by chilling to below this temperature.

(ii) *Correct hanging* Shortly after slaughter the flesh of an animal stiffens in the process of *rigor mortis*. The muscle proteins, actin and myosin, 'lock together' during rigor mortis, giving a dense structure which would lead to tough meat if it was cooked during this period. The weight of the animal during hanging causes stretching of the muscle proteins and causes breaks in the muscle fibres which are apparent after rigor mortis has passed. As a result the meat is more tender.

(iii) *Chemical changes during storage* After slaughter many chemical changes occur in meat. One important effect is brought about by the conversion of *glycogen*, which is the energy storage compound in muscle, into *lactic acid*. This lowers the pH from 7.4 to 5.5 and causes partial coagulation of the meat proteins, increasing tenderness. However, less water is retained in the meat as pH decreases, which reduces tenderness. A compromise between these two opposing factors is achieved if the temperature is held at the level at which the optimum rate of conversion of glycogen to lactic acid occurs.

Other changes that occur during storage are the development of flavour in the meat and the further tenderisation by enzymes within the animal carcase.

The effects of cooking on meat

The quality of meat varies greatly from one cut to another and therefore the method of cooking must be chosen carefully for each type. Table 5.2 summarises the main effects of cooking on meat and should be taken into account when choosing a method of cooking for a piece of meat.

Table 5.2 *Summary of the main effects of cooking on meat*

Constituent of meat	Effect	Observation
Muscle fibres	Coagulate and shrink (the higher the temperature the greater the coagulation)	Tenderness is decreased
Connective tissue		
(a) collagen	Moist cooking causes this to melt into gelatin	Increases tenderness
(b) elastin	Shrinks and toughens	Decreases tenderness
Fatty tissue	Melts and makes the meat 'juicier'	Increases tenderness (unless lost from the meat completely)
Vitamins	B vitamins may be lost into cooking water (moist methods) or may be destroyed by heat	Vitamins lost into cooking liquid may be retained if liquid is served as gravy or in stews/soups
Pigments	Haemoglobin and myoglobin change colour with heat	See Figure 5.3 (p. 72)

One other effect of cooking is the *non-enzymic browning* which occurs on the surface of meat when it is roasted, fried or grilled. This is a complex process which involves reactions between reducing sugars and amino acids in the meat and leads to the production of brown polymers. The breakdown of fat from the meat also contributes to colour.

Tenderisation of meat
The preparation of meat is also important to the tenderness of the finished product. Cheaper cuts of meat can be made more palatable by partial breakdown of the muscle and connective fibres prior to cooking and by increasing the water content of the meat (hydration):

(i) *Mechanical breakdown* This involves cutting or breaking the muscle and connective tissues by scoring, using a mallet, or mincing. Less chewing of the meat is required after cooking.

(ii) *Enzymic breakdown* Various protein digesting (proteolytic) enzymes are available which can be sprinkled onto the meat to partially break down the muscle and connective fibres. Their effect is enhanced by heat which partially denatures (see Chapter 8) the proteins. The two main examples are *papain* from the papaya or paw paw, which is a melon-like fruit, and *bromelin* which is extracted from pineapples. It is necessary to obtain even distribution of the enzymes by scoring the surface or forking in the tenderiser; but it is equally important to avoid over-use, which can result in the meat becoming 'mushy'.

Another way of producing more tender meat is to inject animals with proteolytic enzymes just before slaughtering. Enzymic meat tenderisation is useful because it enables second-class meat to be used for better dishes. For example, tenderised brisket can be used for pot roasting.

(iii) *Marinating* A *marinade* is a liquid in which meat or other animal foods is soaked to increase tenderness and flavour. Marinades usually contain wine, vinegar or lemon, and it is the acid and/or alcohol present which denature the fibres and retain water within the meat to increase tenderness. Marinating times are usually between 2 and 18 hours.

Task 5.3 Buy a piece of second-class-quality beef and divide it into four pieces. Prepare and cook three pieces as described in (i), (ii) and (iii) of this section and cook the fourth piece without tenderising. Assess each piece for tenderness after cooking.

Nutritional value

Meat may be included in the diet for many reasons, one of which is its nutritional content. Beef, pork and lamb contain significant amounts of protein, fat and vitamins of the B group (particularly nicotinic acid and riboflavin). The mineral iron is also provided in useful quantities by meat (see Table 5.3). Note that the figures here and in Table 5.4 are from the 8th edn (1976) of the Manual of Nutrition. The complete breakdown of food composition given in Appendix 2b (p. 259) uses data from the 9th edn (1986).

As seen in Chapters 2 and 4, the protein in meat is of great benefit to the diet, whereas the fat content is considered to be less beneficial. This has led to a decrease in the consumption of meat, particularly red meat, by the consumer over recent years, and a demand for leaner meat. Leaner meat can in fact be produced by altering the breeding and feeding patterns of the animal.

Table 5.3 Nutritional content of beef, port and lamb, per 100g

	Energy kJ (kcal)	Protein (g)	Fat (g)	Carbohydrate (g)	Vit. A (µg)	Vit. B_1 (mg)	Vit. B_2 (mg)	Nicotinic acid (mg)	Vit. C (mg)	Vit. D (µg)	Iron (mg)
Beef (rumpsteak, raw)	821 (195)	19	14	0	0	0.08	0.26	4.2	0	0	2.3
Beef (mince, raw)	919 (219)	19	16	0	0	0.06	0.31	4.0	0	0	2.7
Pork (leg, raw)	1115 (265)	17	23	0	0	0.73	0.20	4.5	0	0	0.8
Pork (loin chop, raw)	1362 (324)	16	30	0	0	0.57	0.14	4.2	0	0	0.8
Lamb (leg, raw)	996 (237)	18	19	0	0	0.14	0.25	5.7	0	0	1.7
Lamb (cutlet, raw)	1593 (379)	15	36	0	0	0.09	0.16	3.9	0	0	1.2

Source: Manual of Nutrition (HMSO, Crown copyright, 8th edn).

Table 5.4 Nutritional content of various offals, per 100g

	Energy kJ (kcal)	Protein (g)	Fat (g)	Carbohydrate (g)	Vit. A (µg)	Vit. B_1 (mg)	Vit. B_2 (mg)	Nicotinic acid (mg)	Vit. C (mg)	Vit. D (µg)	Iron (mg)
Heart (lamb, raw)	498 (119)	17	6	0	0	0.48	0.9	6.9	7	0	3.6
Kidney (lamb, raw)	380 (90)	17	3	0	100	0.49	1.8	8.3	7	0	7.4
Liver (lamb, raw)	748 (178)	20	10	2	18100	0.27	3.3	14.2	10	0.5	9.4
Sweetbread (lamb, raw)	549 (131)	15	8	0	0	0.03	0.25	3.7	18	0	1.7

Source: Manual of Nutrition (HMSO, Crown copyright, 8th edn).

5.3 OFFAL

Amongst the organs of the animal which are separated at slaughter for consumption as offal are the liver, kidneys, heart, pancreas (sweetbread), brain and tongue. There is no common type of structure to these organs, each of which has a totally different function in the animal to any other. Heart and tongue, for example, have a high proportion of muscle tissue, although in the case of heart the muscle does not possess the same fibrous structure as skeletal muscle (see section 5.2). Liver and kidney are both whole organs which have a dense cellular structure permeated with blood vessels. Liver and kidney in particular require careful cooking to prevent over coagulation of the proteins, which would give a hard, chewy texture.

Nutritional value
Offals, as well as being inexpensive, are nutritious foods contributing a wide range of vitamins and minerals in addition to protein. They generally contain less fat than red meat. Liver and kidney, for example, are good sources of protein, B vitamins, iron and vitamin A, as well as providing smaller amounts of vitamin C, vitamin D and calcium (see Table 5.4).

Task 5.4 Using Table 5.4 and Appendix 2, calculate approximately how much liver or kidney would be required to supply an average adult male with his daily requirement of vitamin B_2 if, for example, it were his only source of B_2.

5.4 POULTRY AND GAME

Poultry is the term used for domesticated birds and includes chickens, turkeys, ducks and geese. Chickens and turkeys, in particular, are produced on a massive scale and provide excellent nutrition, economically.

Game refers to the wild animals and birds killed for food by hunting and shooting. This includes deer, hare and rabbits (furred game) and pheasant, partridge, grouse and wild duck (feathered game).

Structure of poultry
The tissue structure of poultry is very similar to the red meats previously described, with one main difference being the colour of the flesh. Poultry has two types of meat: dark meat (from the legs and wings) and light meat (from the breast). The dark meat tends to be

juicier because of the increase in connective tissue. The light meat is usually more tender but can be quite dry.

Poultry often has little flavour prior to cooking and so cooking methods which develop most flavour, such as roasting, are usually preferred.

Nutritional value of poultry
Chicken and turkey provide similar amounts of protein to beef, pork and lamb but less fat than beef, pork and lamb. They also contribute towards dietary iron and B vitamins. Ducks and geese contain a much larger proportion of fat than chickens and turkeys (see Table 5.5).

Game
The animals and birds listed previously as game are usually wild and tend to have leaner, tougher muscles than commercially-bred animals. The meat is also darker in colour. Most game is hung for a period of time, dependant on the season, to develop tenderness and flavour, but care must be taken to prevent bacterial spoilage or poisoning of the meat (see Chapter 11). During the hanging period enzymes within the animal and micro-organisms begin to break down the muscle and connective tissues, so increasing tenderness. Marinating is common with game as another aid to tenderisation and flavour development.

5.5 FISH

There is a wide variety of fish caught for human consumption which can be classified in many ways. The simplest division is into oily fish (between 5 per cent and 30 per cent fat) and white fish (less than 5 per cent fat).

Structure
The main tissues of interest in fish are, as in meat, muscle, connective tissue, fat and blood, although in some cases, as in sardines, the bones may be eaten as well. The muscle fibres are the same as in other meat, but are shorter and are embedded in sheets of connective tissue. There is much less connective tissue in fish and it is quite different from other meat, since it softens easily on cooking, enabling the fibres to separate into blocks, giving the characteristic flaky appearance of cooked fish (see Figure 5.4).

The delicate structure of fish is often protected during cooking by a coating of breadcrumbs or batter, and gentler forms of cooking such as poaching are often used (see plate 5.1).

Table 5.5 *Nutritional content of poultry, per 100g*

	Energy (kJ (kcal)	Protein (g)	Fat (g)	Carbohydrate (g)	Vit. A (μg)	Vit. B₁ (mg)	Vit. B₂ (mg)	Nicotinic acid (mg)	Vit. C (mg)	Vit. D (μg)	Iron (mg)
Chicken (raw)	508 (121)	21	4.3	0	0	0.10	0.16	7.8	0	0	0.7
Duck (raw)	513 (122)	20	4.8	0	0	0.76	0.45	5.3	0	0	2.4
Turkey (raw)	454 (108)	22	2.2	0	0	0.09	0.16	7.9	0	0	0.8

Source: *Manual of Nutrition* (HMSO, Crown copyright, 8th edn).

Figure 5.4   *Structure of fish*

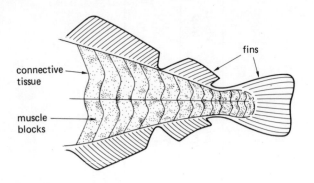

Storage

Storage of fish is much more critical than that of many other foods because of its rapid rate of deterioration. There are large numbers of bacteria in the gut of the fish which are able to break down the flesh quickly because of the lack of connective tissue. Oily fish may also deteriorate if rancidity (see Chapter 10, section 10.2) takes place. Fish should therefore be eaten when fresh, or frozen as soon as possible. During any period of storage – for sale or preparation – they should be kept just above 0°C.

Nutritional value

White fish (which includes cod, haddock, plaice and whiting) are good sources of protein, nicotinic acid and iodine. Oily fish (including herring, mackerel, sardine and salmon) have, in addition, fat (although there is a large proportion of unsaturated fats), calcium, vitamin A and vitamin D (see Table 5.6).

Task 5.5   Using Table 5.6 explain why herring, for example, has approximately three times the energy value per 100 g as cod.

Shellfish

The main groups of shellfish eaten as food are *molluscs* (cockle, mussel, oyster, scallop, clam) and *crustaceans* (shrimp, prawn, scampi lobster, crab). They are a good source of protein and also provide some minerals and vitamins. They do not usually form a large part of the diet, but have interesting flavours and textures, providing variety to the diet.

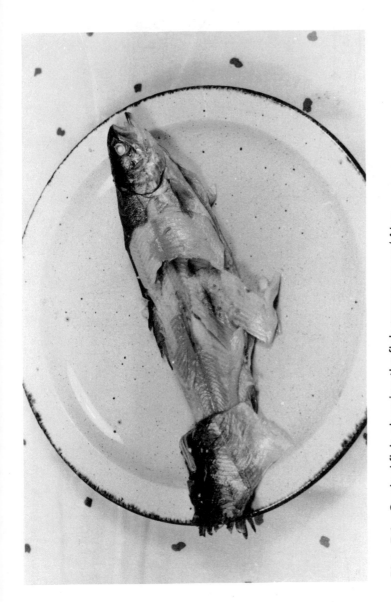

Plate 5.1   Cooked fish, showing the flaky appearance (*Alan Thomas*)

82

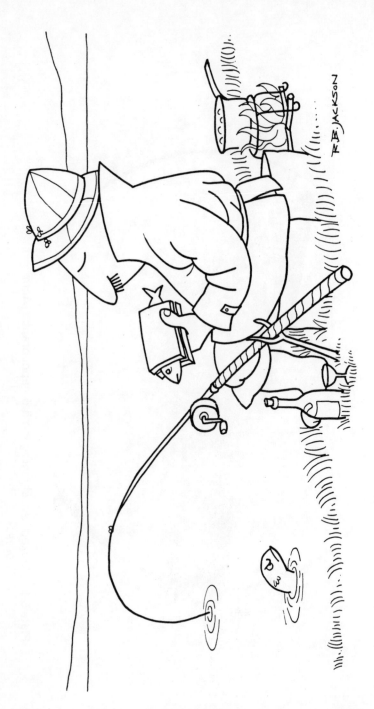

'Fish should be eaten when fresh'

Table 5.6 *Nutritional content of fish, per 100g*

	Energy kJ (kcal)	Protein (g)	Fat (g)	Carbohydrate (g)	Vit. A (µg)	Vit. B₁ (mg)	Vit. B₂ (mg)	Nicotinic acid (mg)	Vit. C (mg)	Vit. D (µg)	Iron (mg)
Cod (raw)	322 (77)	17	0.7	0	0	0.08	0.07	1.7	0	0	0.3
Lemon sole (raw)	343 (82)	17	1.4	0	0	0.09	0.08	3.5	0	0	0.5
Plaice (raw)	386 (92)	18	2.2	0	0	0.30	0.10	3.2	0	0	0.3
Herring (raw)	970 (231)	17	19	0	45	0	0.18	4.1	0	22.5	0.8
Mackerel (raw)	926 (220)	19	16	0	45	0.09	0.35	8.0	0	17.5	1.0
Salmon (raw)	757 (180)	18	12	0	0	0.20	0.15	7.0	0	0	0.7

Source: *Manual of Nutrition* (HMSO, Crown copyright, 8th edn).

84

EXERCISES

1. Describe in simple terms the structure of meat.
2. Why does the composition of meat vary from one cut of meat to another?
3. Suggest the most suitable methods of cooking for (a) neck of lamb, (b) fore-rib of beef.
4. List *five* things that happen to meat when it is cooked.
5. Explain how the process of marinating tenderises meat.
6. Compare briefly the nutritional value of lamb, chicken, liver and herring.
7. What happens to the flesh of game while it is being hung, before cooking?
8. How does the structure of fish differ from that of meat?
9. Suggest suitable methods of cooking for (a) cod, (b) salmon.
10. Which nutrients are present in oily fish but not in white fish?

EGGS, DAIRY PRODUCTS AND FATS

6.1 INTRODUCTION

Some of the commodities discussed in this chapter are of animal origin, others are obtained from plants. They do not possess a common structure, composition or usage, but are grouped together for convenience.

6.2 EGGS

By far the most common type of egg used in catering is the hen's egg, the egg which we are to discuss here. Other eggs that are sometimes used are from ducks, geese and turkeys.

Structure and composition

The hen's egg is made up of a hard porous shell of calcium carbonate which encloses the egg white and egg yolk (see Figure 6.1). There are membranes separating the shell from the white and the white from the yolk; white fibrous proteins, *chalazae*, hold the yolk in place. The composition of the white is quite different from that of the yolk, which explains why some culinary uses of eggs require the use of either yolk or white and others require the whole egg. Table 6.1 shows the main components of the hen's egg.

> **Task 6.1** Using a pair of forceps, a sharp penknife, and scissors, 'peel off' a part of the shell of an egg. This is not as difficult as it sounds! The point of the knife can be used to lever off the shell to reveal the shell membrane at the air sac end. The shell membrane looks like tissue paper and can be cut away to show the egg membrane and the yolk within the

albumen. Cut a large part of the egg shell away and pour out the contents. The chalazae will be visible and the shape of the albumen will vary depending on freshness.

Figure 6.1 *Structure of a hen's egg*

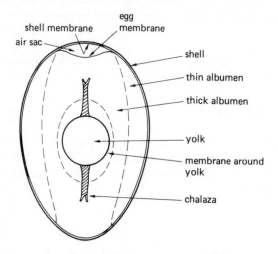

Table 6.1 *Main components of a raw hen's egg*

	g/100g	Notes
Protein	12	More in yolk than in white
Fat	11	Almost all in yolk and containing very high levels of cholesterol
Carbohydrate	0	–
Water	75	–
Vitamins	1	Mainly A, D and riboflavin
Minerals	1	Provides a good source of iron

Storage

The quality of eggs deteriorates during storage in the following ways:

(i)   Water evaporates through the porous shell and is replaced by air. This causes the air sac to increase in size.

(ii) Water from the white moves to the yolk causing the yolk to increase in size and become thinner.

(iii) Thick white is converted to thin white.

(iv) The egg becomes more alkaline, which may affect its culinary properties.

(v) The smell and flavour of the egg change.

In addition to these effects, bacteria may enter through the shell and cause spoilage, eventually leading to the 'bad egg' smell. Since the quality of eggs deteriorates quickly, they should be used immediately or refrigerated, which slows down all of the above processes, and stock rotation should be efficient (see Figure 6.2).

Figure 6.2 *Fresh and stale eggs*

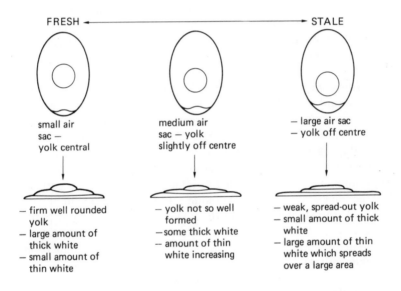

Task 6.2 Take one egg that has been stored for more than two weeks and a fresh egg, preferably laid within the last two days. Place them in a bowl of water and observe. The staler eggs will be more upright or may float because of the larger air space. Break both eggs on to a plate and observe the differences shown in Figure 6.2.

Effect of cooking and uses of eggs

Eggs have many different functions in cooking and are used in a wide variety of dishes. The main aspects of egg cooking depend on the ability of the white and yolk proteins to *denature* and *coagulate* and on the emulsifying properties of *lecithin* (found in the yolk).

(a) *Coagulation* Coagulation of the proteins in eggs gives rise to the *binding* and *thickening* properties of eggs as seen in scrambled eggs, baked custards, cakes, and so on, as well as in boiled, poached and fried eggs, which are dishes in themselves. The white coagulates at about 60°C and the yolk sets over a range from 65°C to 68°C, but in both cases coagulation temperatures are lowered if salt, vinegar or lemon juice is used.

(b) *Foaming* Egg whites are used in meringues, soufflés and some cakes to give a light texture to the finished product. The proteins in the egg white are partially denatured by the mechanical action of beating and trap small bubbles of air to give the characteristic 'foam' structure. In some foams, where denaturation of the proteins is not extensive, the foam may collapse as air escapes, but in others the product is baked into a solid form and retains its shape, for example, in meringues.

(c) *Emulsification* An emulsion is a mixture of at least two liquids which would normally separate if no emulsifying agent were present. Milk, mayonnaise, vinaigrette, margarine and butter are all examples of food emulsions. In the case of mayonnaise, for example, lecithin from the egg yolk enables oil (such as olive oil) and vinegar to mix and remain stable by coating the oil droplets and preventing them from joining together and bringing about separation (see Figure 6.3).

One undesirable effect of cooking eggs is the production of a dark layer of iron sulphide around the yolk in hard-boiled eggs, particularly in eggs that are not fresh. This problem can be reduced or avoided by cooking for the minimum length of time and cooling quickly with cold water.

Figure 6.3   *Lecithin as an emulsifying agent*

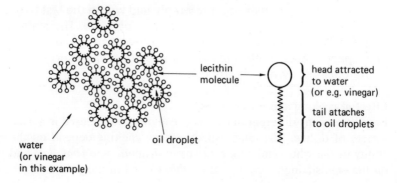

> **Task 6.3** Hard boil two eggs of the same age, cooling one under water immediately and allowing the other to stand. Compare the outside of the yolk of the two eggs.

Nutritional value

Table 6.1 shows that eggs provide useful amounts of protein (of high biological value) and some vitamins and minerals. Iron is the main mineral present in eggs and the vitamins include A, D and riboflavin as well as smaller amounts of other B vitamins.

Although the fat content is only 11 per cent (which equals about 6g in the average egg), it should be pointed out that egg yolk is a very rich source of *cholesterol* (1.26g per 100g).

6.3 MILK

In the UK the milk consumed is usually cow's milk.

Structure and composition

Milk is a white liquid containing water, oil, proteins, salts, lactose, vitamins and minerals. It is an emulsion stabilised by proteins and lipids which coat the oil particles, preventing them from separating out. The exact composition of milk varies according to the breed of cow, the time of year, and the processing the milk undergoes. The average composition of fresh cow's milk is shown in Table 6.2.

Table 6.2 *Composition of fresh cows' milk*

	g/100g
Protein	3.3
Fat	3.8
Carbohydrate	4.7
Water	87.6
Vitamins	1.0
Minerals	1.0

Processing

Most of the milk in the UK is sold in bottles or cartons as whole, liquid milk. However, some is processed to produce evaporated, condensed, dried or skimmed milk. Liquid milk can be obtained in the following ways:

(i)   *Untreated*   This refers to milk taken directly from the cow to the bottle or jug. Any food-poisoning bacteria that are present will not be destroyed during this process.

(ii) *Pasteurised*   This milk has been heat treated to destroy any food-poisoning organisms (see Chapter 12.4).

(iii) *Sterilised*   This type of milk has been treated to destroy *all* micro-organisms and hence greatly extend the shelf life. This category includes traditional sterilised and UHT (ultra high temperature) milk (see Chapter 12, section 12.4).

Heat treatment of the milk has two main disadvantages. It causes some loss of heat-sensitive vitamins such as thiamin and vitamin C and it affects flavour. Up to 30 per cent of thiamin and 50 per cent of vitamin C can be lost during sterilisation of milk. For these reasons it is preferable to minimise heat treatment while ensuring that it is free from food poisoning bacteria.

Homogenisation   is another process used in milk treatment which involves breaking up the fat globules (by passing the milk through a very fine nozzle) to ensure even distribution of the fat throughout the milk and so prevent it separating as a cream layer.

Skimmed milk   has the cream layer removed, which reduces the amount of fat and the vitamins A and D. The reduction in fat makes it more suitable for slimmers and others requiring less animal fat, but it is not suitable for feeding to babies and infants because of the loss of vitamins.

Storage

The storage life of milk depends on the type of processing and heat treatment it has undergone. However, once the container has been opened, the milk should be consumed quickly and refrigerated whenever possible. In the case of untreated and pasteurised milk the process of 'natural souring' takes place during storage because of lactic acid bacteria present in the milk. The bacteria convert lactose, which is present in the milk, into lactic acid, causing an increase in acidity which affects the proteins surrounding the oil droplets in the milk. The proteins may coagulate and the emulsion breaks down, resulting in curdled milk.

Effect of cooking and uses of milk
Milk is used in a variety of dishes to increase nutritional value, appearance and flavour. It can also be used to contribute to the texture of a product and often aids thickening. Examples of dishes in which milk is used are baked custards, creamed soups, sauces, and a variety of puddings. One particular effect of cooking on milk is the coagulation of surface proteins during boiling, which causes a skin to form that traps steam and leads to 'boiling over' of the milk.

Nutritional value
Being the single food for a young animal, milk has a wide variety of nutrients. Although cow's milk does not have the same proportions of these nutrients as human milk, it is nevertheless a good food. It provides useful amounts of protein, calcium, riboflavin and vitamin A, and smaller amounts of iron, vitamin C and vitamin D (see Appendix 2b).

Task 6.4   From the Tables in Appendix 2 calculate for which minerals and vitamins 100g of milk would provide 10 per cent of the daily requirements of an average adult male.

6.4   **YOGHURT**

The production of yoghurt involves the controlled souring of milk by bacteria such as *Lactobacillus bulgaricus* and *Streptococcus thermophilis*. As previously described, the bacteria convert lactose (milk sugar) into lactic acid which causes the milk proteins to coagulate, forming a thicker or more viscous product. The acid produced gives some of the characteristic flavour to yoghurt and has some preservative properties. The most popular commercial yoghurts are those made with low fat milk and with added fruit to give a variety of flavours.

Task 6.5   Make some yoghurt by boiling half a litre of milk, allowing to cool, adding 10ml of natural yoghurt and keeping warm at about 25°C for 24 hours. Describe the changes that must be taking place in the milk during the 24 hours and explain why a warm temperature is required.

6.5 CREAM AND ICE-CREAM

If milk is allowed to stand for a long period, some or all of the fat globules coalesce (join together) and form a layer on the surface called *cream*. Commercially the process is speeded up by *centrifugation* which involves spinning the milk at high speeds to separate the heavier portion from the lighter portion (cream). Cream is classed according to its fat content:

Single cream – minimum of 18 per cent fat – used with fruit, coffee, and so on.
Double cream – minimum of 48 per cent fat – used in cakes and other desserts.
Clotted cream – minimum of 55 per cent fat – used in various desserts and Devon cream teas.

    Whipping cream is also produced, with a fat content of about 35 per cent, to achieve the compromise between cost and the ability to whip (a minimum fat content of 30 per cent is required to enable whipping).

    Ice-cream, whether it is made from vegetable oils (as in the UK), or from milk fat (as in Europe and the USA), is a complex structure containing fat, ice crystals and a sugar solution. These components are combined to form a foam which is stabilised by gelatin or vegetable gums. Ice-cream manufacture is very strictly controlled by law to ensure correct levels of fat, to prevent excessive use of air (used to give the light texture) and to ensure good hygiene.

6.6 CHEESE

Cheese is a food that was originally made from milk that had been produced in *excess* of a community's needs and that could not be preserved. This aspect of cheese manufacture is still of economic importance today, but cheese is also a popular commodity in its own right.

Structure and composition
Cheese is made from milk which has been coagulated and had some or all of the whey (the 'watery' part of milk) removed and has been allowed to ripen. There are many types of cheese and many types of cheese production. The essentials of production are set out below:

(i)   Coagulation of the pasteurised milk is brought about by the addition of lactic acid bacteria or rennet (an enzyme which clots milk) or both.

(ii) The curd (milk solids) is allowed to harden and is separated from the whey which is drained off.

(iii) The curd is pressed, salt is added, and more whey is drained.

(iv) Ripening and maturing take place. This is brought about by:
   (a)   bacteria in the cheese, for example, gruyère and Em-mental,
   (b)   allowing moulds to develop on the surface, for example, camembert and brie,
   (c)   introducing moulds into the cheese, for example, stilton and roquefort.

Table 6.3 shows the variation in composition amongst some cheeses. Note particularly the differences in fat and protein contents.

Table 6.3   *Variation in composition of various types of cheese, per 100g*

Cheese	Energy (kJ) (kcal)	Protein (g)	Fat (g)	Carbohydrate (g)	Water (g)
Camembert	1246 (297)	22.8	23.2	0	47.5
Cheddar	1682 (400)	26.0	33.5	0	37.0
Danish Blue	1471 (350)	23.0	29.2	0	40.5
Edam	1262 (300)	24.4	22.9	0	43.7
Cottage cheese	402 (96)	13.6	4.0	1.4	78.8
Cream cheese	1807 (430)	3.1	47.4	0	45.5

Effects of cooking and uses of cheese

Cheese is used in a variety of dishes such as fondues, omelettes, pizzas and many snacks. It is incorporated into sauces and is also eaten uncooked with bread and biscuits.

When cheese is heated the fat melts and the proteins develop the characteristic 'stringiness' associated with cooked cheese. Stringiness can be reduced by choosing a hard cheese and by avoiding excessive heating.

Nutritional value

Cheese is an excellent source of protein since it is a concentrated form of milk proteins. It also provides large amounts of calcium and is a useful source of vitamin A and riboflavin. Some cheeses contain large proportions of fat (for example, cheddar), but as seen in Table 6.3, this varies considerably from one type of cheese to another.

Task 6.6 Visit a high quality delicatessen shop and make a note of as many cheeses as you can. Next to each name write down how it is ripened.

6.7 BUTTER

Butter is made by removing water from cream until the *liquid* oil-in-water emulsion of cream becomes the *solid* water-in-oil emulsion of butter.

The cream is converted to butter by *churning*, which causes water to be lost and also incorporates small air bubbles into the product which are trapped by denatured proteins from the cream. (This is a similar process to foaming as described in section 6.2.) Prior to churning the cream is usually ripened with lactic acid bacteria.

Butter consists mainly of animal fat, between 80 and 85 per cent, but it also contains water, calcium and vitamins A and D. Table 6.4 shows a comparison of butter and margarine.

6.8 SUET, LARD AND DRIPPING

When an animal is slaughtered the adipose tissue, around the kidneys, for example, becomes solid and can be 'trimmed off' to become *suet*. Suet is usually processed to aid cooking, as in chopped suet, for example, which is used for suet pastry in steak and kidney pudding. Adipose tissue may also be rendered to form *lard*, from pig fat, or *dripping*, from beef or mutton fat.

These fats can be used in cooking for pastry making and frying (in the case of lard), or frying and roasting (in the case of dripping). Lard and dripping both contain 99 per cent fat and are very high in saturated fats.

6.9 MARGARINE

Like butter, margarine is a water-in-oil emulsion. However, it is not manufactured from cream, which is expensive, but from cheaper vegetables oils. The oils used in the UK include groundnut, coconut, palm kernel and palm oil, to which fish and whale oils may be added. The oils are refined and carefully blended to produce a variety of margarines for different functions. The flavour and colour are easily varied, as is the consistency, which needs to be hard for baking and soft for spreading. The process of *hydrogenation* (the addition of hydrogen to an unsaturated fat) is involved to produce fats of the correct consistency for a particular blend. The addition of hydrogen reduces the number of double bonds in the fatty acids causing the melting point to be raised and the softness and plasticity to change to the required levels (see Chapter 2, section 2.10).

One further point regarding the production of margarine is the addition of vitamins A and D in the manufacturing process, which is required by law. Table 6.4 gives a comparison between the composition of butter, margarine and a low fat spread.

Table 6.4   *Comparison of the content of butter, margarine and low fat spreads, per 100g*

	Energy (kJ) (kcal)	Protein (g)	Fat (g)	Carbohydrate (g)	Water (g)
Butter	3041 (724)	0.4	82.0	0	15.4
Margarine	3000 (714)	0.1	81.0	0.1	16.0
Low-fat spread	1506 (359)	0	40.7	0	57.1

It can be seen from the table that the low fat spreads have a much lower energy value when compared with butter and margarine and, as such, are popular with slimmers and other sections of the population. These spreads are not allowed to be referred to as margarine because they exceed the maximum permitted amount of water, which is set at 10 per cent.

Some margarines are made from specific oils such as *sunflower seed oil* and *groundnut oil* and are advertised as 'high in polyunsaturated fats'. They may contain up to 75 per cent unsaturated fatty acids as compared to 51 per cent in other margarines and 28 per cent in butter.

Task 6.7   Construct your own butter versus margarine or low fat spread test. One way of doing this is to use two fats, spread them on crackers and set up a 'triangle test' which involves putting one type of fat on two plates and the other fat on the third. The sampler is asked to pick out the 'odd' one, by tasting blindfolded. Record your results with as many people as possible and decide whether it is easy for people to tell the difference.

6.10   COOKING OILS

Vegetable oils that are available for cooking include the following: corn oil, groundnut oil, soya bean oil, olive oil, sunflower seed oil, cottonseed oil, palm oil, coconut oil and many mixtures of oils.

They are all 100 per cent oil and, as such, represent a high energy source. They often raise the energy value of a fried meal since some oil is absorbed by the food during cooking.

The uses of fats in cooking are discussed in Chapter 2, section 2.10, which explains that fats are used as a heat transfer medium as well as a component of various dishes and salad dressings.

EXERCISES

1. List the ways in which the quality of eggs deteriorates in storage.
2. Describe, with examples, two different functions of eggs in cooking.
3. Distinguish between the two main types of heat treatment used for milk. What is achieved by the two different treatments?
4. Explain briefly how yoghurt is made from milk.
5. Explain how micro-organisms are utilised in the production of (a) gruyère, (b) camembert, and (c) roquefort cheeses.
6. List the three main categories of cream sold in the UK. What legal requirements are stipulated regarding their content?
7. List the main nutrients provided by cheddar cheese.
8. Give examples of ways in which the fatty or adipose tissue of animals is used in cooking (after processing).
9. From what is margarine made? Explain how the process of hydrogenation is involved in margarine manufacture and why vitamins A and D are added to margarine during its production.
10. Choose three of the cooking oils listed in section 6.10 and describe ways in which they are included in the diet.

PLANT FOODS

7.1 INTRODUCTION

Many different plants are used by man to provide food. The part of the plant that is eaten may be the root, bulb, tuber, stem, bud, leaf, flower, fruit or seed. Figure 7.1 gives a few examples of plant foods indicating where they are produced on the plant, using a generalised diagram.

It is difficult to classify plants into satisfactory groups, since the botanical categories are different from the culinary ones. Obvious examples of this are the *tomato*, which is technically a fruit, but is treated as a vegetable, and *rhubarb* which can be classed as a vegetable but is served as a fruit.

In this chapter plant foods have been organised into three groups: cereals, vegetables and fruits.

CEREALS

Cereal grains are the seeds of cultivated grasses. They are probably the most important commodities in the world, forming the bulk of the diet in many underdeveloped countries and having great significance in developed countries, either directly as food for man or indirectly as animal food.

The most important cereals are wheat, rice, maize (corn), oats, rye and barley. In the UK, Europe, North America, Australia and some parts of Asia, wheat is the most significant crop, whereas in most parts of Asia, the Far East, West Africa and some Latin American countries it is replaced by rice and in Latin America and Africa by maize (see Figure 7.2).

Figure 7.1 *Fruits and vegetables come from many parts of a plant*

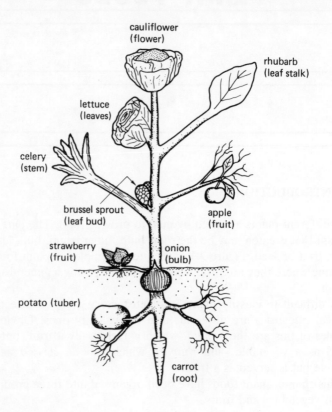

7.2 WHEAT

A grain of wheat consists of a tough fibrous coat which protects the germ or embryo and food reserves found inside (see Figure 7.3).

When the wheat grain germinates, the germ or embryo develops into a new plant using the food reserves in the endosperm, aleurone layer and the germ itself. The bulk of the food reserves are found in the endosperm which contains large amounts of starch as well as protein and B vitamins. The aleurone layer and germ are rich in B vitamins and also contain protein.

Task 7.1 Cut open a single wheat grain with a sharp knife. Observe the powdery starch of the endosperm, the small embryo and the tough, thick outer bran layer.

Figure 7.2 *Important cereal plants*

cereals used for food

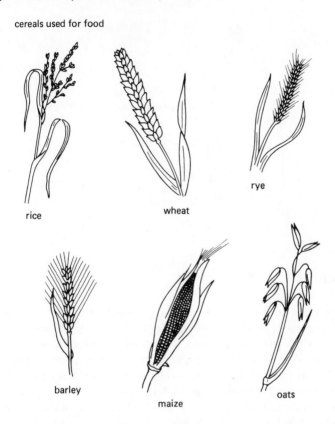

rice   wheat   rye

barley   maize   oats

Different varieties of wheat are produced which have *different* protein contents. The most important protein in wheat is *gluten*, which actually consists of two proteins, glutenin and gliadin. Gluten is important in dough formation and varies from 11 to 15 per cent in hard Canadian and North American wheats to 8 to 10 per cent in the softer English wheats. Durum wheat has a gluten content of between 11 and 13 per cent and is used for the manufacture of spaghetti, macaroni and other pasta.

Task 7.2 Take 50g of several types of flour and mix each type into a ball with a small amount of water. Rinse them one at a time under cold water to wash out the starch until a starch-free gluten ball remains. Compare the gluten content of each type of flour. The gluten balls can then be baked in an oven at approximately 250°C to make a better comparison.

Figure 7.3 *The wheat grain*

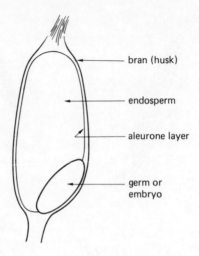

bran (husk)

endosperm

aleurone layer

germ or
embryo

7.3 RICE

The structure of a grain of rice is very similar to that of a grain of
wheat. It consists of a hard outer coat (which is usually removed, as in
polished white rice) surrounding the embryo and food reserves.

Rice grows well in wet, tropical climates and is a very important
crop in many parts of the world, particularly in Asia. Since the milling
process removes the bran and germ, large amounts of thiamin are lost
(along with dietary fibre) and this can lead to the deficiency disease
beri-beri (see Chapter 3, section 3.4). In fact beri-beri is not
uncommon in many parts of Asia, but its occurrence could be
reduced if rice was *parboiled* (soaked and steamed before milling)
because much of the thiamin is then retained in the endosperm.

Brown rice consists of the whole rice grain from which only the
outermost layer of bran has been removed.

7.4 MAIZE

Maize or corn has quite a different structure to the previous two
cereals. It can be eaten as corn-on-the-cob or used to produce corn
oil, corn starch, corn syrup and breakfast cereals such as cornflakes.
Maize is considered to be slightly less nutritious than other cereals
because it has fewer B vitamins and possesses a chemical which
affects calcium and iron absorption in the intestine.

7.5 OATS, RYE AND BARLEY

Oat grains contain more protein and fat than other cereal grains and are used extensively for animal and human consumption. The oat grains are often 'rolled' into flakes and used to produce porridge, muesli, and certain biscuits.

Rye is a cereal with a low gluten content which grows on poor soils. It can be milled like wheat and is often combined with wheat flour to produce bread, as well as being used in the manufacture of whisky.

Barley is another resilient cereal which is used in brewing and distilling as well as for animal foods. The bran can be removed to produce 'pearl barley' which is used in some soups and stews.

A comparison of the nutritional content of cereals is given in Table 7.1.

Table 7.1 *Nutritional content of various cereals, per 100g*

	Protein	Fat	Carbohydrate	Vitamins & Minerals	Water	Fibre
	(g)	(g)	(g)	(g)	(g)	(g)
Wheat	12	2	70	2	12	2
Maize	11	4	69	2	12	2
Rice	7	1	77	2	12	1
Oats	11	9	66	2	10	2
Barley	8	1	75	2	12	2
Rye	8	2	72	2	15	1

7.6 FLOUR

Most of the cereals that have been considered in this chapter are processed in order to make them more palatable. Perhaps the most obvious example of this in the western world is the conversion of wheat into flour and then bread. The manufacture of flour from wheat is a detailed process and includes the following stages:

(i) **Cleaning** the wheat grains.
(ii) **Conditioning** – this produces the correct moisture level in the grain for 'breaking' it.
(iii) **Breaking** – a series of 'break rollers' are used with successively smaller gaps to enable the endosperm to be separated from the bran with increasing efficiency (see Figure 7.4).

Figure 7.4   *Break rollers*

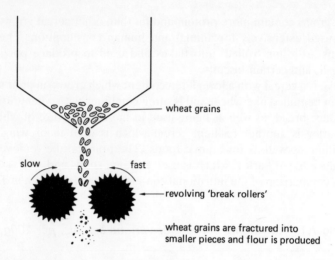

wheat grains

slow   fast

revolving 'break rollers'

wheat grains are fractured into
smaller pieces and flour is produced

There are a series of break rollers with smaller
'teeth' to reduce the particles into finer flour

(iv)   **Reduction** – smooth rollers reduce the particles to a fine flour.

Extraction rate

Wheat is processed into various types of flour which are graded
according to how much of the grain they contain. The main types of
flour are explained in Table 7.2.

In flours of low extraction rate there is a requirement by law to
enrich them with thiamin, nicotinic acid, iron and calcium. These
vitamins and minerals are lost during the milling process as the bran
and germ are removed.

Table 7.2   *Main types of flour*

Flour	Parts of grain included	Extraction rate (%)
Wholemeal	Whole grain – endosperm, germ and bran	100
Wheatmeal	Endosperm, germ and some bran (outer bran layers are removed)	80–95
Wheatgerm	Endosperm and germ, to which extra germ has been added	85
White	Endosperm (germ and bran are removed)	72–75
Patent	Endosperm	40–45

Effect of cooking and uses of flour

The two main components of flour that are affected by cooking and give flour its properties are *starch* and *gluten*. The effects of cooking on starch have been described in Chapter 2, section 2.5, and explain the role of flour in sauces, cream soups, gravies and some puddings. The coagulation of gluten during cooking is another important property of flour and indeed flours are selected for their gluten content. For example, in breadmaking a high gluten content is required to give a strong elastic network capable of holding the gas produced by yeast which gives bread its light structure.

Conversely, in products which do not require gluten development, such as light cakes, shortcrust pastry and biscuits, flour with a lower gluten content is desirable. Table 7.3 shows some of the uses of different types of flour.

Table 7.3   *Some uses of the main types of flour*

Flour		Uses
Wholemeal		Bread, biscuits
Wheatmeal		Bread, biscuits
White:	strong	Bread, puddings, pastries
	soft	Light cakes and biscuits
	self-raising	Some cakes, scones which require a raising agent
	starch reduced	Bread with reduced energy value
	patent	Biscuits, shortbreads, cakes
	durum	Pasta – such as spaghetti, macaroni, noodles

Task 7.3   Compare the qualities of wheat flour, rice flour, arrowroot and cornflour by dissolving 5g of each in 100ml of water and heating. The temperatures at which each thickens can be recorded, as can the resulting degree of thickness and clarity. Relate their properties to functions in cooking.

VEGETABLES

A wide variety of plant structures are eaten and classed as vegetables. Figure 7.1 shows from which part of the plant some vegetables originate and these can be divided into groups for description. The groups are leafy vegetables, underground stems (tubers), root vegetables and pulse vegetables.

7.7 LEAFY VEGETABLES

This group includes cabbage, lettuce, spinach and sprouts (although sprouts are, in fact, buds found between the stem and leaf stalks). These vegetables contain large amounts of fibre as well as vitamin C, carotene (for production of vitamin A) and folic acid. When fresh, leafy vegetables have a firm, crisp texture which is due mainly to the *turgor* of their cells. Turgor refers to the pressure exerted on the cell membrane and cell wall by the water solution inside a cell, and enables vegetables, which contain up to 94 per cent water, to have a firm structure. As the vegetable becomes less fresh, the cell membrane is affected, water is lost from the cells and 'wilting' occurs. This is particularly important in green, leafy vegetables (see Figure 7.5).

Figure 7.5 *Turgor and wilting*

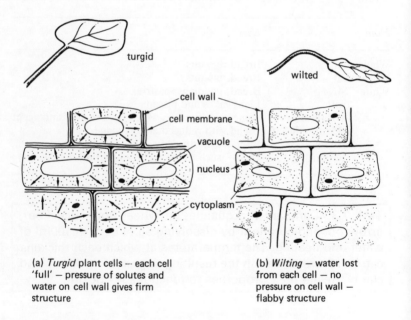

(a) *Turgid* plant cells — each cell 'full' — pressure of solutes and water on cell wall gives firm structure

(b) *Wilting* — water lost from each cell — no pressure on cell wall — flabby structure

7.8 UNDERGROUND STEMS (TUBERS)

Potatoes, Jerusalem artichokes, cassava and yam are examples of tubers. In the UK, as in other parts of Europe and the USA, potatoes are a very important vegetable, forming a significant part of the diet, in one form or another, for many people. Potatoes are rich in starch, therefore providing energy, and also provide the main source of vitamin C in the UK diet, as well as contributing useful quantities of B vitamins, iron and dietary fibre.

Effect of cooking on potatoes
Potatoes need to be cooked in order to become digestible (this applies to many other vegetables as well). The effect of boiling, for example, is to soften the cell walls in the vegetable and to allow water to be absorbed by the starch granules which swell and break. The result is a softer, more digestible product (see Figure 7.6). As an example of how nutrients are lost during the cooking of vegetables, potatoes lose vitamin C quite easily during dry and moist cooking, since vitamin C is heat sensitive, water soluble and oxidises in the air. Table 7.4 shows the amounts of vitamin C in various types of potato.

Figure 7.6   *The cooking of potato, in diagrammatic form*

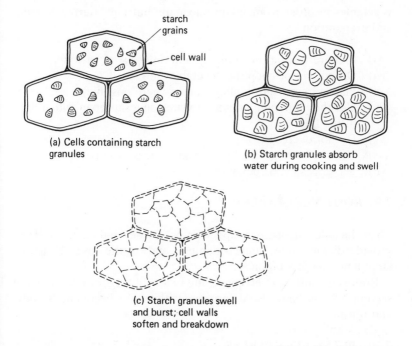

(a) Cells containing starch granules

(b) Starch granules absorb water during cooking and swell

(c) Starch granules swell and burst; cell walls soften and breakdown

Task 7.4   Study Table 7.4 and calculate the percentage loss of vitamin C when old potatoes are (a) stored for 6 months, (b) boiled after 1 month of storage.

Table 7.4 *The vitamin C content of various types of potato, per 100g*

Potato		Vitamin C (mg)
Old,	raw, fresh	30
	raw, 1–3 months storage	20
	raw, 6–7 months storage	10
	boiled, 1–3 months storage	12
	baked, 1–3 months storage	14
	roast, 1–3 months storage	14
	chips, 1–3 months storage	14
New,	raw, fresh	30
	boiled	18
	canned	17

The following is a list of procedures which can be applied to most vegetables in order to maintain maximum nutrients during cooking and preparation:

(i) Prepare just before cooking, and do not soak in water.

(ii) Do not cut or chop the vegetables too small.

(iii) Place directly into boiling water (where possible).

(iv) Use the minimum amount of water, in a saucepan with a tight fitting lid.

(v) Do not overcook.

(vi) Use the boiling liquid for stocks, sauces or gravies.

(vii) Serve as soon as possible.

7.9 ROOT VEGETABLES

These include carrots, parsnips, turnips, swedes and beetroot. They provide dietary fibre, some vitamin C and, in the case of carrots, large amounts of vitamin A.

Root vegetables lose crispness due to loss of turgor as described in section 7.7, and may also deteriorate with age by becoming 'woody' and fibrous.

7.10 PULSE VEGETABLES

Pulses are the seeds of vegetables such as beans, lentils and peas, which are classed as leguminous plants. In the West they are often used before they are mature or dry, whereas in the East they are allowed to mature and may be the staple diet, as in countries such as India and China.

Pulses have a high nutritional value since they are a good energy source, contain significant quantities of protein, are high in dietary fibre and provide vitamins A and B as well as calcium and iron. The composition of some pulses is shown in Table 7.5.

Dried pulses require soaking prior to cooking and make very nutritious soups and stews.

Soya beans, which have been used in the East in the same way as the other pulses, as described above, are now being used extensively in the West to produce *textured vegetable protein (TVP)*. The manufacturing process is complex but involves removing the fat from the beans and producing a dough which is then passed through fine nozzles or 'spinerettes', under pressure. The result is an expanded fibrous material which can be made into mince-like pieces or chunks, that with some final processing resemble meat. TVP is a very palatable foodstuff which can be used as a meat extender in dishes such as Shepherd's pie, spaghetti bolognese and others, or as a meat substitute. In both cases food costs can be greatly reduced.

Task 7.5 Choose a recipe for one of the dishes described above, and prepare the dish in four different ways:

(a) using the stated quantity of minced beef,
(b) substituting 25 per cent of minced beef with TVP,
(c) substituting 50 per cent of minced beef with TVP,
(d) substituting all of the minced beef with TVP.

Present the dishes to a group of people, unlabelled, and make quality judgements for all of them. Are dishes (b) and (c) easy to pick out or unpalatable? Estimate the cost savings that could be made if 50 portions of the dish had a 50 per cent substitution of TVP.

7.11 SUGAR

Sugar, which usually refers to the disaccharide *sucrose* is a commodity which is produced from two different plants: sugar-cane and sugar-beet. It is therefore difficult to group it with any of the other vegetable foods.

Sugar-cane, grown in tropical climates, is a type of grass, whereas sugar-beet, which can be grown in temperate climates such as the

Table 7.5 Composition of some pulse vegetables, per 100g

	Energy (kJ) (kcal)	Protein (g)	Fat (g)	Carbohydrate (g)	Vit. A (µg)	Vit. B_1 (mg)	Vit. B_2 (mg)	Nicotinic acid (mg)	Vit. C (mg)	Vit. D (µg)	Dietary fibre (g)
Beans, haricot, dry	1151 (274)	21.4	1.6	45.5	0	0.45	0.13	2.5	0	0	25.4
" boiled	396 (94)	6.6	0.5	16.6	0	0	0	0	0	0	7.4
Lentils, dry	1293 (307)	23.8	1.0	53.2	0	0.5	0.2	2.0	0	0	11.7
boiled	420 (100)	7.6	0.5	17.0	0	0.1	0.04	0.4	0	0	3.7
Peas, dry	283 (67)	5.8	0.4	10.6	0	0.32	0.15	2.5	25	0	5.2
boiled	223 (53)	5.0	0.4	7.7	0	0.25	0.11	1.5	15	0	5.2

UK, resembles a root vegetable. The cane and the beet contain just below 20 per cent sucrose and undergo detailed processing to produce refined sugar. The uses of sugar in catering are discussed in Chapter 2, section 2.5.

7.12 STORAGE OF VEGETABLES

Vegetables need to be stored carefully to avoid fungal deterioration (see Chapter 10, section 10.3) and wilting. The temperature should be a few degrees above freezing point, that is about 5°C and a dark, clean place is most suitable. To reduce wilting the air should not be too dry, since water will evaporate quickly and the vegetables will become soft and flabby.

FRUITS AND NUTS

Biologically, a *fruit* is the mature ovary of a flowering plant, containing seeds, and *nuts* are dry fruits (as are cereals and leguminous pods such as the pea). However, the culinary definition of fruits usually refers to the fleshy true and false fruits.

7.13 FRUITS

Many types of fruit are used in catering and Table 7.6 outlines some examples.

Table 7.6 *Main types of fruit*

Type	Example	Main uses
Berries	Blackberries, raspberries, gooseberries, cranberries	Jams, jellies, pie fillings
Citrus	Oranges, tangerines, lemons, grapefruit	Breakfast and dessert fruit, jams and jellies
Drupes	Apricots, cherries, peaches, plums	Dessert fruit, jams, jellies
Melons	Watermelon, honeydew, cantaloupe	Dessert fruit, hors d'oeuvres
Pomes	Apples, pears	Dessert fruit, jams, jellies, pie fillings
Tropical/ Subtropical	Banana, avocado, figs, dates, pineapple	Desserts and main courses

Source: G. V. Robins, *Food Science in Catering* (Heinemann).

Like most vegetables, fruits have a very high proportion of water and contain very little protein or fat. They are useful providers of dietary fibre, vitamin A and vitamin C, and contain about 10 per cent carbohydrate. Unlike vegetables, the carbohydrate in ripe fruit is sugar in the forms of glucose and fructose, as opposed to starch. The effect of cooking on fruit is similar to the effect on vegetables, in that the cell walls become softened with heating, making the fruit much softer and very easily digested. To a certain extent this softening occurs during the *ripening* process of fruit, which is why fruits are consumed longer after harvesting than vegetables. (As described in section 7.9, vegetables become tougher and more woody with age.) During ripening the cell walls change chemically and, accompanied by the conversion of starch into sugars, this causes the fruit to become softer and sweeter.

7.14 NUTS

Nuts that are in common use include almonds, brazils, walnuts, hazelnuts, chestnuts, peanuts (which are not true nuts) and coconuts.

Nuts are a good source of protein and energy, most of the energy being provided by fats, and they also contain useful amounts of B vitamins, iron and calcium. Nuts are high in dietary fibre (see Table 7.7).

In a diet that excludes food of animal origin, such as that undertaken by vegetarians, nuts can be very useful in the provision of protein and other nutrients.

7.15 STORAGE OF FRUIT

Fruit should be stored under similar conditions to vegetables, that is cool, dark, but not too dry. However, conditions must be even more strictly monitored to bring about controlled ripening. Normal temperatures are about 5°C, but some fruit, such as bananas, require much higher temperatures of about 13°C. Ventilation is also critical to ensure that moisture levels and carbon dioxide levels (which affect ripening) can be controlled. In some cases other gases such as ethylene are used to aid ripening.

Task 7.6 Visit a vegetarian restaurant and study the menu. Write down the ways in which balanced meals have been created without the use of meat. Which are the most commonly used plant foods?

enttarious nuts, per 100g

	Energy (kJ) (kcal)	Protein (g)	Fat (g)	Carbohydrate (g)	Vit. A (µg)	Vit. B_1 (mg)	Vit. B_2 (g)	Nicotinic acid (g)	Vit. C (g)	Vit. D (µg)	Dietary fibre (g)
Almonds	2336 (556)	16.9	53.5	4.3	0	0.24	0.92	2.0	0	0	14.3
Brazil nuts	2545 (606)	12.0	61.5	4.1	0	1.0	0.12	1.6	0	0	2.21
Peanuts, fresh	2364 (563)	24.3	49.0	8.6	0	0.9	0.10	16	0	0	4.5
Walnuts	2166 (516)	10.6	51.5	5.0	0	0.3	0.13	1.0	0	0	2.0

111

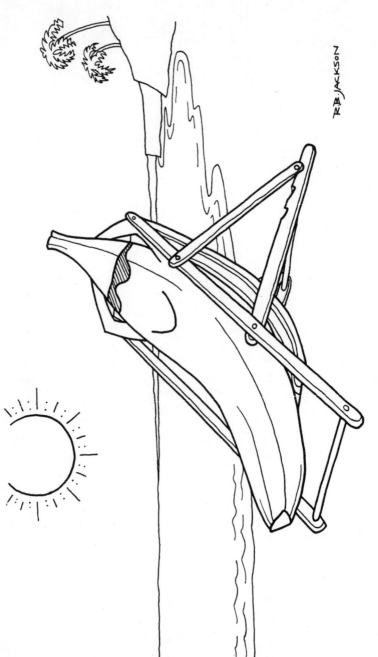

'. . . bananas require much higher temperatures'

R.B. JACKSON

EXERCISES

1. List the main types of cereal grown for man's consumption or animal feed.
2. Describe the structure of a wheat grain, and explain where the various nutrients are contained.
3. Explain why brown 'unpolished' rice is better nutritionally than white 'polished' rice.
4. Explain what is meant by 'extraction rate' and give the extraction rates of four different types of flour.
5. Make a list of points that are important in order to retain the maximum amount of vitamin C when preparing and cooking potatoes.
6. What are pulse vegetables? Explain why pulse vegetables are excellent foods to include in the diet.
7. Explain briefly how TVP is made. What uses are there for TVP in mass catering?
8. Describe the ideal conditions for the storage of vegetables.
9. What is the relationship between turgor, crispness and wilting in fruits and vegetables? Describe the effect cooking has on the texture of fruits and vegetables.
10. Bearing in mind that a vegan will base his/her diet on the types of food described in this chapter, which foods would you suggest were included in his/her diet to ensure a satisfactory protein intake? Can you suggest any meals that would utilise these foods?

PART III

COOKING OF FOOD

HEAT TRANSFER AND
METHODS OF COOKING

8.1 INTRODUCTION

There are three main reasons for cooking food:

(i)   to improve its **digestibility**, that is, to make it easier to eat, break down and absorb,

(ii)   to increase its **palatability**, which means to make it more attractive by improving the taste, smell and colour, and

(iii)   to make it **safe** (or safer) to eat, in relation to food poisoning and food spoilage micro-organisms (see Chapters 9 and 10).

Cooking food requires the transfer of heat to the food or the generation of heat within the food, both of which can be achieved in many ways. In fact, most of the common cooking methods, such as boiling, frying, and roasting, involve more than one of the types of heat transfer which are *conduction, convection* and *radiation*.

In conduction and convection, heat transfer is *indirect*, since it is transferred by a solid, air or a liquid, whereas in radiation (infra-red or microwave) heat transfer is *direct*, requiring no medium for travel.

8.2 CONDUCTION

This is the process by which heat energy flows through an object from a high temperature to a lower temperature. For example, if a cold aluminium saucepan is placed on a hotplate or gas ring, the base of the pan heats up and heat travels to the inner surface of the pan by conduction. The heat is then transferred to the food inside the saucepan (see Figure 8.1).

Different materials have different rates of conduction and are therefore suitable for different functions in catering. Metals are

Figure 8.1 *Conduction through the base of a saucepan*

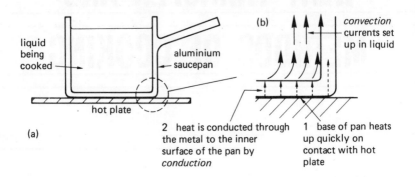

usually good conductors and are used for the manufacture of saucepans, large pots, roasting and baking trays, boilers, and kettles. Where the transfer of heat needs to be slow, as with the linings to ovens and refrigerators, gloves, handles, stirrers and spatulas, poor conductors are required such as air, cloth, wood, rubber and plastic. Table 8.1 shows some good and poor conductors of heat.

Table 8.1 *Conductors and insulators in catering*

	Material	*Uses*
Good conductors	Silver	Expensive. Uses normally involve presentation of food.
	Copper	Pans, pots and kettles. Saucepans often lined with tin (copper pans may be unlined, lined with tin or even lined with silver as in flambé cookery)
	Aluminium	Pans, pots and kettles
	Iron	Fritures, frying pans, baking sheets.
Poor conductors (insulators)	Plastic	Handles, control knobs
	Wood	Handles, trivets, etc. Use is severely restricted now because of fire and hygiene hazards
	Air	Insulating layer in refrigerators and ovens

The choice of metal used for saucepans and other equipment is not just governed by conduction rate, however. The cost, weight and durability of the metal are also important, and lead to the selection of aluminium and copper pans in most cases.

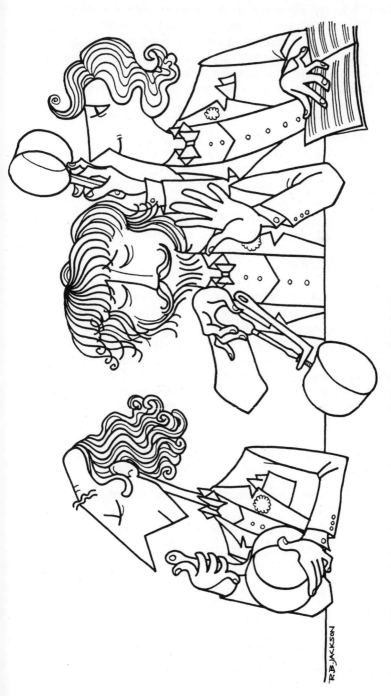

' . . . usually good conductors and are used for the manufacture of saucepans . . .'

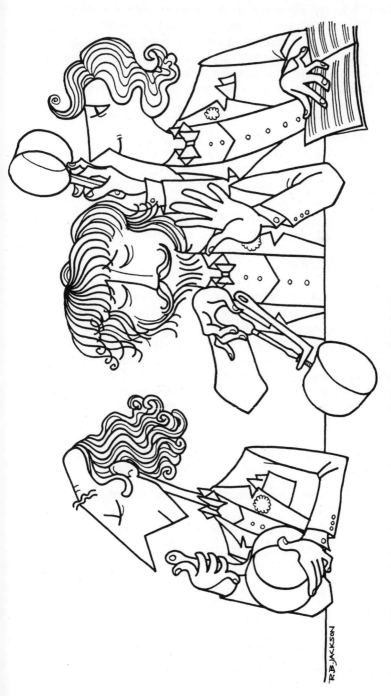

Task 8.1 By referring to a catering theory textbook, or visiting a restaurant kitchen, make a list of the different types of pan used in a restaurant kitchen. Next to each one state which metal(s) is/are used, and explain what the pan is used for, and how the type of metal is suited to its use. Compare the approximate costs for one type of pan if different metals can be used.

Conduction is the main type of heat transfer in two types of cooking: *griddling* and *shallow frying*. However, it is also involved in the transfer of heat to the container in boiling, poaching and stewing, as well as being responsible for the penetration of heat in solid foods. For example, although heat transfer to a roasting chicken is mainly by convection and radiation, heat travels from the outside of the chicken to the inside by conduction.

8.3 CONVECTION

This is the process by which heat energy flows in a fluid (a gas or a liquid), due to temperature differences in it. For example, in a pan of water, if heat is applied to the base of the pan, water at the bottom of the pan expands and becomes *less dense* (that is it has a larger volume but the same mass), causing it to rise to the surface. Cold surface water is displaced and falls, until it reaches the bottom of the pan and is itself heated, causing it to rise and become part of the convection currents that are set up in the liquid. In this way heat energy travels through a fluid and can be transferred to the surface of food, for example in the poaching or boiling of an egg. Convection, as seen in Figure 8.2, is responsible for heat transfer in boiling and poaching.

Figure 8.2 *Heat transfer during the poaching of an egg*

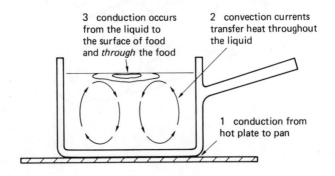

In the same way, convection is the main method of heating in stewing and braising (which involve convection currents in water), steaming (in water vapour), roasting and baking (in air) and deep frying (in oil).

Task 8.2 Observe the convection currents set up in water when it is heated in a glass container, by holding a piece of white card behind the cooking vessel.

8.4 RADIATION

Radiation is the transfer of heat energy from one place to another by electromagnetic waves. The spectrum of electromagnetic waves is shown in Figure 8.3 and includes X-rays, ultra-violet light, visible light, infra-red, microwaves and radio waves.

Figure 8.3 *The electromagnetic spectrum*

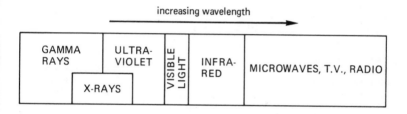

The two types of radiation applicable to catering are infra-red radiation and microwave radiation:

(i) Infra-red radiation
Infra-red rays are produced by grills (and salamanders), electric ovens (in which about 40 per cent of the heat is radiation), toasters and barbecues. The food needs to be near the heat source and is heated directly when infra-red rays are absorbed. It is a fast and efficient method of heat transfer and should be used with 'thin' foods, since the surface of the food heats up quickly but conduction of heat to the centre is slow.

(ii) Microwave radiation
The major difference between microwave cooking and conventional cooking is that *heat is generated within the food itself* in microwave cooking. Microwaves, as can be seen from Figure 8.3, are similar to infra-red and radiowaves. They are produced by converting electrical

energy into radiation, which occurs in the *magnetron* of a microwave oven. Like other radiations, microwaves may be absorbed, transmitted or reflected by different substances; they are absorbed, for example, by food. In particular, the water in food is a good absorber of microwaves. When microwaves are absorbed, the energy is converted into the vibration of molecules in food, leading to the production of heat, which cooks the food (see Figure 8.4).

Metals reflect microwaves and cannot be used in this type of oven, whereas glass, china and some plastics transmit microwaves and are ideal containers.

Unlike conventional methods of heat transfer, microwaves bring about rapid cooking and do not rely on conduction within the food itself, unless the food is particularly 'thick' (microwaves penetrate about 4 cm into the food). It is not true that microwaves cook from the inside out. Because of the speed of cooking, the surface of food does not turn brown as in conventional cooking, although some microwave ovens achieve 'browning' with additional radiation.

Figure 8.4 *The microwave oven*

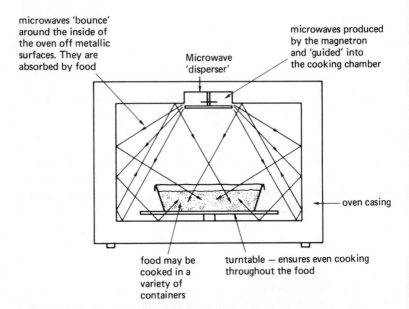

Microwave ovens are useful for defrosting and reheating foods, and are being used increasingly for many dishes originally prepared conventionally.

Task 8.3   Compare the speed of cooking achieved by microwaves and a conventional method, by noting the time it takes
for a set volume of water to boil in identical cooking vessels,
for example, pyrex beakers/dishes or the time it takes for
identical-sized potatoes to cook.

8.5   TYPES OF COOKING

The previous sections have covered the scientific aspects of heat
transfer. It is now necessary to relate heat transfer to the common
cooking methods and to discuss how food is cooked in each case. The
common methods of cooking can be divided into two groups: moist
methods and dry methods:

(i)   **Moist methods** – these include boiling, poaching, steaming,
braising and shallow poaching.
(ii) **Dry methods** – these include grilling, roasting, pot roasting,
baking, shallow frying and deep frying.

8.6   BOILING AND POACHING

These two methods involve cooking in a liquid containing water. In
the case of boiling, the temperature is 100°C, whereas in poaching
lower temperatures of between 75° and 93°C are used, when 'simme-
ring' takes place. Poaching enables delicate foods such as white fish
or eggs to be cooked without being broken up by vigorous action in
the boiling water.

In both cases the minimum amount of water should be used to
prevent dilution of flavour and reduction of nutritional value unless
the liquid itself is required, as in soups or stocks. The nutrients most
likely to be lost are the vitamins B and C, although in the production
of soups and stews, which involves boiling, the nutrients lost from
meat or vegetables are retained in the water.

One consideration to be made when boiling or poaching is whether
to add the ingredients to cold or hot water. Some of the advantages of
both are given in Table 8.2

Task 8.4   After studying Table 8.2 make a list of foods that
should be cooked by being placed directly into hot water and
those that are best cooked from cold.

Table 8.2 *Advantages of cooking from cold or in hot water*

Advantages of placing ingredients directly into hot water and cooking	Advantages of placing ingredients into cold water and heating
1. The nutritional value of the food remains high since fewer water soluble vitamins are lost 2. There is less loss of colour particularly with green vegetables 3. Foods coagulate quicker and retain shape. This is important with eggs and meat 4. Cooking time is reduced 5. There is less chance of burning, for example, with starch thickened foods	1. Impurities (which form a scum and discolour the food(can be removed as the food cooks, giving maximum clarity 2. It is safer than dealing with boiling water since hot splashes can be avoided

Plunging foods, particularly vegetables, into hot water for a very short period of time is called *blanching* and is useful because it inactivates enzymes that break down the food or cause colour changes.

Since the temperature of boiling is quite low in comparison to roasting, baking and grilling, the coagulation of protein, which occurs in meat, for example, is less extensive than at higher temperatures. Boiling or stewing is therefore a good method of cooking less expensive meats.

Examples of dishes or foods that are boiled or poached are: stocks, soups, stews, less expensive cuts of meat and poultry, fish, shellfish, vegetables, jams, sugar products, eggs, rice and pasta.

Boiling and poaching involve conduction through the container, convection in the cooking medium and conduction through the food.

8.7 STEAMING

Food can be cooked using steam at atmospheric pressure (see Plate 8.1) in which case temperatures between 100° and 103°C are likely, or at high pressure (70–105 kN/m or 10–15 psi – pounds per square inch), in which case the temperature can rise to 121°C. (kN/m is a metric unit of pressure – kiloNewtons per metre.) In both cases, cooking occurs more quickly than in boiling and there is a reduction in nutrient loss; less water is used which also reduces nutrient loss.

This method of cooking is applicable to vegetables and some puddings, such as steamed sponge pudding, Christmas pudding and

Plate 8.1   A steam-boiling pan (*Zanussi: CLV Systems Ltd*)

steak and kidney pudding. Meats are generally not steamed because of colour loss which makes them look less attractive. But since there is good nutrient retention, steaming is often used in hospital and school catering.

Heat transfer is by convection of steam and conduction through the food.

8.8 BRAISING AND SHALLOW POACHING

Braising and shallow poaching involve cooking food in a small amount of liquid in a covered container in an oven. The temperatures used are usually between 175°C and 200°C and cooking times vary depending on the type of food. Casseroles and hotpots are cooked in a similar way but contain slightly more liquid and may be uncovered for colour development of the food. However, unlike braised dishes, they are served in the container.

In all cases heat transfer *to* the container involves convection, radiation and conduction, while heat transfer *in* the container is by convection. Cooking with the lid on traps steam which also aids cooking by convection.

Foods cooked in this way include fish, less expensive cuts of meat, offal and vegetables.

8.9 GRILLING

Grilling is a dry, fast, high temperature method of cooking. The heat source may be below the food as in the over-heat grills or above the food as in the under-heat grills or salamanders.

The high temperatures, which may be between 150°C and 210°C on the surface of the food, mean that only thin, tender foods can be grilled satisfactorily. These include fish and tender cuts of meat, poultry and game.

The method of heat transfer is mainly infra-red radiation, but some conduction from the metal grill bars and some convection take place.

8.10 ROASTING AND POT ROASTING

Oven roasting is the cooking of food in dry heat with fat or oil present. The temperatures of roasting vary up to about 240°C, but it would appear that the higher temperatures produce a drier, tougher product due to the greater shrinkage and loss of juices.

The high temperatures of roasting are also responsible for the loss of heat sensitive vitamins.

Heat transfer in roasting is mainly through convection, although radiation plays a significant role, particularly in electric ovens. Conduction from the container to the base of the food which could cause burning is avoided if the food is raised, for example on a bed of vegetables.

Spit roasting is similar to oven roasting but more radiation takes place and heating is less controlled.

Pot roasting is quite different, however, since it occurs in a closed container, which traps steam rather like braising.

Foods suitable for roasting include the better cuts of meat, poultry and game and vegetables, particularly potatoes.

Task 8.5 Obtain a range of meats such as stewing beef, rump steak, pork steak, leg of lamb, and weigh similar portion sizes accurately. Roast them in a tray in an oven at 180°C for 30 minutes. Re-weigh the pieces of meat and calculate for each the percentage weight loss due to roasting:

$$\frac{\text{Weight loss}}{\text{Original weight}} \times 100 = \text{Percentage weight loss}$$

Which type of meat shrank most during roasting?
Variations can be made to this experiment by sealing the meat, by including fish and poultry or by comparing weight loss at different roasting temperatures.

8.11 BAKING

Baking is similar to roasting in that it occurs in an oven with dry heat; however, the food is not cooked in fat, but steam may be produced, by the food itself, and modify the cooking.

Flour products form the bulk of foods that are baked.

8.12 SHALLOW FRYING

Shallow frying, which includes griddling, is a dry method of cooking where thin foods are cooked in a very small amount of fat (sometimes provided by the food itself). The temperatures used may be as low as 95°C, are usually between 150°C and 175°C, but are in some cases as high as 195°C.

One important aspect of shallow frying is the development of colour and flavour in the food, which may be enhanced by using a high quality fat, such as butter.

Shallow frying is a quick method of cooking and is suitable for tender foods such as meat, poultry, fish, shellfish, eggs and fruit.

The amount of fat used is very small, which means that food is in contact with the pan or plate, and conduction is therefore the method of heat transfer.

8.13   DEEP FRYING

This is the immersion of food into hot oil and is a quick, dry method of cooking. High temperatures are often used, up to 195°C, and the food cooks rapidly because there is uniform heating over the whole surface. The average temperatures are between 165°C, which would be suitable for the blanching of French fried potatoes, and 185°C, which would be used to brown French fried potatoes. Care must be taken when deep frying because of the high temperature of the fat, the possibility of splashing, and the risk of rapid water vaporisation when large quantities of watery foods are added. The fat should be changed regularly and should not be used above its smoke point, which is reduced with continuous usage.

Deep frying increases the energy of food since some fat is absorbed during the cooking process. It is a suitable method of cooking for potatoes, other vegetables, fish and white meats.

Convection currents are set up in the oil, which cause conduction to heat the food, in deep frying.

8.14   CHANGES DURING COOKING

It would be impossible to list all the changes that occur during cooking. However, there are three groups of changes that are of interest: structural changes, changes in appearance (colour, flavour and smell), and changes in nutritional value. Some of the more obvious changes brought about during cooking are shown in this section.

(i)   Structural changes

As well as the changes that occur during the preparation of food, such as foaming, and the formation of emulsions, the heat during cooking alters the structure of food quite significantly. Table 8.3 describes some changes to structure.

Plate 8.2(a) A forced air convection oven (*Zanussi: CLV Systems Ltd*)

Plate 8.2(b)   Modular cooking tops (*Zanussi CLV Systems Ltd*)

Plate 8.2(c)   Pressure steamers (*Zanussi CLV Systems Ltd*)

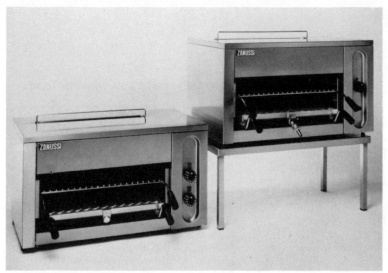

Plate 8.2(d)   Salamander grills (*Zanussi CLV Systems Ltd*)

Table 8.3   *Some structural changes in food brought about by cooking*

Structural change	Examples
Cells soften and separate	Fruits and vegetables
Gelatinisation and gelation take place	Fruits, vegetables and cereals
Thickening due to pectin occurs	Fruits, jams and jellies
Crystallisation and formation of non-crystalline confectionery occur	Sugar
Proteins denature and coagulate	Meat, fish, poultry, cheese, eggs and milk
Collagen (connective tissue protein) melts	Meat, poultry and fish

(ii)   **Changes in aesthetic qualities**
As food is cooked the colour changes, and depending on the skill of the cook, the taste and smell of the food improve (see Table 8.4).

(iii)   **Nutritional changes**
The value of proteins does not usually deteriorate when denaturation and coagulation take place; but other nutrients, particularly vitamins and minerals are affected by cooking (see Table 8.5).

Table 8.4 *Changes in appearance, taste and smell of food*

Change	Example
Browning (Maillard reaction)	The surface of meat, bread and many other foods
Browning (caramelisation)	Sugar when heated in small amounts of water is converted into caramel which is brown
Pigment changes	Various pigments in fruits and vegetables alter as a result of cooking, e.g., green peas become a dull olive green in normal cooking. Meat pigments are also affected by heat
Flavour/aroma	Cooking involves a complex set of chemical changes which involves the production of new substances that stimulate the taste and smell senses of the body

Table 8.5 *Some nutritional losses that occur during cooking*

Nutrient	Losses
Proteins	Some amino acids can be lost if cooking is excessive, and some may be less easily obtained by the body due to changes in the protein structure
Fats	Some essential fatty acids may be lost due to breakdown with heat
Carbohydrates	Cooking usually makes carbohydrates more easily digested by the body
Minerals	Some minerals may be lost from foods such as fish, meat and vegetables into the cooking liquid
Vitamins	Vitamins B and C are lost into cooking water, are also destroyed by heat and may react with oxygen. Vitamin A is also sensitive to heat

In some instances the nutritional value of a food may increase during cooking. This is best illustrated in frying of French fried potatoes for example, where fat is absorbed by the food and the energy value is therefore increased.

EXERCISES

1. What are the main reasons for cooking food?
2. Describe the process of conduction, giving examples of where it occurs in cooking.
3. Explain how convection occurs in a warm liquid and how a boiled egg is cooked in this way.
4. Which types of radiation are used for cooking food? Explain how each type works and make a list of foods suitable for each type.
5. Describe the principles involved in boiling and list foods suitable for boiling.
6. Outline the main differences between boiling and steaming, listing the main advantages of steaming in a commercial operation.
7. List the types of heat transfer at different points when a meat dish is braised in the oven.
8. What types of food are suitable for grilling?
9. Which methods of cooking produce the greatest amount of brown colour on the surface of foods?
10. List some of the safety risks associated with deep fat frying.

PART IV

CARE OF FOOD

CHAPTER 9

137

MICRO-ORGANISMS

9.1 INTRODUCTION

Micro-organisms are living organisms not visible, singly, to the naked
eye. They exist as single cells, groups of cells or large colonies, in
which case they may become visible. They are of relevance to the
catering industry since they are responsible for *food poisoning* and
food spoilage as well as being involved in the production of beer,
wine, bread, cheese, yoghurt and other foods.

There are many different types of micro-organisms but they are
usually divided into five groups: *bacteria, fungi* (this group includes
moulds and yeasts), *viruses, protozoa* and *algae.*

9.2 BACTERIA

The single cells of bacteria are very small, having a diameter of about
0.5 μm to 1.0 μm (see Appendix 1). There are a variety of cell
shapes, some of which are shown in Figure 9.1. Despite the variety of
shapes, the basic cell structure is similar in each case. Bacterial cells
possess a cell wall, cell membrane, cytoplasm, nuclear material and in
some cases a capsule (around the cell wall) and flagella, which bring
about movement. A generalised bacterial cell is shown in Figure 9.2
(see also Plates 9.1, 9.2).

Growth and reproduction
Bacteria obtain food for growth from their immediate surroundings,
by diffusion. The cell continues to grow until a critical size is reached
and then the nuclear material duplicates, the cytoplasm divides and
two new cells are produced in a process called *binary fission* (a type of
asexual reproduction, see Glossary). In this way large colonies of

Figure 9.1 *The shapes of bacteria*

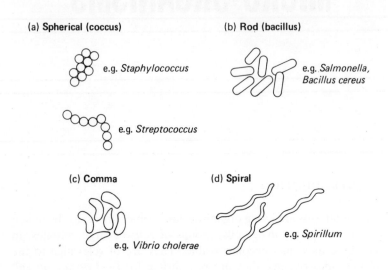

(a) Spherical (coccus)

e.g. *Staphylococcus*

e.g. *Streptococcus*

(b) Rod (bacillus)

e.g. *Salmonella,
Bacillus cereus*

(c) Comma

e.g. *Vibrio cholerae*

(d) Spiral

e.g. *Spirillum*

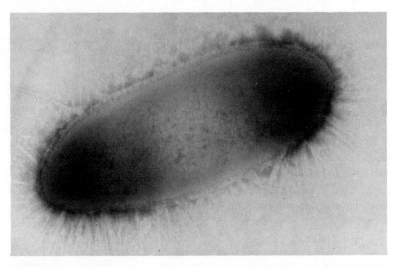

Plate 9.1   An electron micrograph of a single salmonella cell
(× 65,000) – note the 'rod' shape (*C.J. Webb*)

identical cells can be produced in a very short time (see Figure 9.3
and Plate 9.3).

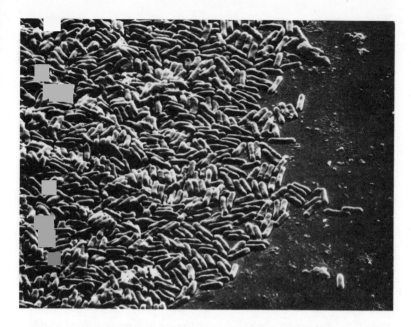

Plate 9.2   An electron micrograph of a colony of rod-shaped
bacteria (× 3000) (*Biophoto Associates*)

Figure 9.2   *Diagrammatic representation of a bacterial cell*

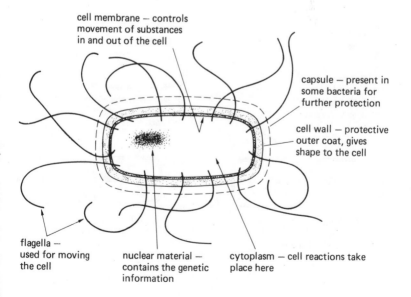

cell membrane — controls
movement of substances
in and out of the cell

capsule — present in
some bacteria for
further protection

cell wall — protective
outer coat, gives
shape to the cell

flagella —
used for moving
the cell

nuclear material —
contains the genetic
information

cytoplasm — cell reactions take
place here

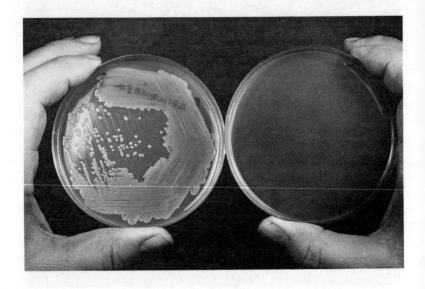

Plate 9.3   Agar plates showing colonies of bacteria (left) and a
control plate with no growth (right) (*C.J. Webb*)

Figure   9.3   *Bacterial   reproduction   (binary   fission – asexual
reproduction)*

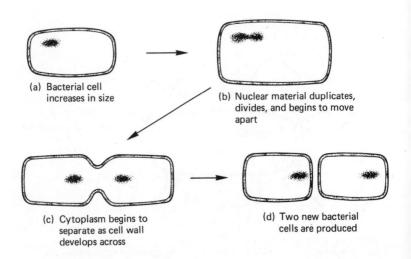

(a) Bacterial cell
increases in size

(b) Nuclear material duplicates,
divides, and begins to move
apart

(c) Cytoplasm begins to
separate as cell wall
develops across

(d) Two new bacterial
cells are produced

Some bacteria have the ability to produce a 'dormant' stage in their life cycle called a *spore*. The production of spores enables a bacterium to withstand unfavourable conditions, such as high or low temperatures, and to 'germinate' when conditions improve (see Figure 9.4).

Figure 9.4 *Spore formation in bacteria*

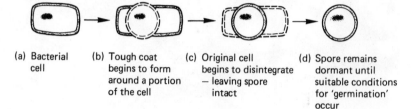

(a) Bacterial cell

(b) Tough coat begins to form around a portion of the cell

(c) Original cell begins to disintegrate — leaving spore intact

(d) Spore remains dormant until suitable conditions for 'germination' occur

Living (vegetative) bacteria and spores are present in almost all environments of the soil, air and water and become established on or in the tissues of plants and animals, including man.

A few examples of bacteria and their relevance in catering are given in Table 9.1.

Table 9.1 *Bacteria of relevance to the catering industry*

Name of bacteria	Relevance
Salmonella spp	Food poisoning and food-borne diseases
Staphylococcus aureus	Food poisoning
Lactobacillus spp	Some species are involved in the production of cheese and yoghurt. Others cause food spoilage
Streptococcus spp	Production of yoghurt and cheese
Acetobacter	Spoilage of food and vinegar production

9.3 FUNGI

This group contains non-microscopic organisms, such as mushrooms and toadstools, as well as the much smaller moulds and yeasts.

Moulds

Although moulds can exist as single cells, they are more likely to be growing as a threadlike mass on dead or living organic matter. If a single cell lands on a food source, branching structures called *hyphae* grow from it, eventually forming a dense mass called a *mycelium* (see

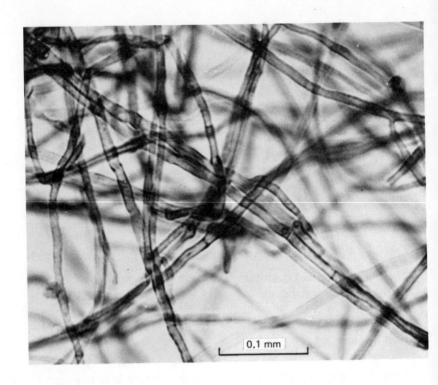

0.1 mm

Plate 9.4 A fungal mycelium showing hyphae (*C.J. Webb*)

Plate 9.4). The nutrients for growth are obtained in a similar way to bacteria, that is, diffusion occurs from the surrounding material. However, in moulds the hyphae are able to penetrate into plant or animal tissue and increase the efficiency of diffusion. Moulds can reproduce *asexually*, which involves one hyphae, or *sexually*, which requires two separate hyphae. In both cases spores are produced which are dispersed (or distributed) by air, water or animals (see Plate 9.5). New mycelia are formed if spores land in a favourable environment. Figure 9.5 shows asexual reproduction in two types of moulds.

> **Task 9.1** Leave a small selection of fruits and/or vegetables and a slice of bread on a windowsill for a day or two. Observe through a magnifying glass, if possible, the fungal growth that occurs after a certain period of time. (Note – the food should be disposed of properly and as quickly as possible after the investigation.)

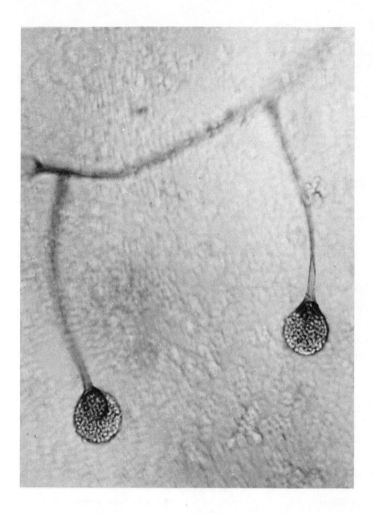

Plate 9.5   Fungal spores. These structures are the sporangia of the fungus Mucor (*C.J. Webb*)

Yeasts

Yeasts are smaller than moulds and are single celled. They are usually oval in shape and measure between 5 μm and 10 μm in diameter. The cells have a cell wall, cell membrane, cytoplasm and a nucleus.

The pattern of reproduction is different in yeast from other fungi, since new cell are produced by 'budding'. Normal growth results in a general increase in the size of the cell, and a bulge appears

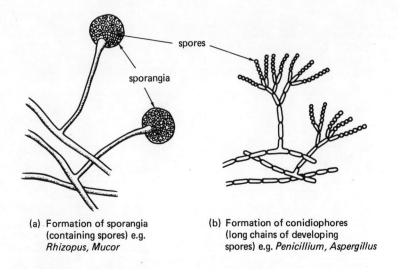

(a) Formation of sporangia
   (containing spores) e.g.
   Rhizopus, Mucor

(b) Formation of conidiophores
   (long chains of developing
   spores) e.g. *Penicillium, Aspergillus*

Figure 9.5   *Asexual reproduction in fungi*

on one side. The cell continues to grow and the nucleus divides, providing a nucleus for the bud. Finally the cell wall and cell membrane close up and separate the bud from the original cell. Table 9.2 shows some fungi and their effects in catering.

Table 9.2   *Fungi of relevance to food and catering*

Name of Fungi	Relevance
Penicillium roqueforti	An example of a *Penicillium* involved in cheese-making
Penicillium spp	Several species cause food spoilage or poisoning
Saccharomyces cerevisiae	The yeast which produces alcohol from sugar
Various mushrooms	Larger fungi used as food for man (and some are poisonous to man!)

9.4   VIRUSES

Viruses are very much smaller than the other micro-organisms, being only 20 to 300 nm in size (this may be one-hundredth the size of a bacterium!) They are unable to reproduce by themselves but can direct 'host' cells to produce virus material for them.

Viruses are responsible for causing diseases such as the common cold, influenza, measles and chickenpox, which are spread by contact, and infectious hepatitis and poliomyelitis, which may be spread by contaminated food or water. Recently viruses have been discovered to be responsible for several types of infections of the gut, causing diarrhoea and vomiting. One possible source of the viruses may be certain shellfish.

9.5 PROTOZOA

Protozoa are single-celled, water-dwelling micro-organisms capable of movement. They have little relevance to the catering industry with the exception of the species that cause food- and water-borne diseases. Perhaps the most important example is *Entamoeba histolytica*, which causes amoebic dysentery.

9.6 ALGAE

Algae are organisms that can produce their own food by photosynthesis (see Glossary). They range from microscopic forms such as *Chlorella* to the much larger seaweeds. Few of them are important to catering, although one recent development is the use of algae to produce protein food for animal or human consumption. As yet the process has not been perfected.

9.7 WHAT MICRO-ORGANISMS NEED IN ORDER TO GROW

All living things require certain conditions in order to grow well. If any of the conditions is unsatisfactory, for example, if there is insufficient food, then growth will slow down or stop.

Micro-organisms require the following if they are to grow well:

  (i)   the correct **temperature**,
 (ii)   sufficient **food.**
(iii)   sufficient **water**,
 (iv)   correct conditions for **respiration** (that is, they may, or may not need oxygen),
  (v)   suitable **environmental conditions**, and
 (vi)   sufficient **time.**

It is interesting to note that **food preservation** relies on altering one or more of the above conditions to prevent microbial growth (see Chapter 12).

(i) Temperature

There is no single temperature at which micro-organisms grow best. Some micro-organisms (*psychrophiles*) grow well in cold conditions, many grow best at temperatures around man's body temperature, 37°C (*mesophiles*), and a few prefer temperatures up to 60°C (*thermophiles*).

Food spoilage micro-organisms are usually psychrophiles causing deterioration in foods at room temperature (around 20°C) and in refrigerated conditions. *Pathogenic* or disease-causing organisms are usually mesophilic, growing best at body temperature; some bacteria that are thermophilic can cause problems in the food preservation industry, for example, in the canning process (see Figure 9.6).

Figure 9.6 *The effect of temperature on the growth of micro-organisms*

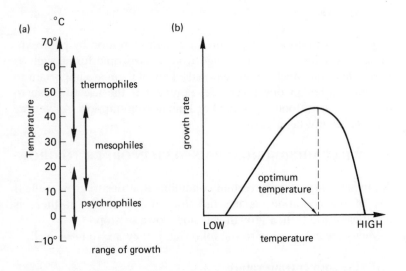

Figure 9.6 (b) shows how temperature affects the growth of one group of micro-organisms. At lower temperatures growth is poor, this increases until the *optimum* temperature is reached, and as the temperature continues to rise, growth slows down and stops. Table 9.3 illustrates some important temperatures relating to the growth of bacteria.

Task 9.2 Imagine that you have to build a fence in your garden and can choose a frosty day in January, an average day at the end of May or a hot humid day in August. Which day would you choose? Which conditions would you describe as optimum for you to carry out physical work?

Table 9.3 *Important temperatures for bacterial growth*

Temperature (°C)	Importance
−18	Domestic freezer – very few bacteria can live at this temperature – growth rate is very slow
0	Freezing point – growth rate is slow
1–5	Refrigeration temperature. More bacteria, particularly spoilage bacteria can survive at this temperature
18–30	Room temperature (winter – summer). Growth rate is much higher and increases with temperature
63	Vegetative (living) bacteria are destroyed
100	Boiling point of water – vegetative bacteria are destroyed, some spores may survive

(ii) Food

Micro-organisms require a source of food containing the necessary materials for growth, that is, energy, raw materials and various vitamins and minerals. They obtain food by diffusion from the surrounding material and may produce enzymes to break down organic matter into smaller units which can be absorbed more easily. In most circumstances food that is eaten by man is also suitable for micro-organisms and is subject to spoilage or poisoning.

(iii) Water

Water is necessary for all living things to grow and function normally. Chemical reactions in the cell take place in water as do many other processes such as digestion and excretion.

The water content of food is therefore important for microbial growth. However, not all of the water is *available* to micro-organisms since some of it is 'held' within the food's structure. Fresh fruit and vegetables have a high proportion of available water (referred to as having *high water activity* – Aw), whereas dried foods have a low proportion.

Some micro-organisms, particularly some fungi, have adapted to exist in foods with low water activity and may cause spoilage even in very dry foods.

(iv) Availability of oxygen

In order to respire, that is, to release energy from nutrients, some micro-organisms require oxygen while others do not.

Organisms requiring oxygen are referred to as *aerobic*, those that do not are *anaerobic*. Some micro-organisms can respire with or without oxygen and are called *facultative* aerobes or anaerobes. It follows that exclusion of oxygen from a product, as occurs in vacuum packing, does not prevent food spoilage or poisoning since some micro-organisms can exist with no oxygen. Vacuum-packed and canned foods employ other methods of microbiological control in addition to the removal of air.

(v) Environmental conditions

The immediate environment is critical to micro-organisms and two factors in particular are of importance:

(a) *pH* – this refers to how acidic or alkalinic a substance is (see Glossary). Most micro-organisms grow best in neutral conditions, between pH 6 and 8, which is the pH range of the majority of foods. However, some micro-organisms, mainly yeasts and moulds, can tolerate acid conditions and are therefore able to spoil foods such as fruit and fruit juices.

The pH values of some common foods are shown in Table 9.4.

Table 9.4 *pH values of some foods*

	pH value	Foods
acid	2–3	Lemon
	3–4	Apple, rhubarb
	4–5	Orange, tomato, banana
weak acid	5–6	Bread, white fish, potatoes, cheese
	6–7	Milk, egg yolk, chicken
neutral	7	Water, fresh meat
weak alkali	8–9	Baking soda
	9–10	Egg white

(b) *osmotic conditions* – strong sugar solutions (such as jam and confectionery) and strong salt solutions (such as foods stored in brine) have the effect of restricting the amount of available water to micro-organisms. The solutions may even draw water from the cells of the micro-organisms, causing death.

(vi) Time

Quite simply, if food is not contaminated with micro-organisms and is consumed immediately, there is no *time* for spoilage or poisoning to take place. However, foods supplied to the caterer, for example, chickens or vegetables, are often contaminated with micro-organisms. They are often stored for some time, and if the conditions outlined in (i) to (v) are satisfied, then large numbers of micro-organisms can be produced.

The growth rate of micro-organisms varies from type to type, but bacteria, for example, can reproduce by *binary fission* (see Glossary) every 15–20 minutes, if ideal conditions are present. This means that *1 000 000 000* bacteria *could* be produced from one single cell in 10 hours in ideal growing conditions.

Figure 9.7   *Growth of a bacterial colony from one bacterial cell*

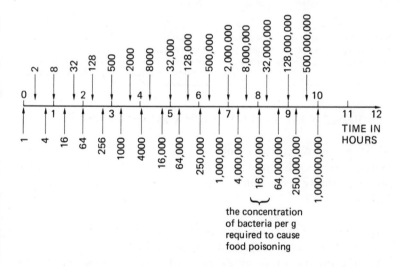

the concentration of bacteria per g required to cause food poisoning

The growth of a bacterial colony increases in the way that Figure 9.7 shows and follows a similar pattern each time, with the *extent* of growth depending on the availability of food, water and the other things previously mentioned. Figure 9.8 shows the different phases in the growth cycle of a bacterial colony.

Task 9.3   Make a list of different *types* of preserved foods and explain which of the growth factors for micro-organisms have been exploited.

Figure 9.8 *Growth pattern of a bacterial colony*

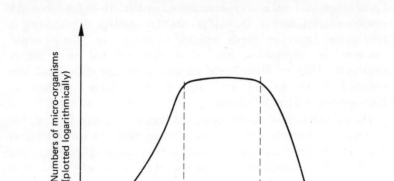

9.8 BENEFICIAL EFFECTS OF MICRO-ORGANISMS

Although many micro-organisms cause disease and spoilage, the majority are not harmful to man and may in fact be exploited to produce useful effects. Some of these uses are not related to catering, such as:

(i) the use of micro-organisms to break down and recycle organic material, as in sewage treatment, and

(ii) the production of antibiotics to be used in medicine for the control of infection.

In catering the main examples rely on the process of *fermentation*, which is the anaerobic breakdown of organic chemicals.

The most obvious food fermentations fall into three categories:

(i) beer, wine and vinegar production,

(ii) bread and cake manufacture, and

(iii) the production of dairy products such as cheese, yoghurt and butter.

The fermentation reactions are similar in each case and although they are not as simple as Figure 9.9 suggests, they can be represented by a single equation.

Figure 9.9 *Fermentation*

$$\text{SUGAR} \xrightarrow[\text{bacteria}]{\text{yeast/}} \text{INTERMEDIATE PRODUCT} + \text{CARBON DIOXIDE (CO}_2)$$
(e.g. sucrose)   (e.g. alcohol/lactic acid)

Task 9.4 Make as detailed a list as you can of foods that depend on the presence of micro-organisms at some stage in their production.

(i) Beer, wine and vinegar
The organism used in the manufacture of beer and wine is the yeast *Saccharomyces cerevisiae*. There are many 'strains' or types of this yeast which are used for the different varieties of beer and wine. The yeast is used to ferment *malted barley* (in beer production) or *grapes* (in wine production); the products are alcohol and carbon dioxide in each case. The qualities of the beverage produced depend on the blend of ingredients used.

Vinegar is produced by the further breakdown of alcohol by aerobic bacteria such as *Acetobacter*. The alcohol is converted into acetic acid and water.

(ii) Bread and cakes
The same type of yeast is used in breadmaking as in the production of alcoholic beverages, that is *Saccharomyces cerevisiae*. However, in this case it is the carbon dioxide which is important and not the alcohol (which evaporates during baking). The carbon dioxide acts as a raising agent, expanding the gluten network in the dough, giving a light, open texture. The dough is then baked in position and the carbon dioxide escapes.

(iii) Dairy products
Several dairy products rely on micro-organisms in their manufacturing process. The main examples are butter, yoghurt and cheese.

In *butter* manufacture certain species of the bacterium *Streptococcus* are added to produce the acids which give butter its characteristic flavour.

In *yoghurt* (see Chapter 6, section 6.4) *Streptococcus thermophilis* and *Lactobacillus bulgaricus* are added to convert lactose sugar into

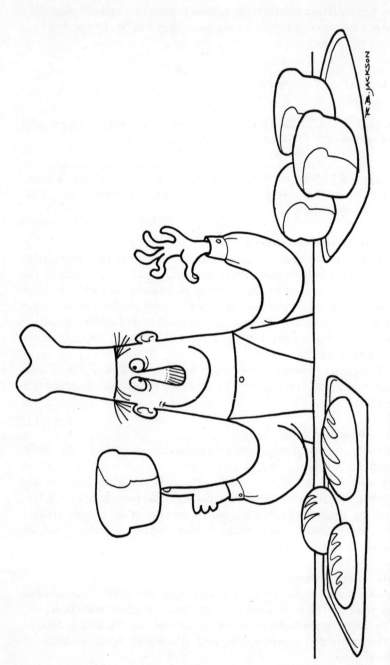

'. . . alcohol . . . evaporates during baking'

lactic acid, which brings about coagulation of the milk proteins and the production of yoghurt.

Bacteria and moulds are involved in *cheese-making*. Cheshire, Cheddar, Wensleydale and Gruyère are ripened by bacteria; in Gruyère the bacteria produce propanoic acid to give a distinctive flavour and create 'holes' in the structure with carbon dioxide. Examples of cheeses ripened by mould growth are Stilton and Danish Blue, where moulds grow inside the cheese, and Camembert and Brie which have mould growth on the surface. Penicillium is an example of a mould used in cheese-making.

New protein food

One further beneficial effect may be derived from micro-organisms if present research into the production of protein from algae, such as *Spirulinium* and *Chlorella* can be perfected. These micro-organisms are grown intensively (growing by photosynthesis), are harvested, and are then converted into a high protein food. However, there are still many problems to be overcome if this is ever to become a viable commercial proposition.

EXERCISES

1. What are the functions of the following structures in bacterial cells: (a) cell wall, (b) flagella, (c) nuclear material?
2. How do bacteria obtain their nutrients?
3. What is a bacterial spore?
4. Using the text and the Glossary describe what the following terms mean: (a) pathogen, (b) saprophyte, (c) toxin.
5. What is a 'mycelium'?
6. Describe the process of reproduction in yeasts.
7. What is the optimum temperature and temperature growth range of mesophilic micro-organisms?
8. Which micro-organisms are able to grow in dried foods?
9. What number of bacteria could be produced from one cell in 8 hours if conditions were ideal and reproduction occurred every 15 minutes?
10. Describe one useful effect of micro-organisms which is exploited by man in the food industry.

CHAPTER 10

FOOD SPOILAGE AND FOOD POISONING

10.1 INTRODUCTION

Food spoilage is the reduction in quality of food, caused by micro-organisms, pests, chemical change and/or enzymic activity and is usually detectable by sight, smell or taste.

Food poisoning is an illness caused by eating food which is naturally poisonous or has been contaminated with toxic chemicals or pathogenic micro-organisms.

10.2 FOOD SPOILAGE

Food spoilage is responsible for a significant amount of economic loss, due to wastage, in the food and catering industry. If profits are to be made, it is important to keep wastage to a minimum, which can be done by storing and handling food carefully to reduce spoilage.

(i) Microbial spoilage
This is by far the most important type of food spoilage in catering and may be due to bacteria or moulds. The micro-organisms may be present on or in the food itself, or may contaminate it during the period of storage. They are able to break down the organic material of the food, using the chemicals produced as food for growth and reproduction. This process is made much easier by the fact that *autolysis* takes place in the food at the same time (see next section). Examples of microbial spoilage in foods are given in Table 10.1.

Task 10.1 Make a detailed inspection of your own domestic kitchen and the storage cupboards of your college/works store*, perhaps first thing on a Monday morning, to see if you

'Food spoilage . . . is usually detectable by sight, smell or taste'

can find any traces of food spoilage beginning. Refer to Table 10.1 before doing so.

If you would like to look around someone else's store, make a very tactful request and explain exactly what you are doing!

Table 10.1   *Some types of microbial spoilage of food*

Food	*Type of spoilage*
Bread	Mould growth; ropiness
Fruits and vegetables	Mould growth producing slime or rot
Milk	Souring
Meat	Slime on surface
Sugar and sugary foods	Fermentation
Canned foods (improperly processed)	Gas production

As seen in Chapter 9, section 9.7, micro-organisms that spoil food grow at lower temperatures than pathogens, for example, and therefore spoilage can occur at room temperature and even in the refrigerator (see Plates 10.1, 10.2). Stock rotation is therefore very important.

Plate 10.1   Spoilage of fruits and vegetables caused by moulds (*C.J. Webb*)

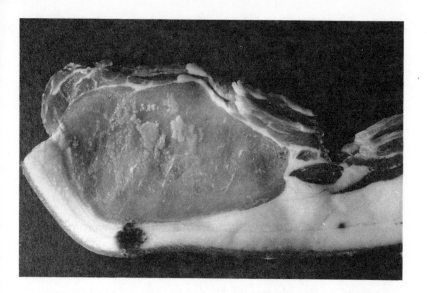

Plate 10.2   Microbiological spoilage of bacon (*C.J. Webb*)

(ii)   Autolysis

This is the process of '*self-breakdown*' which occurs in plants and animals after harvesting or slaughtering. Enzymes are released after death which begin to break down the cellular structure of plants and animals and enable the nutrients present to be 'recycled' to other organisms. As seen in the previous section, this process is coupled with the breakdown by micro-organisms.

(iii)   Chemical spoilage

Many chemical changes occur in food during its storage which affect palatability and some changes render the food inedible. One important type of chemical process which can take place is the development of rancidity in fats and oils and foods containing large amounts of fat or oil. In fact there are two types of rancidity:

(a)   *Oxidative rancidity*   This involves the reaction of *oxygen* from the atmosphere with unsaturated double bonds in the fatty acids of a fat (see Chapter 2, section 2.7). A chain reaction takes place, which results in the production of several unpleasant chemicals which give the characteristic rancid taste and smell (see Figure 10.1).

Figure 10.1   *Oxidative rancidity*

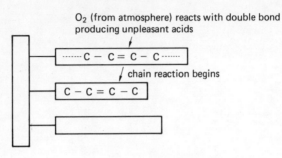

(b)   *Hydrolytic rancidity*   This is less common than oxidative rancidity. It occurs if *enzymes*, either from the food, or micro-organisms present in the food, break down the triglyceride structure of the fat into glycerol and fatty acids. Some of the fatty acids produced are unpleasant and make the fat taste and smell rancid (see Figure 10.2).

Since both types of rancidity are due to chemical reactions, several factors which slow down or stop the reactions can be exploited to reduce or prevent both types of rancidity (see Table 10.2).

Table 10.2   *Factors affecting rancidity in fats and oils*

Factor	Ideal storage conditions	Type of rancidity
Temperature	At low temperature, such as a refrigerator or cold store	Oxidative and hydrolytic
Oxygen	In wrapping or containers to exclude atmospheric oxygen	Oxidative
Ultra-violet light	Dark place or wrapped to exclude light	Oxidative
Metallic ions	Avoid the use of metal containers and utensils where possible	Oxidative
Enzymes	Storage free from contamination by micro-organisms, which may produce enzymic breakdown	Hydrolytic

Task 10.2   Divide a small slab of butter or margarine into two portions. Leave one piece covered in opaque greaseproof paper, in a refrigerator and the other exposed to sunlight at room temperature. Check regularly and note how long it takes for the signs of rancidity to appear in each. I would suggest that smell is the best method of detection in this case!

Figure 10.2 *Hydrolytic rancidity*

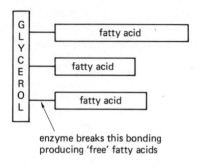

enzyme breaks this bonding
producing 'free' fatty acids

(iv) **Physical spoilage**
This includes:

(a) damage, such as bruising, caused to food during harvesting, slaughtering and storage. This may occur in fresh fruits, vegetables, meat, fish, and so on, as well as preserved foods in cans, packets and other containers, and
(b) damage caused to food or food containers by pests such as rats (which may gnaw foods or their containers or soil foods with faeces and urine) or insects (which may invade foods such as cereals), for example the flour mite.

10.3 THE PREVENTION OF FOOD SPOILAGE

In order to restrict or prevent food spoilage there needs to be good management of stock within an establishment. The storekeeper has the difficult task of holding sufficient food in stock for the needs of the catering staff to carry out their work, and to allow for the economy of bulk buying. But he/she cannot hold excess food that is likely to spoil before it is used. One important responsibility is the checking of goods as they arrive at the store from the supplier. The quality of food must be examined carefully, and substandard goods, which would obviously spoil quickly, should be rejected.

The storekeeper should keep exact records of the amount of each type of foodstuff with the dates of purchase and should ensure its usage in the correct order, to achieve satisfactory stock rotation. Regular checks on stock are necessary.

Obviously different foods require different storage conditions, some of which have already been discussed. A summary of the main principles of storage is given in Table 10.3.

Table 10.3 *Food storage*

Type	Examples	Storage conditions
Perishable	Fruits and vegetables	Low temperature (4°C–10°C), not too dry (because of wilting), dark
	Meat, poultry	Chilled (4°–6°C), covered, in clean hygienic conditions, away from any contamination
	Fish	Chilled (0°–2°C), clean and used as quickly as possible
	Milk, eggs, cream, yoghurt	Chilled (2°–4°C), well wrapped, good stock rotation
	Butter, margarine, cooking oils	Chilled (4°–7°C), wrapped, dark, airtight containers
	Bread	Room temperature, away from contamination, well-wrapped, ventilated
	Frozen foods	Below −18°C, in labelled packages, no re-freezing should take place
Non-perishable	Cereals	Cool, dry, strong airtight containers. Stock rotation is essential
	Dried foods	Cool, dry, airtight containers
	Canned and bottled foods	Cool and dry, containers regularly checked, good stock rotation

10.4 AN INTRODUCTION TO FOOD POISONING
Food may be poisonous, or cause illness, for several reasons:

(i) Some foods are *naturally* poisonous. For example, some mushrooms and toadstools, plants such as 'deadly nightshade', red kidney beans (if not cooked sufficiently), and some fish, contain chemicals that are poisonous to man.

(ii) Food may contain or become contaminated with *toxic chemicals*. Heavy metals such as lead, copper, tin and mercury, agricultural pesticides and herbicides, and chemicals such as disinfectants, can contaminate food during its growth, storage, preparation or cooking.

(iii) Food may become contaminated with *pathogenic micro-organisms* or *toxic chemicals produced by micro-organisms*. This is by far the most important type of food poisoning and usually involves bacteria.

Trends in the numbers of food-poisoning cases
The main reasons for the occurrence of food poisoning are bad temperature control and incorrect storage (see Figure 10.3). Food

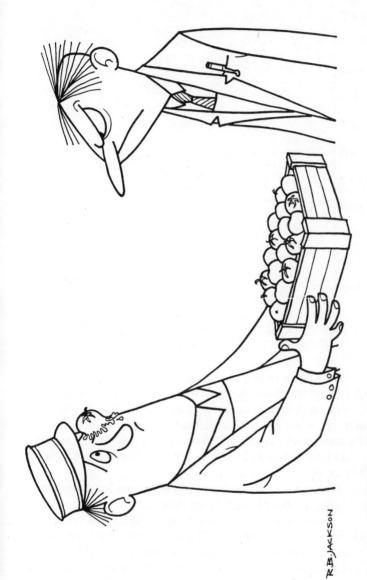

'Substandard goods should be rejected'

R.B.JACKSON

Figure 10.3 *Numbers of cases of food poisoning in England and Wales between 1970 and 1984*

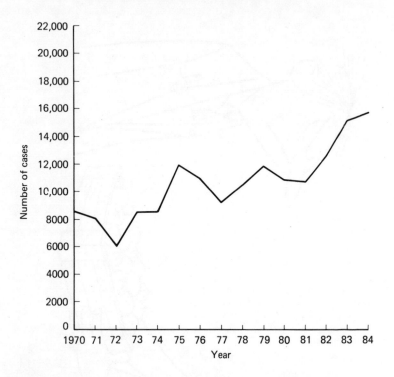

hygiene studies have shown that most cases of food poisoning arise from food being prepared too far in advance of service, being stored at too low or too high a temperature (see Chapter 11), being cooled too slowly, not being reheated sufficiently, or from incorrect thawing of frozen food before cooking. However, in many of the *Staphylococcus* food poisoning cases, an infected food handler was to blame (see Chapter 11).

Bearing these points in mind, some of the reasons for the *continued increase* in the number of cases being reported are:

(i)   The actual number of cases being reported has increased. Greater public awareness of food poisoning, better reporting procedures in the medical and environmental health services, and improved laboratory techniques, enable more cases to be accurately recorded.

(ii) The percentage of meals 'eaten out' continues to increase. This means that more food is prepared in commercial establishments where faults in hygiene can occur more easily and where one fault affects many people.

(iii) The percentage of convenience foods used is rising in commercial and domestic catering. A greater understanding of temperature control and storage is required with these foods and there is therefore a greater chance of mistakes being made.

(iv) Increasing numbers of 'take-away' food establishments, where food is often kept at serving temperature (or just below!) for long periods of time. This may lead to numbers of bacteria increasing to an extent which could cause food poisoning.

(v) Mass catering in the public sector. Often the finances available in hospitals and schools are restricted, which can lead to small staff numbers and a basic standard in facilities and equipment.

(vi) Larger factories producing pre-packed foods. This means that more pre-packed foods are being eaten and once again, one mistake can affect many people.

(vii) Advancing technology and new systems in mass catering.

Centralised cooking operations (see Chapter 12, section 12.10) produce large quantities of food and require a longer distribution chain than traditional cooking. This gives more chance for mistakes to be made. Cook-chill and cook-freeze systems, employed with centralised cooking, require a high level of understanding by the staff involved in order to ensure good hygiene standards.

It cannot be stressed enough that in nearly all the above cases good education in food hygiene for the staff involved would dramatically reduce the cases of food poisoning.

Task 10.3 Research back copies of a national daily newspaper in your local library for an important recent outbreak of food poisoning. Note how the story of the outbreak unfolds over several days and write a brief summary of how it came about.

10.5 BACTERIAL FOOD POISONING

There are a great number of bacteria that cause food poisoning in man. The main groups are *Salmonella* (of which there are over 1500 types), *Staphylococcus aureus*, *Clostridium perfringens*, *Campylobacter jejuni*, *Bacillus cereus* and *Vibrio parahaemolyticus*. The

164

disease, botulism, caused by *Clostridium botulinum*, is rare in the UK, but is important because it is usually fatal. (In fact, many food preservation processes are designed to ensure the destruction of this bacterium in particular.)

The symptoms brought about by the different bacterial groups vary, but they include some or all of the following: vomiting, abdominal pain, diarhoea, headache, fever and nausea. However, botulism is quite different from other food poisoning diseases, since most of its effects are on the nervous system (see Table 10.4).

The symptoms depend mainly on whether the food poisoning is of the *infective* or *toxic* type:

(a) Infective food poisoning

This includes *Salmonella*, *Campylobacter* and *Vibrio* and is brought about by the release of poisonous chemicals (endotoxins) from the breakdown of bacterial cells *in* the gut. Obviously there needs to be a large number of organisms ingested in order to form a colony in the gut. The symptoms of food poisoning begin to appear when sufficient bacterial cells are broken down, liberating endotoxins. The *incubation period*, which is the time lapse between consumption of the contaminated food and the onset of symptoms, is quite long in infective food poisoning.

Figure 10.4 *Infective food poisoning*

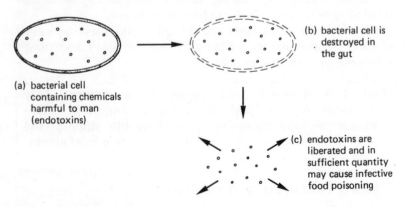

(a) bacterial cell containing chemicals harmful to man (endotoxins)

(b) bacterial cell is destroyed in the gut

(c) endotoxins are liberated and in sufficient quantity may cause infective food poisoning

(b) Toxic food poisoning

This occurs with *Staphylococcus*, *Bacillus cereus* and *Clostridium botulinum*.

These bacteria each produce poisonous chemicals while growing in or on the food (exotoxins). This means that food is already

Figure 10.5 *Toxic food poisoning*

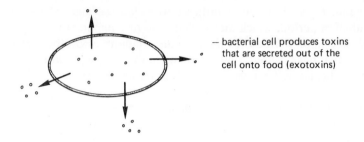

— bacterial cell produces toxins that are secreted out of the cell onto food (exotoxins)

'poisoned' before it is eaten and leads to a much shorter incubation period than occurs in infective food poisoning.

In the case of *Clostridium perfringens*, a toxin is released when the vegetative form of the organism produces spores while it is actually living in the gut of man.

Salmonella(e)   There are many different types of salmonellae, for example, *Salmonella typhimurium* and *Salmonella enteritidis*. Salmonellae are rod-shaped bacteria that do not form spores and do not produce toxins. This means that if food contaminated with salmonellae is cooked thoroughly, no poisoning occurs. This is not necessarily true of some of the bacteria that *do* form spores or toxins.

The organism is found mainly in the intestines of humans, and animals such as cattle, pigs, poultry, pets and pests. It is therefore present in faeces and anything that comes into contact with faeces. One important aspect of hygiene is the necessity to wash hands thoroughly after visiting the toilet, since bacteria from faeces can be transferred to food by the hands.

Salmonellae are responsible for the largest portion of food poisoning incidents reported, although this does not always mean that they cause most incidents; rather that the symptoms are severe enough to cause most cases to be reported. Foods that have been associated with salmonellosis (food poisoning caused by *Salmonella*) include meat and meat products such as sausages, poultry, cream and egg products.

Salmonellosis is one of the more severe types of food poisoning and in some cases can be fatal, particularly if contracted by infants or elderly people. Details of the disease are given in Table 10.4.

Campylobacter jejuni *Campylobacter jejuni* is an organism which was only recognised as a food poisoning organism a few years ago, but has quickly grown in importance. It is thought to be as common as *Salmonella* but the techniques for its identification are not fully developed yet. It is often difficult to isolate because of its long incubation period, which means that food or equipment causing the disease cannot be traced by the time the symptoms show themselves. Foods that have caused food poisoning in this way are poultry, some red meats and milk which has not been pasteurised.

Vibrio parahaemolyticus   This is an important food-poisoning organism particularly in Japan. It is found to be common in fish, and shellfish such as prawns, cockles and oysters. Frozen prawns are imported in large quantities and if contaminated can represent a health risk, since they may not be recooked and may be prepared in advance of service, as in prawn cocktail. It is most important to buy fish and shellfish from a reliable source. Details of the disease are in Table 10.4.

Staphylococcus aureus   The symptoms caused by this organism are quick to arise and are usually short-lived. In fact it is thought that many cases of this type of food poisoning are not accounted for in the statistics, because people do not bother to report them. In most cases there is a good chance that the illness was caused by bad hygiene on behalf of the cook, because staphylococci are naturally found on the skin, in the nose and throat and in cuts, sores, boils and scratches of humans. It is therefore very easy for the organism to be transferred to food during preparation and if temperature control and storage are inadequate, poisoning can result. Unpasteurised milk can be another source of staphylococci. Important foodstuffs in this case are cream and milk and dishes incorporating them, such as custards, trifles and bakery products and also cold meats.

Staphylococcus forms a toxin which is quite resistant to heat, being able to survive up to 30 minutes of boiling. For other details see Table 10.4.

Clostridium perfringens   This organism is found in human and animal intestines and also in dust and soil. This means that meat, poultry and vegetables may be contaminated when they reach a food establishment; it explains why food poisoning caused by *Clostridium perfringens* is quite common.

One major feature of this bacterium is that it forms a highly resistant spore which can survive many cooking processes. This is important when food is reheated because the surviving spores may germinate and multiply during storage and cause food poisoning if

Organism	Incubation period	Duration of illness	Symptoms	Source	Observations
Salmonella	6–48 hours	1–7 days	Diarrhoea, abdominal pain, vomiting, fever	Farm animals, poultry, pests, humans	Easily destroyed by heat (does not form a spore or toxin). Can be fatal in young or old
Campylo-bacter jejuni	2–10 days	5–7 days (or more)	Abdominal pain, diarrhoea, general illness (vomiting is uncommon)	Poultry and farm animals. Often in milk	Long incubation period – only recently recognised as a food poisoning organism
Vibrio para-haemolyticus	2–48 hours	2–5 days	Severe diarrhoea, abdominal pain, vomiting, fever	Fish and shellfish	Particularly important in Japan
Staphylo-coccus aureus	2–6 hours	6–24 hours	Vomiting, diarrhoea, abdominal pain, sometimes collapse	Humans (particularly nose, throat & skin), farm and domestic animals, and milk	Important because of its presence on the food handler, easily passed on to food. Rapid recovery (therefore many cases not reported)
Clostridium perfringens	9–12 hours	12–24 hours	Diarrhoea, abdominal pain, nausea. (vomiting is rare)	Farm animals, pets, humans, dust & soil	Forms a spore which is difficult to destroy by heat. Important in reheated dishes
Bacillus cereus	1–16 hours	6–24 hours	Abdominal pain, diarrhoea, vomiting, nausea	Soil, water & the surface of vegetables. Rice is often affected	2 types: 1 – short incubation period, produces diarrhoea; 2 – longer incub. period – mainly vomiting
Clostridium botulinum	18–36 hours	Death in 1–8 days, or slow recovery over 6–8 months	Difficulties with vision, speaking & swallowing. General paralysis of muscles. Respiratory failure	Soil, water, surface of vegetables	Spores are formed. The toxin affects the nervous system leading to the different symptoms shown here. Fatal in most cases

not destroyed during reheating, which often does not reach high temperatures. Since *Clostridium perfringens* does not require oxygen it is able to grow in rolled joints, stews and casseroles, mince dishes and sausages, many of which are popular reheated dishes (see Table 10.4).

Bacillus cereus *Bacillus cereus*, of which there are two similar types, produces symptoms quickly that do not last long, recovery usually being within one day. The organism is found in soil and water and affects one commodity in particular, rice. *Bacillus* is a spore former and produces a toxin; it is associated with the food poisoning that arises from inadequately reheated boiled or fried rice. Details of the two types of *Bacillus cereus* are shown in Table 10.4.

Clostridium botulinum This organism forms a highly resistant spore and produces a powerful toxin which affects the nervous system. It is often fatal if ingested. Although it is not common in the UK, it is important because of this. The disease *botulism*, caused by this organism, can be brought about if canned or bottled foods are insufficiently heated during processing. This enables spores to germinate and produce the toxin which only needs to be eaten in small quantities to give the symptoms shown in Table 10.4. Most cases of botulism have resulted from home preserving of meat products and vegetables. Death occurs in about 70 per cent of cases.

A summary of the main types of food poisoning organisms is given for quick reference and comparison.

The Table can be used to learn about the specific types of food poisoning which can then be related to the general principles of food hygiene which are discussed in Chapter 11.

Task 10.4 Read through the following three accounts of fictional food poisoning incidents and identify which bacterium was responsible in each case. Give reasons for your answers.

(a) A large number of people in three neighbouring villages were taken ill with diarrhoea and abdominal pain. It was discovered later that four days previously these villages had been supplied with unpasteurised milk as a result of a mechanical failure at the local dairy. Most of the people were ill for just under one week.

(b)   Out of a family of four who ate out in a restaurant on a Saturday evening, two of the people were vomiting and had diarrhoea by 11.30 p.m. (23.30 hours) the same evening. After investigation it was found that the only course on the menu that both people ate was the egg mayonnaise starter. Bacteriological samples from their vomit and faeces were taken, which were compared several days later with bacteriological samples from the nose and throat of the chef preparing the hor d'oeuvres. How long were the two people likely to be ill?

(c)   A group of people attending a barbecue all suffered the following day with food poisoning. The symptoms lasted several days and included diarrhoea, vomiting, severe stomach ache and some people had a very high temperature. On the evening of the barbecue the food had been consumed quickly and a second 'round' of sausages were taken from the freezer and cooked to 'feed the hungry'.

10.6   FOODS CARRYING A HIGH RISK OF FOOD POISONING

In very general terms, food containing a high proportion of protein and water are suitable for the growth of the micro-organisms causing food poisoning. Of course this does not mean that all the foods listed below will lead to illness, because other factors such as the temperature and length of storage are obviously important.

Foods that are a 'high risk' and that require careful treatment are:

(i)   **Meat** (beef, pork, lamb, poultry)
Dishes made with meat, such as stews, casseroles, sausages, beefburgers, meat pies and minced dishes.

(ii)   **Fish and shellfish**
This should include dishes that contain fish and shellfish.

(iii)   **Dairy products and eggs** (milk, cream, cheese, ice cream and eggs)
Also all the sweets that contain milk, cream and eggs, for example, trifles, cream pastries, meringues, and so on.

(iv)   **Rice** (boiled or fried)

10.7 FOOD- AND WATER-BORNE DISEASES

Unlike food poisoning, the food- and water-borne diseases involve transmission of pathogenic organisms to man via food or water which is *not* the medium for growth of the organism causing the disease.

Examples of this group of diseases include: typhoid and paratyphoid fever, dysentery, cholera, brucellosis, tuberculosis and parasitic worms.

The food-borne diseases differ from food poisoning in the following ways:

(i) Food or water is only a means of transport for the bacteria, not a medium for growth.

(ii) Only a small number of bacteria are required to cause an infection.

(iii) There is a much longer incubation period involved (up to three or four weeks).

(iv) There is no requirement for multiplication time in the food/water.

(v) Water is often the vehicle for transmission (unlike food poisoning).

(vi) The symptoms are much more varied than in food poisoning (possibly as a result of the organism entering the bloodstream and causing a more general illness).

Table 10.5 describes some of the more important food-borne diseases.

EXERCISES

1. Distinguish between food spoilage and food poisoning.
2. Describe the process of autolysis.
3. Name one type of chemical spoilage that can occur in food, stating which types of foods are likely to be affected and precautions that can be taken to reduce this type of spoilage.
4. Describe the role that should be played by the storekeeper to keep food spoilage to a minimum.
5. List *four* reasons why the incidence of food-poisoning cases continues to increase.
6. Name five bacteria that can cause food poisoning.
7. Using one of the organisms listed in Question 6 describe: the incubation period, duration of illness, symptoms, source, effect

Table 10.5 *Food-borne diseases*

Disease	Symptoms	Notes
Enteric fever (typhoid & paratyphoid)	1–3 weeks incubation period. Fever, diarrhoea, headache, general weakness	Caused by organisms of the *Salmonella* group. Transmitted by water or food contaminated directly or indirectly with faeces. Paratyphoid is the less severe.
Cholera	Incubation period of 1–6 days. Vomiting, diarrhoea and dehydration.	Caused by contamination of food or water with faeces. The organism responsible is *Vibrio cholerae*.
Dysentery (bacillary)	2–4 days incubation period. Diarrhoea and fever.	The organism, *Shigella*, is passed on by food or water contaminated with human faeces.
Brucellosis (undulent fever)	1–4 weeks incubation. Fever, general pains in muscles and joints. The symptoms are recurrent over a long period of time	Transmitted by contact with animals or by consumption of contaminated water or untreated milk.
Tuberculosis	Fever, general illness, intestines and other organs affected.	Not common now, but often transmitted by raw milk 30–40 years ago.
Parasitic worms	Symptoms include: fever, nausea, abdominal pain, muscular pain, weight loss.	Two main worms: *Trichinella spiralis* and the tapeworms *Taenia saginata* and *Taenia solium*. Passed on by infected meat. Thorough inspection of meat has greatly reduced this problem.

of cooking and any other important points you consider are relevant.

8. Describe the difference between infective and toxic food poisoning.

9. Make a short list of foods that you would treat carefully in a catering establishment because they were a 'high risk' in terms of food poisoning.

10. Name three *food-borne* diseases.

FOOD HYGIENE

11.1 INTRODUCTION

It is the role of the caterer to provide food which is not only nutritious and palatable, but is also *safe* for the consumer. This can be achieved if food is stored, prepared, cooked and served *hygienically*. It is therefore necessary for all catering personnel to have a thorough understanding of micro-organisms, their role in food poisoning and how food should be handled hygienically to prevent disease.

11.2 HOW FOOD IS CONTAMINATED

Food may already be contaminated when it arrives in the kitchen, or may become contaminated by the food handler, by cross-contamination from equipment or utensils, or by pests (and domestic animals) in the kitchen or store.

In each of these cases, the risks of contamination and the subsequent possibility of food poisoning must be reduced in as many ways as possible.

11.3 FOOD WHICH IS CONTAMINATED 'ON ARRIVAL'

Much of the food that arrives in the kitchen, particularly raw and fresh foods, is already contaminated with bacteria, some of which may be pathogenic. For example, fresh fruit and vegetables contain bacteria from the soil and from the air and can become contaminated during storage. Cattle, pigs, sheep and poultry all contain large numbers of bacteria, including *Salmonella* and *Clostridium perfringens*, in their intestines, which may be transferred to the meat during even the most careful slaughtering processes (see Figure 11.1).

174

Figure 11.1 *Food contaminated 'on arrival' in the kitchen*

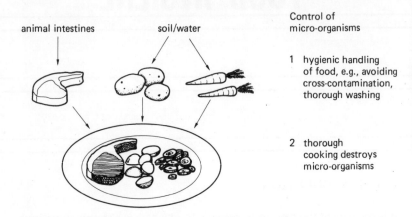

animal intestines   soil/water

Control of
micro-organisms

1 hygienic handling
of food, e.g., avoiding
cross-contamination,
thorough washing

2 thorough
cooking destroys
micro-organisms

It is the role of the butcher and caterer to ensure that the bacteria present on or in the food are not given the chance to increase in numbers to a level which could cause food poisoning.

It is obviously *not* the fault of the caterer that food is contaminated on arrival in his kitchen. However, he is at fault if he does not *treat* it as contaminated and does not create conditions for storage, preparation and cooking which minimise the risk of food poisoning.

11.4 THE FOOD HANDLER

Certain of the food-poisoning bacteria, *Staphylococci* in particular, are present on or in the human body. The surface of the skin and the linings of the nose, mouth and throat often contain large numbers of staphylococci which can easily be transferred to food during its preparation and cooking if there is poor hygiene (see Plate 11.1).

Bacteria of the *Salmonella* group and *Clostridium perfringens* species may also be present in humans, in the intestine. A person who 'carries' pathogenic bacteria in this way but who does not experience the symptoms of food poisoning is called a *healthy carrier*. Carriers are a risk in catering, since food can become contaminated easily, for example, if hands are not washed properly, preferably with an anti-bacterial soap, after visiting the toilet; this could lead to a food-poisoning incident. (In a person who is recovering from food poisoning, pathogenic bacteria may still be present in his or her intestines, although the symptoms have cleared up. This type of person, a *convalescent carrier*, should not return to work in catering until he or she is free from pathogenic bacteria.)

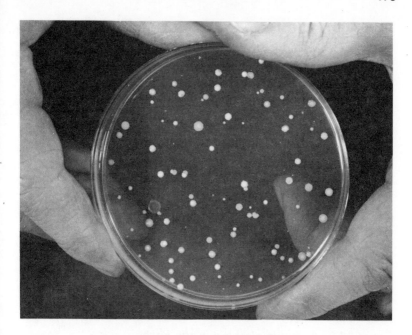

Plate 11.1   Cultures of staphylococci grown from the skin
surface of a human (*C.J. Webb*)

Personal hygiene
Since the food handler is likely to be contaminated with pathogenic
bacteria, good personal hygiene is essential. The food handler should
reduce his direct contact with food as much as possible and observe
the general rules of food handling set out in the *code of practice* which
follows.

A Code of Practice for Food Handlers
1. Maintain a high standard of general bodily hygiene by washing,
    bathing or showering regularly. This reduces the number of
    bacteria on the body and also prevents the breakdown of sweat
    by bacteria, which leads to offensive body odour.
2. Wash hands thoroughly and regularly. This should be done
    automatically when entering a food preparation area, after
    visiting the toilet, after smoking, coughing, sneezing and any
    other action which is likely to contaminate the hands with
    bacteria.

***

Task 11.1   Record over one day, preferably when you are
working in a kitchen, how many times it was necessary to
wash your hands. List the different reasons why.

3. Finger nails should be kept short. This reduces the amount of dirt, grease and bacteria that collect under the nails.

4. Avoid sneezing and coughing on to food *or* on to the hands, since they may then come into contact with food.

5. Avoid habits which involve the hands coming into contact with the nose, ears, hair, beard or any other part of the body likely to be contaminated with bacteria.

6. Do not smoke in a food room and wash hands after smoking before returning to a food room. Smoking may involve the transfer of food-poisoning bacteria from the mouth to the fingers.

7. Handle food as little as possible. This can be achieved by using tongs, spoons and other utensils wherever possible. Fingers should *never* be put into food, for example, when tasting food before final seasoning.

8. Wear the correct protective clothing. Figure 11.2 shows some of the items of clothing worn by a chef, and their role in good hygiene.

Figure 11.2 *Suitable clothing in the kitchen*

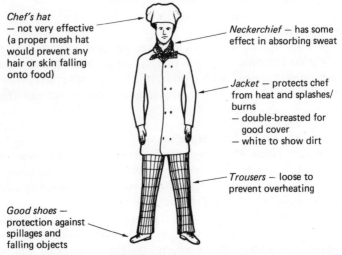

Chef's hat — not very effective (a proper mesh hat would prevent any hair or skin falling onto food)

Neckerchief — has some effect in absorbing sweat

Jacket — protects chef from heat and splashes/burns — double-breasted for good cover — white to show dirt

Trousers — loose to prevent overheating

Good shoes — protection against spillages and falling objects

9. Do not wear jewellery (plain wedding rings are often allowed but should be kept very clean). All jewellery is capable of trapping dirt, grease, soap and sweat, which can support the growth of bacteria.

10. Cuts, grazes and spots on the skin's surface should be covered with waterproof dressings, preferably coloured so that they would show up in food if lost.

11. The management should be informed if a person (or a close family member) has any important bowel illnesses, such as food poisoning, or any infectious diseases of the respiratory system or skin.

Task 11.2   Read through the above list, ask yourself questions and make notes as to whether *you* have any room for improvement. For example:
point 1 – Approximately how many baths or showers do you have a week?
point 3 – How long are your finger nails?
point 5 – What are *your* bad habits in the preparation of food? (We all have them!) It is interesting to ask a friend to watch you for a while and note what hygiene mistakes you make.
point 9 – List the items of jewellery you normally wear. Do you take them *all* off?

11.5   CROSS-CONTAMINATION

Cross-contamination is the transfer of pathogenic bacteria from a contaminated source to an uncontaminated source. It is of most importance when the food contaminated is ready to be eaten and is to receive no further cooking.

The source of bacteria in cross-contamination may be: other food (see section 11.3), the food handler (see section 11.4) or food pests (see section 11.6). However, there are many other *indirect* ways in which cross-contamination can occur in the kitchen. The majority of these examples involve contaminated equipment, utensils and work surfaces in the kitchen. For example, if a knife is used for cutting raw food and is later used with cooked food, having not been washed thoroughly in between, then bacteria can be transferred from the knife to the cooked food. For this reason kitchen equipment, utensils, chopping boards and work surfaces should be thoroughly washed in between different cooking and preparation processes (see Figure 11.3).

Table 11.1 groups some of the main examples of cross-contamination and outlines how they should be prevented.

Task 11.3 Have a detailed look at your kitchen, domestic or commercial and list the specific incidences in which cross-contamination *could* take place.

Figure 11.3 *Cross-contamination*

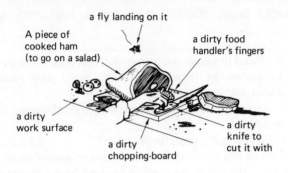

Table 11.1 *Cross-contamination and its prevention*

Source	Examples	Prevention
Contaminated utensils	Knives, whisks, etc.	Thorough cleaning
Contaminated equipment	Slicers, mincers	Thorough cleaning
Dirty cloths	Dishcloths, towels	Discourage use, but regular cleaning if used
Contaminated work surfaces	Chopping-boards, tables	Thorough cleaning
Incorrect storage conditions	Raw food next to cooked in refrigerator	Correct storage, e.g. separation of raw and cooked foods
The atmosphere	Air currents, draughts	Good ventilation system
Food handler	Hands, coughing, sneezing	Thorough hand washing, hygienic practices
Food pests	Insects, rodents	Prevent entry

11.6 PESTS

Animal and insect pests can cause a problem to the caterer because of the spoilage they may cause to food and because many of them carry pathogenic bacteria, such as *Salmonella*, on their bodies or in their intestines. The most important pests to the catering industry are: rats, mice, cockroaches and flies, although domestic pets such as cats and dogs are also a hazard and should not be allowed near food preparation areas. In addition to these there are also many species of moths, beetles and mites that may be introduced into an establishment with food ingredients or packaging.

Rats and mice

Two species of rat, the Brown (Common) Rat and the Black (Ship) Rat, and the house mouse are the main rodents associated with catering establishments in the UK. They are capable of causing considerable damage to food premises and to food in storage by their gnawing and chewing habits. They are likely to contaminate food with which they have been in contact, with urine, with bacteria such as salmonellae from their intestines (and therefore their droppings) or from contamination on their feet or fur (see Plates 11.2, 11.3).

Plate 11.2   A Brown Rat, becoming more contaminated with bacteria! (*Rentokil Ltd*)

The signs of a rat or mouse infestation include: droppings, urine stains, greasy smears on walls, skirting boards and other surfaces (from their fur), damage to woodwork, plastic, plumbing pipes, food containers, and signs of gnawing, such as shredded cardboard, paper and wood shavings (see Plates 11.3, 11.4).

The best method of control for pests in a catering establishment is prevention rather than cure. This can be achieved if the premises are

Plate 11.3   House mice feeding on food remains (*Rentokil Ltd*)

basically sound and if regular maintenance is carried out to seal holes
in wood and brickwork. Repairs should also be made to windows,
doors, and so on, as soon as is necessary, to ensure that they are as
pest proof as possible. The premises should possess a good, safe
drainage system which prevents the entry of rodents, while the
disposal of waste should be carefully controlled. Refuse or waste
should be regularly removed to the outside of the premises, where it
should be stored away from the building in strong bins with tightly
fitting lids. Regular collection to match the needs of the establishment should be arranged with the local authority or a private
collector. Inside the premises, food should be stored in strong,
closed, metal or plastic containers on shelves raised from the floor.
This discourages nesting of pests and aids cleaning. There should also
be careful inspection of incoming ingredients and rotation of stock.

However, if an infestation of rodents *is* discovered, then immediate
action should be taken to eradicate it. To do this, expert advice
should be sought, either from the local Environmental Health Officer
(EHO) or from a private Pest Control Company. The usual method
of control is to leave small bait boxes of poison in strategic places
along the rodent 'run', which the rodents will eat over a period of a
few days. Anti-coagulant poisons (which prevent the blood from
clotting) are usually preferred in food premises, and these are

Plate 11.4   Mouse droppings in a catering store (*Rentokil Ltd*)

available as a gel, paste or contact dust to be used according to circumstances, by the specialists described above.

Cockroaches

The two main species of cockroach which affect catering establishments in the UK are the Oriental or Common Cockroach, and the German Cockroach or Steamfly. They are very important pests in that they are difficult to eradicate since they live in dark, warm, humid places that are often inaccessible. They are rarely seen during the day, emerging to search for food at night, and it is therefore difficult to assess the extent of an infestation. Their reproduction rate can be very fast, and in favourable conditions a single pair of German cockroaches can produce an infestation of several thousands in a year.

Cockroaches are usually contaminated with pathogenic bacteria, of which *Salmonella, Staphylococcus, Streptococcus* and *Escherichia coli* are common examples; these can be transferred to food when the insect is feeding or walking over it. Cockroaches also produce a foul smell which can taint food and is one of the signs of a cockroach infestation. Once again the control should be by prevention. This involves keeping the structure of the building in a sound condition, paying particular attention to the sealing of cracks, crevices and holes around pipework, ventilation systems, and so on. Food should be correctly stored and food debris properly disposed of.

In the event of an infestation, the EHO or Pest Control Company should be contacted for eradication, which usually takes the form of a series of sprayings with insecticidal chemicals, the use of insect powder, and the placing of adhesive traps to detect and monitor any insects present.

Flies

The housefly and blowfly are both common pests to the caterer, particularly in warmer weather. Both types of fly feed on waste and refuse and therefore become contaminated with pathogenic bacteria. They transfer these bacteria to food when they land on it, by walking over the surface and also be secreting their saliva on to the food (the saliva begins to digest food and the liquid produced is sucked up by the fly).

Control methods are available for killing flies when they are inside the catering establishment, but in each case there are disadvantages. Table 11.2 describes the common methods of fly control.

The only satisfactory method of control for flies is to prevent them from entering the kitchen by the use of mesh screens over doors and

Plate 11.5　A Common Cockroach (*Rentokil Ltd*)

Fig 11.6   A house fly (*Rentokil Ltd*)

Table 11.2 *Fly control*

Type	Method of control	Comments
Fly screens and meshes over windows and doors	Prevents entry of flies	Most suitable method
Ultra-violet electrocutors	Attracts flies with UV light and electrocutes them on contact with an electric grid	Very effective. Important to include emptying and cleaning of fly tray in cleaning schedule
Insecticidal paints on walls and ceilings	Contains chemicals that kill flies	Dead flies need to be regularly cleaned away, otherwise they may pose a hygiene hazard
Aerosols	Contains chemicals that kill flies	As above
Fly papers	Consist of a resin strip to trap flies	Regular removal of dead flies is required

windows and to avoid leaving waste food exposed in the kitchen. Any potential breeding sites must be eliminated or treated to destroy the maggots.

11.7 THE DESIGN OF FOOD PREMISES

The design of food premises has an important part to play in good hygiene and in fact food premises must comply with the Food Hygiene Regulations (see section 11.8).

The first consideration of design should be the *site*, which must be away from obvious sources of contamination such as slaughterhouses and refuse tips. The size of the building or buildings should be adequate for the operations that are likely to take place, without causing overcrowding. The layout of rooms and equipment should also be carefully planned.

Several important aspects of design and planning follow:

(i) Ventilation
It is important to ensure that temperature and humidity are controlled in food premises to minimise the growth of micro-organisms and create good working conditions for staff. A good ventilation system will produce a rapid turnover of air, thereby removing smells, grease, steam, dust and airborne micro-organisms.

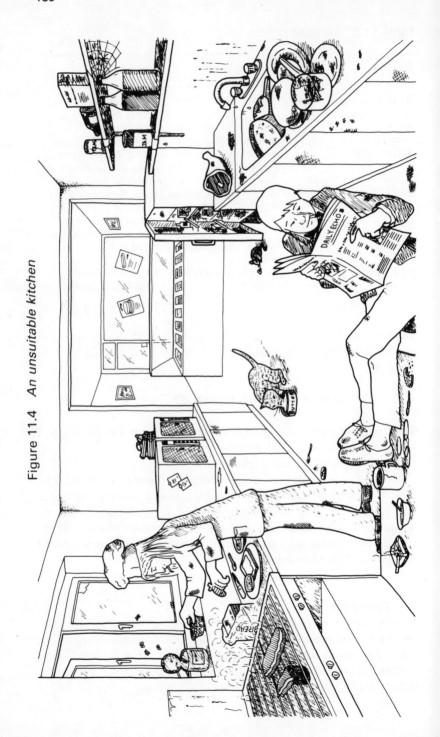

Figure 11.4 *An unsuitable kitchen*

Figure 11.5 *Ventilation flow in a kitchen*

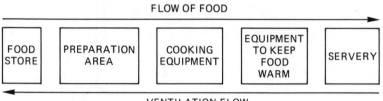

The ventilation system should be constructed to flow in the opposite direction to the flow of food, wherever possible, and in this way cross-contamination will be minimised.

(ii) Lighting

Adequate lighting is necessary for safe and efficient working conditions to enable thorough cleaning to take place. The lighting should be carefully sited in relation to work surfaces and equipment, and should not produce shadows. Fluorescent striplights are preferred to tungsten since they give more evenly distributed light and are more economical to run. The light fittings should be covered with light diffusers to prevent glare.

(iii) Water supply, drainage and sanitation

There should be a good, clean supply of hot and cold water for the purposes of handwashing, cleaning, and food preparation. Waste water must be able to flow away easily into the main sewer and floors in the kitchen should contain gulleys for drainage and cleaning.

The sanitary facilities in an establishment should be of a high standard if good personal hygiene amongst the staff is to be maintained. Facilities should include separate male and female changing rooms with individual lockers for the safe storage of personal items. Toilets should be provided and these should be away from the food preparation areas, separated by a ventilated room as specified by law. Wash-handbasins should be sited next to the toilets and also in the food preparation areas, and should be equipped with soap or detergent (preferably anti-bacterial), a nail brush and a method of hand drying. A correctly-used paper towel system of hand drying is probably the most suitable method, although hot air dryers are very efficient but not hygienic in food preparation areas.

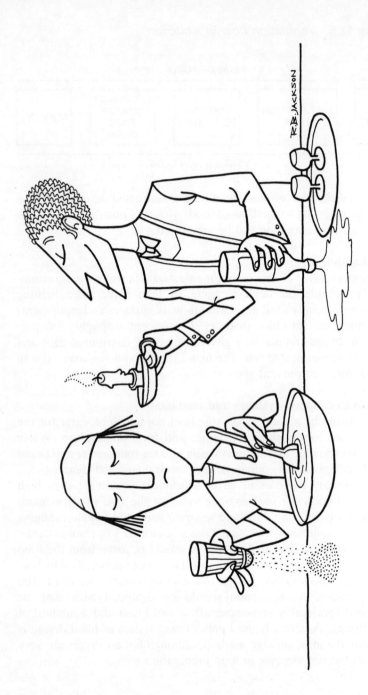

'Adequate lighting is necessary . . .'

> **Task 11.4** Wash-handbasins in the toilets of a food establishment are required by law to have a 'wash your hands' notice displayed next to them. Explain why.

(iv) **Refuse disposal**

Many of the points regarding refuse disposal have been dealt with earlier in this chapter. However, when planning a new kitchen, disposal can be made much more hygienic if waste disposal units are fitted into sinks, if good bins are sited correctly in the kitchen, and if a proper refuse storage area is constructed outside the premises with concrete floors and walls and plastic or steel bins. Polythene refuse sacks are not suitable on their own because they tear easily and can be 'gnawed' or chewed through by pests.

(v) **Floors, walls and ceilings**

The floors and walls of a kitchen should be made of hard wearing, impervious, relatively smooth and easy-to-clean materials.

In addition, floors need to be relatively non-slip, which means that a compromise between 'easy-to-keep-clean' and 'non-slip' has to be reached. The actual choice of material for a floor depends on many factors concerned with its intended use. But in general terms, in preparation areas which require a heavy duty covering, quarry tiles, ceramic tiles, vinyl sheeting or granolithic concrete are suitable. In dry areas terrazzo, vinyl and thermoplastic tiles are satisfactory.

Wall coverings should be light in colour to show dirt and should be coved at the joints with the floor and ceiling. Examples of suitable surfaces include thermoplastic sheeting and stainless steel sheets, although both may prove expensive. In many establishments good quality plaster coated with gloss paint is sufficient and is less expensive. Wall tiles, although giving the appearance of a good covering, may not be hygienic because of the porous grouting which is often used.

In the case of floor and wall coverings it should be stressed that the quality of *fitting* is as important as the type of material.

Ceilings should be constructed with adequate space for ventilation and should be smooth and easily cleaned. Absorbent plaster, to avoid condensation, with an emulsion covering, is very suitable.

(vi) **Work surfaces**

Many types of work surface are suitable for the different tasks to be performed in a kitchen. Each surface, once again, should be smooth, hard wearing and easily cleaned. Stainless steel and hard plastic laminates are the most suitable surfaces for most tasks, but for chopping, hard compressed rubber is often used. Wooden surfaces are to be avoided because they are absorbent and develop cracks and crevices into which food and bacteria become trapped, making effective cleaning very difficult.

(vii) **Equipment**
A new kitchen should be designed to contain sufficient sinks, basins and work surfaces to meet the demands of the work being carried out. It will also contain equipment for specialised tasks, such as mincers, mixers and slicers, which must be suitably maintained and cleaned regularly.

Task 11.5 Obtain permission to look around a college or restaurant kitchen and make a list of the different surfaces present. What materials have been used? How well do you think they are suited to the work that takes place?

11.8 **FOOD HYGIENE LAW**

The present law concerning food in the UK is the Food Act 1984. This act was based upon the earlier Food and Drugs Act 1955, which covered many aspects of food and its sale, and in particular gave rise to the specific hygiene legislation: The Food Hygiene (General) Regulations 1970. These regulations are applicable under the Food Act 1984 and are enforced by Local Authorities (The Environmental Health Department) to ensure the correct storage, preparation and sale of food in all food premises.

The law covers three broad areas of food control:

  (i)   Control of chemical additives and the chemical composition of food.
 (ii)   Control of the health of food animals and their adequate inspection at time of slaughter.
(iii)   Control of the conditions under which food is processed and sold and the actions of personnel at this stage.

It is the role of the Environmental Health Officer (EHO) to ensure adequate sampling, analysis and inspection of food. This enables areas (i) and (ii) to be covered in a relatively straightforward manner. However, area (iii) is a more difficult area to control. The EHO has the responsibility of ensuring that food premises are in good condition, that there are good facilities and that the use of the premises and facilities by staff is satisfactory. It must be explained, however, that the EHO has many other responsibilities as well as the control of food and these include: health and safety, pollution control, housing and many other aspects of environmental health.

Although food hygiene law is complex and is constantly being revised to cover new or different aspects of food hygiene, a summary of some of the important implications of the Food Hygiene (General) Regulations 1970 are shown in Table 11.3. The actual regulations are written in relation to (i) premises, (ii) equipment, (iii) food handlers,

Table 11.3 *A summary of some of the important regulations from the Food Hygiene (General) Regulations 1970*

Regulation	Summary
6	Catering or other food processes must not take place in insanitary premises.
7	Articles and equipment used in food preparation and storage must be clean and in good condition.
9	The food handler must protect food from the risk of contamination, e.g., food kept covered, stored off the ground, separated from animal food, etc.
10	Food handlers should have a high standard of personal cleanliness, e.g., clean clothes, no bad habits, etc.
11	Food handlers should have adequate overclothing.
12	Food handlers should wrap and transport food in a satisfactory manner.
13	A food handler *must* inform the management (who then contacts the Medical Officer for Environmental Health) if he is suffering from intestinal infection, e.g. typhoid, salmonellosis, or other food poisoning.
16	Sanitary conveniences should be in good condition and clean.
17	A clean and adequate water supply must be provided.
18	Adequate handwashing facilities must be provided.
19	Suitable first aid equipment must be provided.
20	Accommodation should be provided for storage of outdoor clothing.
21	Suitable sinks should be provided for the washing of food.
22	The lighting for food rooms must be adequate.
23	Ventilation in food rooms must be adequate.
26	Waste food should not be allowed to accumulate in a food room.
27	This deals with the temperature control of food in storage, preparation, cooking and service.
29	This states that the food handler is guilty of an offence if he fails to comply with the regulations.

(iv) services (for example, water supply, lighting, etc.) and (v) practices (that is, specific restrictions on food handling).

11.9 CLEANING

Good cleaning procedures and a well-organised cleaning schedule are essential to good hygiene. Regular cleaning of surfaces, utensils and equipment keep the numbers of micro-organisms to a minimum, thereby reducing the risk of food poisoning and food spoilage.

The cleaning schedule should be simple but well organised to ensure regular cleaning of surfaces (floors, walls and ceilings), drains and gulleys. It should enable work surfaces, ovens, refrigerators, specialist equipment and utensils to be cleaned daily, at the end of each use or as often as necessary.

Detergents

The process of cleaning can take several forms. However, the most common form of cleaning involves hot water and a *detergent*. The hot water is able to dissolve or suspend grease and dirt and depending on the temperature, may destroy some or all of the micro-organisms present. The detergent is required to enable the water to 'wet' the material being cleaned, which it does by reducing the surface tension. Detergents should be odourless, tasteless and non-toxic to man. The action of a detergent is shown in Figure 11.6.

Figure 11.6   *Diagrammatic representation of detergent action*

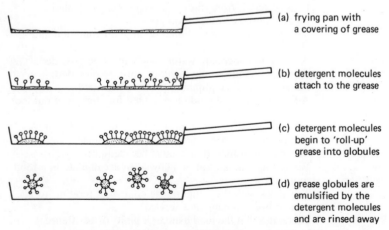

(a) frying pan with a covering of grease

(b) detergent molecules attach to the grease

(c) detergent molecules begin to 'roll-up' grease into globules

(d) grease globules are emulsified by the detergent molecules and are rinsed away

NB   These diagrams are *not* to scale — detergent molecules and grease globules would be microscopic!

In many cleaning operations chemicals may be used to help in the destruction and removal of micro-organisms. A range of chemicals is available which may act as:

  (i) antiseptics,
 (ii) disinfectants,
(iii) sterilants.

In fact, some chemicals used in this way may fall into two or more of the above categories, depending on the concentration in which they are used. Table 11.4 explains the differences between antiseptics, disinfectants, sterilants and sanitisers and gives examples of their uses in the catering industry.

Disinfectants
There are many instances when a chemical disinfectant is suitable or necessary, for example, laminated plastic work surfaces should be disinfected after preparation of raw meat and poultry.
    There are several important points to bear in mind when using a chemical disinfectant:

  (i) The manufacturer's instructions should be adhered to *exactly* – for example, dilutions must be accurate.
 (ii) Disinfectants require *time* to act, for example, 2 minutes, 5 minutes. A quick wipe over is not sufficient.
(iii) Good contact must be made between the disinfectant and the surface to be cleaned.
 (iv) There are many types of disinfectants and so the right chemical must be chosen for a particular job. In catering, for example, a 'wide spectrum' disinfectant, which is one that is capable of killing a *wide range* of micro-organisms, is most suitable.
  (v) It must be rinsed away effectively.
 (vi) Food debris must be rinsed away prior to use because it may inactivate the disinfectant.
(vii) Disinfectants deteriorate with time. Therefore new solutions must be made up regularly.
(viii) It is often necessary to alternate two disinfectants to prevent the development of resistant bacteria to one disinfectant.

Table 11.4 *Antiseptics, disinfectants, sterilants and sanitisers*

Type	Effect	Uses	Examples
Antiseptic	Reduce the number of micro-organisms present	Reduce infection or possibility of infection on human skin	Savlon, Dettol, TCP
Disinfectant	Kills living (vegetative) micro-organisms, although some spores may survive	General cleaning	Savlon, Dettol, Domestos, Bettadine, Stericol
Sterilant	Kills living micro-organisms and spores	Cleaning where sterilisation is necessary (not particularly relevant to catering)	Stericol, Domestos
Sanitiser	Contains a disinfectant *and* a detergent	In processes where cleaning and disinfection are required, e.g., washing up	Steriplus, Shield, Odex A3

There are five main types of chemical disinfectant:

Hypochlorites (bleaches) are inexpensive and quick to act but are easily inactivated by food debris and are corrosive to many metals.
Iodophors are effective and stable although may be expensive.
Quaternary ammonium compounds (QAC) are safe, non-corrosive, stable and odour/taint-free, but may not be effective against all bacteria.
Phenols There are several types of which some are unsuitable for food premises.
Pine disinfectants are strong smelling and should not be used in food premises.

The chemicals used in detergency and disinfection are often classified as cationic, anionic, non-ionic or amphoteric and should therefore be explained. In simple terms this refers to the *electrical charge* of the chemicals used and can be positive or negative. Negatively charged is referred to as *anionic*, positively charged is *cationic*, no charge is *non-ionic* and a chemical which alters from positive to negative depending on conditions is *amphoteric*. The main point is that solutions should not be mixed unless they are *compatible*, for example, an anionic detergent with an anionic disinfectant, since opposites could cancel each other out.

Task 11.6 Look at some of the common cleaning agents in a supermarket or wholesale supply shop and note which ones are antiseptics, disinfectants, sterilants and sanitisers. Do any of them fall into two categories? If so explain how their use is adapted for the different functions.

Perhaps the most common, the most useful, and possibly the cheapest, disinfectant is hot water, above 63°C, since at this temperature vegetative micro-organisms will be destroyed. This fact can be exploited in many cleaning situations, such as washing up.

Washing-up
The process of washing-up can be a simple operation as in the domestic single sink system, or it can involve expensive and sophisticated dishwashing equipment, as in some large hotels.
Washing-up should consist of the following stages:

(i) *Preparation* Prior to washing, plates, pans, utensils, and so on, should have food debris and grease removed so that the detergent used in the washing stage works efficiently.

(ii) *Washing* The hot water and detergent remove grease and dirt from the articles with the aid of mechanical action.

(iii) *Rinsing* Dirty water, detergent and 'suspended particles' are removed from the articles being cleaned.

(iv) *Drying* Any remaining rinse water is removed.

Washing-up is achieved either *manually* or with the aid of *specialised equipment*.

(a) *Manual washing-up* If a *single sink* is used, then hot water (40°–45°C) and a detergent are used, but there is usually no rinse stage. This is an unsatisfactory method of washing-up and often involves drying with a towel or cloth which may re-contaminate dishes, pans and utensils. If a *double sink* is available, then the main wash can be carried out in the first sink (at 40°–45°C), followed by rinsing and disinfecting in the second sink (at 80°C). At such high temperatures the articles being washed may dry in the air, since evaporation occurs very quickly. In some cases the second sink may contain cooler water with a chemical disinfectant.

(b) *Mechanical washing-up* There are several types of dishwashing machines available. Simpler models involve rotating brushes in a sink of hot water or open sinks with turbulent hot water. The most popular models use high pressure jets of water, which pass over the dishes, and so on, that are in a stationary or moving rack. Most machines incorporate a pre-rinse, a detergent wash (60°–65°C) and a disinfectant rinse (75°–80°C). Drying is often by air (see Plate 11.7).

Cleaning schedules
Washing-up is a specific example of a cleaning procedure that takes place regularly in a catering establishment. As indicated at the beginning of this section, the other cleaning procedures should be accurately designed and preferably written down and displayed. A simple kitchen cleaning schedule might consist of several of the areas or items of equipment to be cleaned with a step-wise set of instructions detailing the procedure, to include: floors, walls, work surfaces, sinks, handbasins, cupboards, ovens, refrigerators, grilles, mincers, can-openers, and so on. Three examples are shown in Table 11.5.

Task 11.7 Draw up a cleaning schedule for one or two of the other areas or equipment in the list.

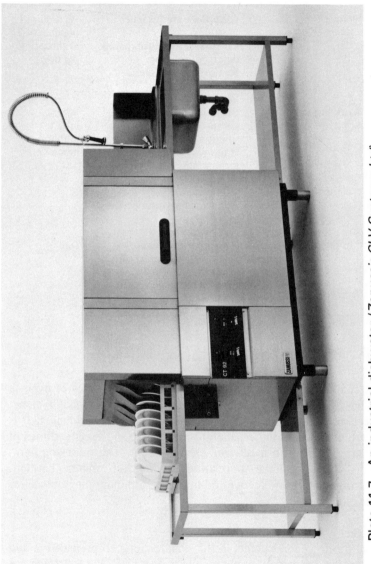

Plate 11.7   An industrial dishwater (Zanussi: CLV Systems Ltd)

Table 11.5 *Examples from a cleaning schedule*

Area or equipment		Details	Frequency
(a) Floor	(i)	Clear floor area as much as possible	As required possibly two or three times per day
	(ii)	Clean with freshly prepared detergent solution	
	(iii)	Remove excess detergent with sponge mop	
	(iv)	Rinse with fresh water	
(b) Work surfaces	(i)	Clear debris away	After each food preparation process
	(ii)	Clean with fresh detergent solution	
	(iii)	If surface has been used for meat, poultry, fish, etc. then clean with fresh disinfectant solution	
	(iv)	Allow time for disinfectant to act	
	(v)	Rinse with clean water	
(c) Can-opener	(i)	Remove from socket	Daily
	(ii)	Scrub with hot detergent solution	
	(iii)	Rinse in hot clean water	
	(iv)	Air dry	

11.10 PRACTICAL FOOD HYGIENE

This chapter has so far dealt with the general principles of hygiene and has described the main points regarding food, personal hygiene, cross-contamination, design of premises, the law and cleaning. It is important to relate these general principles to the specific duties of the different staff in a catering establishment. The following paragraphs discuss hygiene in relation to the chef, waiter, barman, porter/assistant, storekeeper and manager, although they only show *some* examples.

The chef
Many of the general points in this chapter refer to preparation and cooking, and therefore apply mainly to the chef. The following are useful points.

199

'The Chef'

The chef should:

(i) Have a very high standard of personal hygiene (see section 11.4), paying particular attention to the hands.

(ii) Avoid any bad habits such as picking the nose, scratching the beard.

(iii) Be aware of being a responsible member of the kitchen team and lead by example.

(iv) Work in a clean, tidy and organised manner, clearing away and cleaning surfaces, utensils and equipment along the way.

(v) Be aware of the risks of cross-contamination, such as storing raw next to cooked foods, not using separate knives, using cloths to wipe surfaces, etc. (see section 11.5) and work to reduce the cross-contamination as much as possible.

(vi) Be aware of the need to cook, thaw or reheat food *thoroughly*.

(vii) Have good quality, clean dress.

(viii) Undergo any food hygiene education that may be available, passing any knowledge gained on to others as appropriate.

The waiter

Once again the waiter or waitress must have a very high standard of personal hygiene, as described in section 11.4. The points listed there will be of particular importance if silver service is involved, as the waiter may need to prepare food in front of the customer, as in filleting fish, preparing steak tartare, serving chateaubriand, etc. There is also the responsibility of ensuring the cleanliness of equipment, such as serving trolleys, and of cutlery, which should be handled correctly. Separate serving spoons should be used for different dishes and food waiting to be served should be kept warm on a hot plate. Cold sweets and puddings should be served hygienically using tongs, spoons or other implements and should be refrigerated and covered in between servings.

The barman

With the increasing popularity of bar meals and snacks, the barman now has to deal with food as well as drinks. At peak drinking times the turnover of glasses can be very high. Hygiene is extremely important since infection can easily be passed on by a glass that has not been cleaned properly. Glass washing can take place using a double sink (see section 11.9) preferably with a disinfectant or anti-bacterial agent in the wash, or specialist glass washing machines may be used. Drying should be by air and should not involve cloths or towels. The handling and storage of glasses are also important. They should never be picked up with fingers inside the glass and they should be stored on regularly cleaned shelves. They should not be stored upside down above the bar where customers' smoking could contaminate them. The drinks' optics should be washed down and checked regularly; as in other drinks' service, the use of a new glass at the optic reduces the risk of cross-contamination. Many drinks, particularly cocktails, require the use of lemon, cherries, mint, and so on, and therefore associated equipment, chopping-boards, knives and so on. The general rules of hygiene and cleaning apply. If the duties of the barman do extend to more food preparation, then the section entitled 'The chef' becomes more applicable. However, the barman has the added disadvantage of handling money contaminated with bacteria, while dealing with food.

Task 11.8 Explain why the practice of leaving open dishes of peanuts, crisps, olives and so on on the bar could be considered to be unhygienic.

The kitchen porter

The duties assigned to the kitchen porter vary from one business to another. However, he may be involved in some cleaning, disposal of food waste, some vegetable preparation and many other tasks. He should follow the cleaning schedules set out and ensure the effectiveness of the cleaning agents being used, by careful dilution, regular replacement, and correct use. It is important to select the right cleaning agent for the right job, for example, to ensure no corrosion of aluminium equipment. Regular removal of food waste, hygienic use of the disposal unit, efficient emptying of bins and disposal of refuse sacks are all essential for good hygiene in the kitchen. Any tasks involving preparation or pre-preparation of food such as potatoes and other vegetables demand the same rules of good hygiene as any other food preparation in the kitchen.

The storekeeper

Many of the important points relating to good storekeeping are dealt with in Chapter 10. A summary of those points and some other aspects are listed here.

The storekeeper should:

(i) Check the quality of goods as they arrive and reject if necessary. The storekeeper has some control over which suppliers to use and should be aware of the standard of delivery person, refrigerated vans and so on.

(ii) Keep accurate records of stock and ensure efficient rotation.

(iii) Make regular checks on food likely to deteriorate or become infested with pests, for example flour and cereals.

(iv) Assess the efficiency of ventilation in the store and monitor the temperature, in order that goods are kept in optimum conditions for storage.

(v) Maintain the division of separate areas of food storage such as raw foods away from cooked foods if they share a refrigerator.

(vi) Use the hand washing facilities provided, particularly before handling food when issuing it to kitchen staff.

(vii) Ensure that the disposal of waste food and food packaging is conducted hygienically.

In addition to these points the storekeeper should obviously adhere to the points regarding personal hygiene and have good, clean overalls.

The chambermaid

General room cleaning, hygienic replacement of bed linen, correct use of the right chemical cleaning agents (see section 11.9) for washbasins, toilets, baths and showers are all the responsibility of the chambermaid. Many rooms also have limited refreshment facilities and so dirty crockery and food waste need to be dealt with hygienically, and supplies of tea, coffee and biscuits topped up.

The management

The management has a very significant role to play in the maintenance of good standards of hygiene. A good manager has a working knowledge of all aspects of his business and this should include food hygiene. He or she must set good standards and must check the quality of food preparation, cleaning, personal hygiene of staff, standard of repair of the building and so on. He should encourage staff to attend food hygiene courses and make it easy for them to do so, by perhaps allowing time off for attendance.

EXERCISES

1. Explain why many raw foods, such as meat and vegetables, already possess significant numbers of bacteria when they arrive at a food establishment.

2. Make a list of points that you could give to a new food handler that would help him or her achieve a high standard of hygiene and reduce the risks of food poisoning.
3. Describe three ways in which cross-contamination of foods might occur in a kitchen.
4. List the main pests associated with food premises.
5. Describe what preventative measures can be taken to ensure that the pests listed in your answer to Question 4 do not infest food premises.
6. What should you do if you discover an infestation of pests in your establishment?
7. Discuss the qualities required of the following items in a kitchen: (a) the floor, (b) the work surfaces, (c) the ventilation system.
8. Briefly explain how the refuse disposal system can be made as hygienic as possible.
9. Name the law that covers the production and sale of food and *very briefly* outline what it sets out to achieve.
10. Describe one cleaning process in the kitchen that would benefit from the use of a disinfectant. Explain how the disinfectant should be used and what it would achieve.

SUGGESTED PRACTICAL WORK

The tasks set throughout this book can be attempted by the student with little or no equipment or supervision. If experiments are to be carried out in Food Hygiene, equipment and supervision *are* necessary.

The following experiment demonstrates in a simple way why a knowledge of food hygiene is essential to all people handling food.

Experiment: To investigate the presence of micro-organisms on the food handler and in the kitchen.

Apparatus: petri dishes, nutrient agar, cottonwool, markers, clear tape, incubator.

Method:

(a) The petri dishes should be sterilised and nutrient agar poured in, made to the manufacturer's specifications, and stored upside down (see Figure 11.7).
(b) A list of sites for sampling of the food handler and kitchen are made, for example: hands, finger nails, jewellery, hair, coughing; sinks, work surfaces, bins, floors, and so on.
(c) Petri dishes are labelled appropriately with initials, date, sampling place, medium for growth, and incubation temperature.

Figure 11.7 *A petri dish containing nutrient agar*

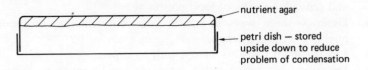

(d) Sterile cottonwool is wiped over the surface to be sampled and then, opening the petri dish as briefly as possible, smeared across the nutrient agar.

(e) The petri dishes are taped, to keep them closed.

(f) The petri dishes are incubated for 72 hours at 40°C.

(g) Without opening them, the petri dishes are observed and the approximate number and types of microbial growths are recorded.

(h) Conclusions are drawn.

Note: Many other experiments can be carried out with the use of agar plates. The effect of temperature can be investigated by inoculating agar plates (that is the deliberate transfer of bacteria from one place to another) with known bacteria and incubating at different temperatures, for example, 0°C, 20°C, 40°C, 60°C, 80°C. The effect of the medium for growth can be investigated by inoculating plates with different types of agar. The effect of disinfectants can be investigated by inoculation of agar plates which contain troughs for holding a small amount of disinfectant.

Many specialised microbiology books are available with practical details of these types of experiments, if further study is required.

FOOD STORAGE

12.1 INTRODUCTION

The techniques of food storage have been developed over thousands of years to enable food to be eaten when it is not in season or after the point at which it would have become inedible, if it had not been preserved. The techniques involve controlling microbial breakdown and chemical or enzymic changes that occur in food itself as it is stored.

This chapter is divided into two sections which look at:

(a) **Short-term storage** – this refers to storage periods of a few hours up to a few days and includes the preparation and cooking of food.

(b) **Longer-term storage** – this covers the commercial food preservation processes such as canning, freezing and dehydration which allow food to be stored for a few days up to two or three years.

In both sections the 'life' of the food is extended by controlling one or more of the conditions required for the growth of micro-organisms described in Chapter 9, section 9.7.

SHORT-TERM STORAGE

Most short-term storage relies on temperature control of food. The Food Hygiene Regulations (Chapter 11, section 11.8), which are designed to reduce the risk of food poisoning and spoilage, state that food (such as meats, fish, gravy, imitation cream, egg products, milk and milk products, and so on) shall be kept *above 63°C* or *below 10°C* and when it is cooked or partly cooked it shall be served immediately or returned to a temperature below 10°C or above 63°C until service. These temperatures ensure that bacteria are destroyed or are dormant.

> **Task 12.1** Describe what happens to bacteria (a) above 63°C, and (b) below 10°C.

12.2 HIGH TEMPERATURE CONTROL

Normal cooking methods such as boiling, roasting and frying should raise the temperature of food well above the 63°C specified in the Food Hygiene Regulations. However, the control of temperature *after* cooking is very important, particularly if food is to be kept for a long time before service. Thermostatically controlled bain-maries, hot plates, hot trolleys or servery counters are essential to keep the food above 63°C, and these pieces of equipment must be checked and maintained regularly to ensure no faults arise in temperature control.

12.3 LOW TEMPERATURE CONTROL

Below 10°C the 'shelf-life' of food is extended by a few days (and sometimes longer), since the growth of micro-organisms is reduced and chemical changes occur more slowly. The development of the *refrigerator* has therefore led to significant improvements in food storage. However, it must be stressed that cross-contamination can occur in a refrigerator and foods do deteriorate; they may even spoil or cause food poisoning. As with all equipment, it should be used correctly and its limitations should be clearly understood.

The normal range of temperatures for a refrigerator is between 1° and 5°C, which should stop the growth of pathogens and greatly reduce the multiplication of spoilage organisms. However, it must be remembered that once foods are removed from the refrigerator any micro-organisms present may grow and reproduce at their normal rate. The following points should be observed when using a refrigerator:

   (i) The temperature should be checked regularly with a thermometer.
  (ii) It should be kept clean.
 (iii) It should be defrosted regularly to prevent the build up of ice which reduces efficiency.

(iv) Warm or hot foods should not be placed directly into a refrigerator, because they raise the internal temperature.

(v) Good stock rotation is essential.

(vI0 Foods should be stored to avoid cross-contamination, for example, cooked foods should be stored away from and above raw foods.

(vii) Foods should be covered whenever possible.

(viii) In the event of a breakdown in refrigeration, food should be used immediately or thrown away.

Task 12.2 Using a domestic or commerical refrigerator, monitor the temperature range over which it operates by placing a thermometer inside the cabinet and altering the settings. Does the lowest setting keep the food cool enough? You may like to experiment by placing a hot table jelly in the refrigerator to see just how high the temperature is raised; but this of course must not be done if there is a significant hygiene risk.

Particularly with foods that have a short shelf-life, it is important for the caterer, and the consumer, to know what the life of the food is. Therefore many foods are now labelled with information, such as a date or code that indicates when it should be sold, the 'sell-by date', or when the quality begins to fall, the 'best-before' date (see Chapter 13, section 13.6).

Task 12.3 Choose two or three food commodities: yoghurt, biscuits, tinned beef, for example, and determine the average length of time you could keep the food according to the 'sell-by' or 'best-before' dates.

LONGER-TERM STORAGE

Food can be preserved for long periods of time by commercial processing. Processing may involve high or low temperatures, packing in specialised containers, drying, the use of natural and artificial chemicals and irradiation. In some cases a combination of several techniques is used.

12.4 HIGH TEMPERATURE TECHNIQUES

High temperatures are used in many processes such as *canning* and *bottling*. The temperature used depends on the foodstuff and the type of process. One important factor is the pH value of the food. If this is acidic, such as in some fruits and vegetables, the temperature required to sterilise the food is lower than in neutral foods. The reason for this is that pathogens cannot tolerate the acid conditions in the food and a limited heat treatment is therefore sufficient. However, in foods above pH5.3, such as meat, fish, and milk, high temperatures are required to achieve sterilisation. A temperature of 115°C for several minutes is average for the canning process of most neutral foods. Recently the HTST (high temperature-short time) process has become common because a slightly higher temperature, for example 120°C, can be used, for a much shorter time, perhaps a few seconds. Commercially this process is more economical.

The canning or bottling process varies considerably across the range of foods and drinks processed in this way.

The process may involve sealing the vessel before treatment or heat treating in the vessel before final sealing under aseptic conditions, that is, in conditions that prevent re-contamination by micro-organisms (see Figure 12.1).

In some cases sterilisation is not possible, or not desirable, since the high temperatures used have a significant effect on the texture and taste of the food. The compromise of *pasteurisation* can be used in which lower heat treatment temperatures are used which destroy pathogens but do not affect the palatability of the food to the same effect. Examples of foods which are commonly pasteurised are milk,

Figure 12.1 *Structure of a can*

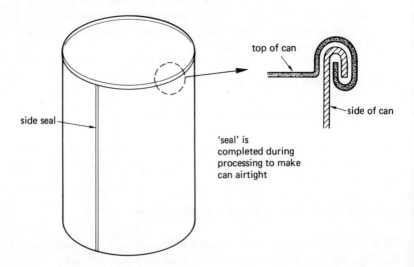

top of can

side of can

side seal

'seal' is
completed during
processing to make
can airtight

milk derivatives such as yoghurt and cream, and some of the cooked meats such as ham or luncheon meat. The texture and taste of the cooked meats would be altered significantly if subjected to excessive heat treatment. In fact, they do not need very high temperatures because they contain salt and other chemicals which act as preservatives.

Table 12.1 shows a summary of the main types of heat treatment used for milk.

Table 12.1   *Heat treatment of milk*

Type	Treatment	Effect
Untreated	None	Any pathogenic bacteria present will not be killed. There is therefore a possible health hazard.
Pasteurised (Holder Process)	62.8°C for 30 minutes – rapid cooling to 10°C	Pathogens are killed, rendering the milk safe.
Pasteurised (HTST (high temperature–short time))	71.7°C for 15 seconds – rapid cooling to 10°C	Processing does not affect palatibility and nutritive value excessively.
Sterilised in bottle	105°C–110°C for 20–40 minutes	The milk is sterile but the nutritive value, appearance and taste are affected.
Sterilised (UHT (ultra high temperature))	135°–150°C for 1–3 seconds	

Spoilage of canned and bottled goods can occur if either the heat treatment process or the container is faulty (or is damaged in storage). In canning the most common faults arise when the seal is incorrectly formed or is incomplete, allowing entry of micro-organisms. This can lead to the formation of unpleasant substances within the food and may involve the production of gases. If gases are produced the can will bulge and may become 'blown'. In any of these circumstances the food and container must be disposed of immediately.

12.5   LOW TEMPERATURE TECHNIQUES

Section 12.3 described 'chilling', which extends the life of food by a few days. If temperatures are reduced beyond chilling and the food is *frozen*, then the storage life can be greatly extended, often for months and even years. The temperatures used in freezing have an effect on:

(a) **Micro-organisms** – very few types of micro-organisms can grow at temperatures below 0°C, and are restricted by the shortage of available water (much of the water is converted to ice).

(b) **Enzymic activity** – autolytic enzymes present in the food may continue to function but at a much slower rate.

Task 12.4 Explain why even food that has been frozen for several months may still represent a food-poisoning hazard. (Do not include in your answer the risks of contamination from other sources after thawing.)

The quality of frozen foods is high and is often regarded as being the closest to fresh food because in most cases there is little nutritional loss and the texture and taste of the food is less affected than in canning, for example. An exception to this is the freezing of foods with high water contents such as strawberries and raspberries, which become very 'mushy' on thawing.

Task 12.5 Obtain one food commodity in as many different forms as possible, for example, strawberries: fresh, frozen, tinned or in jam. Assess each of them in terms of: taste, smell, texture, over-all palatibility. (Remember that some processes will have used sugar, etc., that affect these qualities.)

The storage time for frozen foods depends on the temperature at which the food is stored. The lower the temperature, the longer the storage (see Table 12.2).

Table 12.2 *Length of storage for refrigerated foods*

Type of freezer	Storage temperature	Length of storage
Freezer compartment of domestic refrigerator	−6° to −12°C	1 week to 1 month
Domestic freezer	−18°C	About 3 months
Commerical freezer	−30°C to −40°C	Several months, sometimes years

Important in the freezing process is the *rate* at which food is frozen. If food is *quick frozen*, the ice crystals formed are small and tend not to destroy the cell structure. This means that on thawing less water is lost (*drip*) and the food is not 'mushy'. Quick freezing is mainly suitable for small foods, where extraction of heat from the food is easy. In *slow freezing* much larger ice crystals are formed which damage the cell structure, causing water to be lost and 'mushyness' to occur when thawed. Larger items, particularly meat, which are frozen this way, experience *drip* on thawing, which results in nutritional loss and a deterioration in palatability (see Figure 12.2).

Figure 12.2   *Freezing of food*

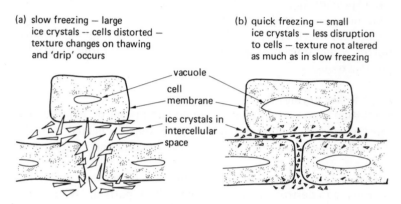

(a) slow freezing – large ice crystals -- cells distorted – texture changes on thawing and 'drip' occurs

(b) quick freezing – small ice crystals – less disruption to cells – texture not altered as much as in slow freezing

vacuole

cell membrane

ice crystals in intercellular space

The main types of commerical freezing are *plate freezing* which involves refrigerated metal plates between which the food is placed (fish and meat for example) and *blast freezing* which utilises a flow of cold air over the food (peas and other vegetables, for example). *Cryogenic freezing*, in which food is placed into liquid nitrogen at $-200°C$ can be used for delicate foods such as strawberries and raspberries to reduce the damage caused during freezing; but the process is expensive.

12.6   DEHYDRATION

The drying of food has a preserving effect because it reduces the level of available water to below a point at which micro-organisms can grow. Early methods of drying were developed to preserve fish, meat and fruit, and relied on the evaporation of water caused by the heat of the sun. Other traditional methods of food preservation, such as *smoking*, also rely on the fact that water is driven out of the food (although smoking involves drying in the presence of anti-microbial chemicals that preserve the food). *Salting* can be considered to have a drying effect since it reduces the amount of water osmotically (see Chapter 9, section 9.7).

Modern commerical drying can be extended to many types of food, which are dried in the following ways:

(i) **Air drying**
Food is placed on perforated trays and hot air is blown over it. A more recent adaptation of this is *fluidised bed drying*, in which warmed air is circulated around the food.

(ii) **Spray drying**
This method is used for liquid or semi-liquid foods (milk, eggs, beverages) which are sprayed through a fine nozzle into a stream of hot air. Water quickly evaporates from the droplets formed and a fine powder remains.

(iii) **Roller drying**
Semi-solid food such as cooked potato and instant breakfast cereals can be dried by being poured as a paste on to a heated revolving drum. The paste dries on the surface of the drum and is scraped off.

In the above techniques heat treatment is often necessary before processing to destroy micro-organisms. This is particularly important with milk and egg products.

(iv) **Accelerated freeze drying**
In *accelerated freeze drying* food is frozen and then heated slowly to convert the ice directly into water vapour. (The liquid stage is missed out and the process is called *sublimation*.) The effect is that there is little disruption to the food structure, and addition of water during cooking gives a product which is similar to the original in flavour, colour and nutritional value. The process is slightly more expensive than the other drying techniques, but is widely used for meat, shellfish, fruits and vegetables, and coffee.

Task 12.6 Make a survey of a range of dried foods. Can you tell which of the commercial drying techniques has been used? If so, do the different processes affect price considerably?

12.7 CHEMICAL CONTROL

Amongst the many chemicals added to food are those that are added to preserve it. Chemicals may be natural or synthetic and are used to prevent:

(i) microbial breakdown, and

(ii) deterioration by oxidation (anti-oxidants).

(i) Microbial preservation

(a) *Sugar and salt* – These are common substances in food and have a preserving effect by restricting the amount of water available to micro-organisms. The water is 'bound' to the sugar or salt by *osmosis*. Examples of foods preserved in this way are *jams* which have a high sugar content and *meat and vegetables* which can be preserved with salt.

(b) *Curing* – This is a traditional method of food preservation used with bacon and ham, which involves soaking or injecting meat with a solution of salt, sodium nitrite and potassium nitrate. The process alters the texture and flavour of the food, but is considered acceptable by many people.

(c) *Smoking* – Some foods are preserved by being subjected to wood smoke which contains *aldehydes* and *phenols* which are organic chemicals that prevent the growth of micro-organisms. Smoking has the additional effect of partially drying the food. Bacon and cheeses are treated in this way.

(d) *Natural acids* – Since micro-organisms cannot grow in low pH conditions, the presence of acid in food has a preserving effect. Two examples are *pickling* of vegetables, such as onions in vinegar (containing acetic acid) and the production of lactic acid in yoghurt.

(e) *Other chemical additives* – Many of the processes described so far are traditional methods of preserving food and have involved the use of the same chemicals for many years. At the present time any new chemicals required by a manufacturer to preserve food are governed by strict legislation (see Chapter 13). Some of the common preservative chemicals in use today that are permitted by law are shown in Table 12.3.

(f) *Antibiotics* – An antibiotic is a chemcial produced by one micro-organism which is harmful to another micro-organism. Antibiotics are probably best known for their use in medicine to treat infection. They can have a preserving effect on food by reducing microbial growth. However, their use is very limited because they are likely to reduce resistance to disease in food, and in man as the consumer.

214

Table 12.3 *Chemical preservatives*

'E' number	Chemical	Foods
E220	Sulphur dioxide	Fruit based foods and drinks, beers, ciders, wine, sausages and many convenience foods
E200 E210	Sorbic acid ⎱ Benzoic acid ⎰	Yoghurt, fruit juices, soft drinks and many convenience foods
E249 E250 E251 E252	Potassium nitrite Sodium nitrite Sodium nitrate Potassium nitrate	Cured meat, processed meats, sausages
E280	Propionic acid	Baking and dairy products

Nisin is the only remaining antibiotic in use, since it is not used in medicine. It is found in canned meats, cream and cheese.

(ii) **Anti-oxidants**
Many foods deteriorate in quality during storage because of chemical changes in the food. The most important changes occur due to reaction of the food with oxygen from the atmosphere, leading to *oxidation*. Anti-oxidants, whether found naturally in the food or added, function by preventing oxygen from combining with the food, usually by reacting with oxygen themselves. However, the fact that the anti-oxidants react with oxygen means that they become 'used up' in time and the food will eventually deteriorate. Vitamin E and vitamin C are naturally occurring anti-oxidants in plants; two synthetic anti-oxidants are BHA (butylated hydroxyanisole) and BHT (butylated hydroxytoluene). The latter chemicals are often added to oils and fats to reduce or prevent rancidity.

12.8 **IRRADIATION**

Ionising radiation such as X-rays and gamma-rays (see Figure 8.3) can be used to kill or reduce the numbers of micro-organisms in food. As with heat treatment, several levels of irradiation can be used to produce different effects. High doses of radiation are required to produce sterilisation and have been used with meat and seafood, while pasteurisation can be achieved with a lower dosage to extend the shelf life and prevent spoilage in meat, poultry, fish, seafood, fruit, vegetables and cereals.

The food is treated by passing it on a conveyor belt through a chamber containing a radiation source, such as cobalt or an electron-beam machine. The dose of radiation can be accurately measured and is related to the length of time it is exposed to the radiation.

There is, of course, controversy over the use of irradiation in this way, and although it is permitted for restricted use in the USA, France, Holland, Japan and other countries, it is not, at the time of writing, permitted in the UK. The present discussion in the UK about the irradiation of foods concerns advantages and disadvantages, some of which are shown in Table 12.4. One point that is probably agreed on is that while irradiation may be used for pasteurisation of foods, it will almost certainly not be used for sterilisation of human food, because of the high doses required.

Table 12.4 *Some advantages and disadvantages of the irradiation of food*

Advantages	Disadvantages
Irradiation: – could reduce food spoilage and food poisoning. – could reduce food wastage because of the above point. – can be used to control ripening in fruits and prevent sprouting in vegetables. – could extend the shelf life of fruit and vegetables because of the above point.	Irradiation: – may not be *necessary*, since many other food preservation methods are suitable. – is thought by many people to alter texture and palatability of food significantly. – is alarming to many people. Although scientific testing has shown no health risks, people are slow to be convinced.

12.9 PACKAGING

Packaging plays an important part in the preservation of food. As well as protecting against damage, the package should prevent the entry of air, moisture and micro-organisms, all of which would cause deterioration of the food.

Cans, bottles, boxes and simple bags have been used for many years to package food but recent technology has led to the development of very sophisticated packages made of plastic or plastic and metal. Plastics such as cellulose, polythene, polypropylene and polyvinyl chloride are used frequently, particularly for individually packaged convenience foods. *Retortable pouches* which contain plastic and metal sandwiched together provide a strong but flexible container that enables heat treatment of the food to be achieved more easily and cheaply than in canning.

Task 12.7 Next time you walk around a supermarket or wholesale food shop make a list of as many different types of package used for food as you can.

Many packaging procedures involve the removal of air from the container during processing, creating a *vacuum*. This has the advantage of preventing the growth of aerobic micro-organisms, although anaerobic bacteria, for example *Clostridium perfringens* and *Clostridium botulinum*, would be able to grow if they survived the processing phase.

12.10 STORAGE OF COOKED MEALS IN MASS CATERING OPERATIONS

Technological advances in equipment design, and an increase in the knowledge of food microbiology, have enabled some mass catering operations to move over to more economical *centralised cooking systems*. These systems which operate a 'cook-chill' or a 'cook-freeze' process are dependant on a high degree of understanding of hygiene and microbiology, in order to ensure the production of safe food.

Cook-chill and cook-freeze systems are similar in that they involve mass production of food in a central kitchen, which is then portioned, chilled or frozen, stored, removed from store when required, transported to the required place, reheated and then served. IT IS IMPERATIVE THAT TEMPERATURE CONTROL OF THE FOOD IS *ACCURATE* AND IS *MONITORED* AT EVERY STAGE. (Chapter 11 has indicated that most food-poisoning cases arise from incorrect storage and reheating of food, therefore temperature control is most important. If any fault is discovered in the temperature control, *all* the food should be *discarded*.) The main advantages of cook-chill and cook-freeze systems are the savings in cost, reduction in manpower, and creation of better cooking conditions, for example, working hours and the production of a more standard product. The main disadvantage is the risk of errors being made in the production system.

Staff training and education are essential aspects when introducing a cook-chill or cook-freeze system.

Figure 12.3 shows the main stages in cook-chill and cook-freeze systems.

Figure 12.3 *The main stages in cook-chill and cook-freeze operations*

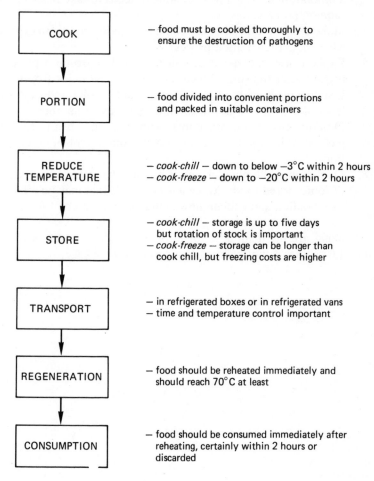

COOK
— food must be cooked thoroughly to ensure the destruction of pathogens

PORTION
— food divided into convenient portions and packed in suitable containers

REDUCE TEMPERATURE
— *cook-chill* — down to below −3°C within 2 hours
— *cook-freeze* — down to −20°C within 2 hours

STORE
— *cook-chill* — storage is up to five days but rotation of stock is important
— *cook-freeze* — storage can be longer than cook chill, but freezing costs are higher

TRANSPORT
— in refrigerated boxes or in refrigerated vans
— time and temperature control important

REGENERATION
— food should be reheated immediately and should reach 70°C at least

CONSUMPTION
— food should be consumed immediately after reheating, certainly within 2 hours or discarded

EXERCISES

1. Describe how you would ensure that a curry and rice dish was kept below the maximum legal temperature if it was produced 90 minutes before service. Assume that it must be stored in the

kitchen, transported to the restaurant and kept in the restaurant while the first course is being eaten.

2. Describe briefly the main points concerning the care and use of a refrigerator.

3. Explain why the pH of a food that is to be canned affects the temperature at which heat treatment needs to take place in the canning process.

4. Make a list of foods that are commonly pasteurised and explain what the pasteurisation process does.

5. Explain how the speed at which a food is frozen affects its texture after thawing. Which foods cannot be quick frozen?

6. List the types of food preservation that involve reducing the level of available water in food, in one way or another.

7. Describe two ways, other than with synthetic chemical additives, in which food can be preserved from microbial deterioration.

8. Oxidation is the main chemical process that affects the quality of some stored foods. Make a list of foods that may be affected by oxidation and explain how manufacturers attempt to reduce it.

9. What are the main advantages of the irradiation of food?

10. List some of the qualities of a good food package.

FOOD ADDITIVES AND FOOD LABELLING

13.1 INTRODUCTION

Many chemicals are added to food during processing for a variety of reasons. One group of additives, the *preservatives*, has been studied in the previous chapter and will be considered again here with the other important groups.

13.2 E NUMBERS

As we have seen in the preceding chapters, there is strict legislation governing the production and sale of food in order to protect the consumer and ensure that he receives food of a high standard. In addition to the general rules laid down by the Food Act 1984 there is specific legislation controlling the use of additives in food in the UK which is based on the country's dietary needs, but is also in line with the European Community directives. The legislation has led to the compilation of a list of permitted additives which are given E numbers for easy identification. The E number system enables information regarding the additives in a food to be coded on the food package, within the list of ingredients. This allows the consumer to identify what he is eating and to make a choice between a food with additives and one without (see Figure 13.1).

Task 13.1 Survey a range of common food packages and make a list of as many different E numbers as you can. Which are the most common numbers?

220

Figure 13.1 *A foodstuff with many additives!*

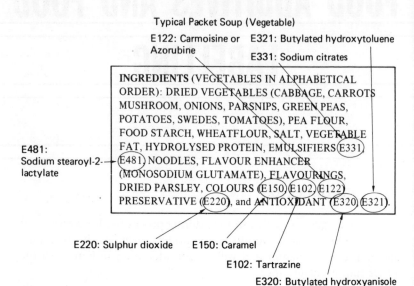

Typical Packet Soup (Vegetable)

E122: Carmoisine or E321: Butylated hydroxytoluene
Azorubine
E331: Sodium citrates

E481:
Sodium stearoyl-2-
lactylate

INGREDIENTS (VEGETABLES IN ALPHABETICAL ORDER): DRIED VEGETABLES (CABBAGE, CARROTS MUSHROOM, ONIONS, PARSNIPS, GREEN PEAS, POTATOES, SWEDES, TOMATOES), PEA FLOUR, FOOD STARCH, WHEATFLOUR, SALT, VEGETABLE FAT, HYDROLYSED PROTEIN, EMULSIFIERS (E331) (E481) NOODLES, FLAVOUR ENHANCER (MONOSODIUM GLUTAMATE), FLAVOURINGS, DRIED PARSLEY, COLOURS (E150) (E102) (E122) PRESERVATIVE (E220), and ANTIOXIDANT (E320) (E321).

E220: Sulphur dioxide   E150: Caramel

E102: Tartrazine

E320: Butylated hydroxyanisole

Source: M. Hansenn, *E for Additives* (Thorson, 1984).

13.3 THE USE OF ADDITIVES

Recently consumers in the UK have questioned the use of additives in food and some claim that their use is excessive. This may be true, particularly of additives that are present just to improve colour or add artificial flavour. Consumer concern may be well founded since risks have been shown to exist with some of the chemicals used. However, it must be pointed out that some of the chemicals not covered by legislation that have been added to food for a very long time, such as sugar and salt which are foods themselves, are also associated with health risks (see Chapter 4). Labelling of foods enables consumer choice in both cases.

In order for a chemical to be a permitted additive it has to undergo a rigorous scientific testing. The additive is investigated in great detail and is fed to animals in abnormally high doses in order to identify any possible affects to health. If there is any evidence to suggest that the chemical would be harmful to man, then it is not permitted to be used. Even before an additive is considered, the manufacturer who wishes to use it must demonstrate the need for a new chemical and prove that an existing equivalent is not available. Even after extensive testing some additives have been permitted that have subsequently been shown to be harmful to man. Some additives have been shown to cause allergies, others are thought to cause hyperactivity in children, while a few are linked with certain types of cancer. What is certain is that many additives are safe and have an important part to play in food processing, preserving the quality of food and also enabling costs to be maintained at a minimum.

13.4 THE TYPES OF ADDITIVES

The European Community directives cover four of the main groups of additives which are anti-oxidants, colourings, emulsifiers and stabilisers and preservatives. Flavourings and enzymes are not yet significantly controlled by regulations, but are subject to the general provisions of the Food Act 1984. Other miscellaneous chemicals which may be added to food include (i) sweeteners, (ii) fortifying agents, (iii) solvents, (iv) mineral hydrocarbons, and (v) modified starches.

Colourings
Colourings are added to food to improve its appearance. The appearance may need to be improved for several reasons:

  (i) Processing and storage can often result in colour being lost and foods appearing 'dull'. For example, the process of canning involves high temperatures which destroy many plant pigments. Since it has been shown that the consumer is reluctant to buy 'dull' coloured food, preferring to see it brightly coloured, most manufacturers add colour to tinned fruit and vegetables, for example.
 (ii) To increase the colour of foods which have ingredients added, such as yoghurts and fruit drinks. Often the added ingredient does not colour the food sufficiently itself and so colours are added. Strawberry·yoghurt, for example, would appear pale pink without added colour, instead of the deeper red colour of most commercial yoghurts.
(iii) To give colour to foods which would otherwise be colourless, such as boiled sweets, jellies and fizzy drinks.

Many of the permitted colours are natural, for example, caramel, turmeric and chlorophyll, while some are artificial. However, the list of permitted artificial additives is decreasing as more questions are raised about their safety.

Foods to which colour cannot be added are fresh meats, poultry, fish, fruits and vegetables, tea, coffee and dried milk.

Task 13.2 Prepare two types of garden peas for tasting. One set to be cooked from fresh in slightly salted water but with no chemicals that would affect colour. The other peas to be commercially preserved and brightly coloured. Ask a number of people to indicate which they prefer, (a) after looking at them but before tasting them, and (b) after tasting. Is there a consensus?

Flavourings

The flavourings that are added to food, of which there are over 1500, are used for similar reasons to the colourings. They are used to replace flavour lost during processing and storage, to improve flavour in foods where ingredients are added that may not be highly flavoured and to give synthetic flavour to foods that would be flavourless. Unlike the colourings, they are not covered in the additives legislation and no E numbers have been assigned to flavourings. Flavourings may be natural in their origin such as herbs, spices, essences of vanilla, lemon, almond, mint or extracts of fruits and vegetables that are commonly used, or they may be synthetic chemicals which are manufactured specifically to resemble popular flavours.

Preservatives

These prevent microbiological spoilage and poisoning, leading to an extended shelf life for many foods. Their use is beneficial in keeping costs down, due to reduced wastage and also thereby increasing the convenience of food storage. There are three main types of preservatives found in food:

(i) *Natural preservatives* – These are not controlled by the specific additives legislation because they are classed as foods in their own right and have been used in food preparation for centuries. They include, salt, sugar, alcohol, lactic acid, acetic acid (in vinegar) and spices.

(ii) *Chemical preservatives* – This group contains the organic acids sulphur dioxide, benzoic acid, propionic acid and sorbic acid, and the curing salts sodium nitrate, sodium nitrite, potassium nitrate and potassium nitrite. The two types of chemical preservatives work in different ways but both are effective in preventing microbial growth. The use of curing salts is carefully controlled to ensure that concentrations are not great enough to lead to the production of nitrosamines in the food, which may be formed when nitrites react with meat, since these are carcinogenic.

(iii) *Antibiotics* – Although these are efficient preservatives, their use is restricted because liberal use of antibiotics leads to the development of resistant bacteria which would severely reduce the effectiveness of antibiotics in medical treatment. The main antibiotic used in the UK is *Nisin* which is found in some canned meats and cheese. Tetracyclines are still permitted in the USA.

Anti-oxidants

These chemicals are used to prevent processes such as oxidative rancidity (see Chapter 10, section 10.2) in fats and oils by preventing oxygen from taking part in the reaction, or at least delaying it. They are particularly important in cooking oils and margarines and products which contain fat or oil, such as crisps.

Vitamin C and vitamin E are examples of naturally occurring anti-oxidants, while BHA and BHT (see Glossary) are two examples of synthetic chemicals used in this way.

Emulsifiers and stabilisers

An emulsifier is a substance that enables two immiscible liquids to mix and a stabiliser is one that helps to prevent that emulsion from breaking down or separating. Emulsifiers and stabilisers are therefore important additives in commercial fats, salad creams, salad dressings, sauces, and many instant and convenience foods. Some of the chemicals used are natural, such as the emulsifier lecithin from egg yolk, now produced from soya beans, and the starches and sugars that are used as stabilisers. Polyoxyethylene monostearate (emulsifier) and sodium carboxymethyl cellulose (stabiliser) are synthetic chemicals in use.

Sweeteners

There are various ways of making foods sweet. Sucrose, glucose, fructose and lactose can be included and are not covered by specific additives legislation. But often it is preferable to use alternatives, for example, if a substance with no energy value is required. Saccharin and cyclamates are examples of sweeteners with no energy value; but cyclamates are not permitted and saccharin is used less and less, since serious questions were raised over their safety.

The only sweeteners that have been given E numbers are sorbitol and mannitol and these are commonly used in confectionery, ice-cream and cakes and pastries.

Solvents
These chemicals enable other ingredients to be included in food as part of the structure, usually by dissolving them. One example is glycerol, which is used in confectionery, icing and liqueurs.

Mineral hydrocarbons
The use of these chemicals is not extensive, but they have proved beneficial in preventing some foods from drying out during storage, preventing dried fruits from sticking together, and producing a shiny surface to sweets and other confectionery.

Modified starches
Several starch-based thickening agents are used to improve the texture of some dairy products.

Miscellaneous additives
Many other chemicals are added to food that do not fall into any of the above categories. Some of these are explained below:

(i) *Flavour enhancers* – The most common example of these is monosodium glutamate which is used in many convenience foods and features in Chinese cookery. It has the effect of increasing the flavour of the food to which it is added.

(ii) *Fortifying agents* – These are nutrients added to food either to replace those lost in processing or to increase the nutritional value of a food. Some fortifying agents must be included by law. These include the B vitamins, calcium and iron that are added to white flour, and the vitamins A and D that are required in margarine to ensure that it is nutritionally equivalent to butter. Others, such as those vitamins and minerals that are used to enrich breakfast cereals and the addition of vitamin C to drinks, are used to increase the nutritional appeal of the food.

(iii) *Humectants* – These are added to prevent drying out in dried fruits and cakes.

(iv) *Releasing agents* – These may be used to prevent the sticking of food to processing equipment, containers and cooking utensils.

(v) *Anti-foaming agents* – These are used to prevent difficulties in processing that may occur when boiling milk, fruit juices, and so on.

(vi) *Bulking agents* – These are added to slimming foods to increase volume without increasing energy value.

(vii) *Raising agents* – Chapter 9, section 9.8 described the use of yeast to produce carbon dioxide for raising in breads and cakes. Chemical raising agents, such as baking powder, are added to some products for the purpose of aeration, which is brought about by the production of carbon dioxide. Baking powder usually contains *sodium bicarbonate* and an acid, which react when water is added to give a salt, water and carbon dioxide:

sodium bicarbonate + an acid = a salt + water + CO_2

Task 13.3 Obtain two types of orange squash, one with as few additives as possible, the other with additives. Ask a group of people to assess the colour, smell and flavour and their individual preferences. (One way to do this is to ask each person to give a score from 0 to 5 and obtain a total score for each one). Do people prefer orange squash with or without additives? **Note any difference in price for the two drinks. Can you explain the difference?**

Table 13.1 shows a summary of the additives in the preceding section, for easy reference (see also Figure 13.2)

Task 13.4 Obtain three different food labels which show a list of ingredients containing several chemical additives. List the ingredients for each package and indicate the main function of each of the ingredients, including the additives.

13.5 HARMFUL EFFECTS OF ADDITIVES

The harmful effects that have been shown, or are suspected, of additives are varied, ranging from minor skin rashes to cancer. Many of the conditions are *allergenic*, that is they are caused by an *allergy* to one or more additive chemicals. An allergy develops when a foreign particle, called an *antigen* enters the body and causes the body to produce an *antibody* to combat it. These antibodies circulate in the blood and attack any further antigens. If there are greater numbers of antigens than antibodies the extra antigens may set up a reaction in one of the tissues of the body. In the alimentary tract this leads to abdominal pain, vomiting and diarrhoea; in the respiratory system breathing difficulties such as asthma may arise; if it involves the skin various rashes may result.

Table 13.1 A summary of the common chemical additives to food

Type of additive	Function	Chemical examples	Food examples	Comments
Colourings	To improve appearance of the food	Tartrazine (E102)	Fizzy drinks, piccalilli, sweets, chewing gum, rind of cheese, tinned processed peas	Thought to be involved in hyperactivity in children and various allergic conditions. Very common
		Sunset yellow (E110), Carmoisine (E122), Amaranth (E123), Ponceau 4R (E124)	Packet soups, orange squash, marzipan Packet jellies, brown sauce, blancmange Gravy granules, liquid vitamin C drinks Dessert toppings, tinned strawberries	Allergic reaction may be caused in some people
		Caramel (E150)	Biscuits, prepacked cakes, Scotch eggs	Safety is in question
Flavourings	To improve taste of food	Herbs, spices, extracts and essences (no E numbers)	Mustards, sauces, pickles	Legislation regarding their use is expected
Preservatives	To preserve food	Sorbic acid (E200) Benzoic acid (E210)	Yoghurt, soft drinks, frozen pizza Jams, beers, pickles	May affect asthmatic people
		Sulphur dioxide (E220)	Dehydrated vegetables, beer, wine, cider	May cause irritation of the alimentary canal
		Potassium nitrite Sodium nitrite (E250) Sodium nitrate (E251) Potassium nitrate (E252)	Cooked meats, sausages Cured meat, bacon, ham Bacon, cheese, canned meat Cured meats, sausages, bacon	May be carcinogenic (cancer forming)
Anti-oxidants	To prevent spoilage by oxidation	Ascorbic acid (E300) Butylated hydroxyanisole (BHA) Butylated hydroxytoluene (BHT)	Butter, fruit, jams, preserves Raisins, cheese spread ,beef stock cubes Savoury rice, packet convenience foods	Not used in foods intended for young babies/children

Emulsifiers and stabilisers	To maintain the structure of the food	Lecithin (E322); Citric acid (E330); Tartaric acid (E334); Sodium alginate (E401); Tragacanth (E413); Pectin (E440a)	E322 – soft margarine, vermicelli; E330 – ice-cream, frozen fish; E334 – jellies, jams; E401 – puddings, packet cake mixes; E413 – processed cheese, cake decorations; E440a – flans, puddings, desserts	
Sweeteners	To sweeten food	Sorbitol (E420) Mannitol (E421)	Chocolates, pastries, confectionery Sweets, ice cream	These are the only two sweeteners with E numbers
Solvents	Enable some ingredients to be incorporated into food	Glycerol (E422)	Liqueurs, confectionery, cake icing	
Mineral hydrocarbons	To prevent drying out of some foods and produce a shiny surface	Chemical manufactured mineral derivatives	Dried fruits, some confectionery, and sometimes eggs	
Miscellaneous additives	To enhance flavour	Monosodium glutamate	Various	May cause heart palpitations headaches, dizziness, etc. (Chinese restaurant syndrome)
	Increase nutritional value	Vitamins, A, B, C, D, calcium, iron	Flour, margarine	
	Humectants, releasing agents, bulking agents, anti-foaming agents	Various	Various	

Source: M. Hanssen, *E for Additives* (Thorsons Publishing Group, 1984).

Figure 13.2 *A selection of ingredient lists from common foods*

(a) *Instant custard*

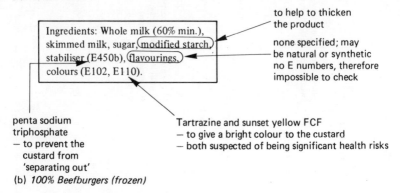

Ingredients: Whole milk (60% min.), skimmed milk, sugar, modified starch, stabiliser (E450b), flavourings, colours (E102, E110).

to help to thicken the product

none specified; may be natural or synthetic no E numbers, therefore impossible to check

penta sodium triphosphate
— to prevent the custard from 'separating out'

Tartrazine and sunset yellow FCF
— to give a bright colour to the custard
— both suspected of being significant health risks

(b) *100% Beefburgers (frozen)*

Ingredients: Beef (minimum 99%), salt, pepper, polyphosphates, preservative E223

This manufacturer has decided to reduce the number of additives and has not used colours or flavours.
The preservative is sodium metabisulphite.
Beware — the addition of polyphosphates is often to enable water to be 'hidden' in the food!

(c) *Tinned baked beans*

Ingredients:
Beans, Water,
Tomatoes, Sugar,
Salt
Modified starch,
Spirit vinegar,
Spices

Free from artificial colours and preservatives

Many manufacturers are aware of consumer demands and the last phrase in this label will influence many consumers

(d) *'Healthy' crunchy biscuit bar*

Ingredients: Rolled oats, Raw Sugar, Vegetable oil, Sultanas (11%), Wheat Flakes, Hazelnuts (4.1%), Honey, Dried Skimmed Milk, Salt.
Free from artificial flavours, colouring and preservatives

Once again the manufacturer has avoided additives and has made a determined effort to compete with the 'junk food' snacks by providing a different type of product

This packet also included additional nutritional information

It is thought that hyperactivity in children can be caused or aggravated by some additives, particularly synthetic colourings and flavourings. It is alleged that these additives cause some children to be overactive, require little sleep and have difficulties in speech, balance and learning. Often asthma and other conditions are linked with the hyperactivity. Some of the conditions that can be caused by, or it is *thought* can be caused by, additives are hyperactivity, asthma and other breathing problems, hayfever, headaches, dizziness, blurred vision, gastric upsets, vomiting, skin rashes, tissue swelling, hypertension and cancer.

In many cases if an additive is suspected of causing a reaction of some sort it is difficult to identify the exact additive. Under medical supervision the patient may be put on a diet which has had a complete group of foods omitted. These are then replaced one at a time until the reaction takes place and the additive is identified. A list of foods containing the offending additive can then be made and these foods are removed from the patient's normal diet.

Task 13.5 Construct a simple questionnaire with a sample of the general public to determine:
(a)   their attitude towards additives in food, or
(b)   their knowledge of what types of chemicals are added to food, or
(c)   their knowledge of the types of health risks sometimes associated with additives.

13.6   FOOD LABELLING

Food labelling is another topic which has become more important in recent years, as processing and technology have progressed. The buyer, whether purchasing food for home use or a large catering establishment, has the right to know exactly what he is buying in packaged foods. There are, of course, regulations governing what should and should not be on a food label. This section describes the information that must be clearly marked on a foodstuff.

A food package must display:

(i)   **The name of the food** – This must be clear and accurate. The name will either be that of a commodity such as salt or pepper or of a specific product such as beefburgers or doughnuts. It must not mislead. For example a 'chocolate-flavour*ed*' biscuit must have a coating whose flavour comes mainly from chocolate, whereas 'choco-late flavour' denotes that the flavour is mainly from an artificial source.

(ii) **The net quantity of food** – This must be clearly shown on most foods and usually shows the weight or volume. Occasionally the number of units is sufficient, as in some breakfast cereals.

(iii) **A complete list of ingredients** – These must be listed in descending order of percentage weight. It is always interesting to note where water, which is used by some manufacturers to 'bulk out' the food, appears on the list. Sugar and salt often appear quite high up. Additives must also be listed in the ingredients, although most of them appear at the end of the list, since only small quantities are used.

'A complete list of ingredients'

(iv) **A date mark** – This is used to give the buyer an indication of the food's freshness and its remaining shelf life. The dates specified on the packet take into account a period of time after expiry, during which the food is still in good condition, enabling the purchaser to store the food for a *sensible* period. Two main types of date are used. The 'sell by' date is for foods which will not last for more than three months and these must be labelled with the day and the month. 'Best before' dates are used with items that can be kept between three and eighteen months and only require the month and year to be specified.

(v) **The conditions for storage** – If foods are to be consumed after the 'sell by' or 'best before' date, they must be stored correctly by the consumer. Guidelines are given on the packet such as 'store in a cool, dry place' or 'refrigerate and eat within 3 days'.

(vi) **Instructions for use** – Details of how to prepare or cook a food are often important in order to ensure optimum palatibility and good hygiene. These should be simply explained on the package.

(vii) **The origin of the food** – Clearly marked should be the place where the food came from or was made.

(viii) **The manufacturer's address** – The name and address of the manufacturer or retailer is important so that the consumer knows who to contact, if further information is required or a complaint is to be made.

Some foods do not have to show all of the above information Fresh unwrapped foods obviously do not need instructions for use or details of storage. However, some manufacturers are beginning to include more information than is legally required, by stating the nutritional content of the foods they have produced.

Figure 13.3 *A modern food package with additional nutritional information*

LOW FAT FRUIT YOGHURT

clearly marked accurate label

net quantity in metric and imperial units

142 g   5 oz

Name of Food

FREE FROM ARTIFICIAL ADDITIVES

KEEP REFRIGERATED
Best before – see lid

storage details

information regarding 'sell by' date which is stamped on lid

Typical Nutritional value per 100 g

Fat	1.1 g
Protein	3.8 g
Carbohydrate	10.5 g
Energy	65 kcal

Added ingredients: Fruit, Demerara sugar, Natural Flavouring

Manufacturers address

additional nutritional information to enable consumer to make more informed food choice

ingredients, excluding the yoghurt, in descending order of weight

accurate 'claim'

necessary for complaints, further information

232

Task 13.6 Survey a range of foods to obtain a food label containing all other types of information described in this section.

EXERCISES

1. List the main groups of additives to food.
2. Explain what the E numbers are.
3. Describe the procedures a chemical additive has to go through before it is permitted to be used in food. What must the manufacturer prove in order to have it accepted?
4. For which main reasons are colourings and flavourings used in food?
5. Describe the main advantages associated with the widespread use of preservatives in our food.
6. Give examples of the following groups of preservatives, indicating foods in which they may be used: (a) natural preservatives, (b) chemical preservatives, (c) antibiotics.
7. What is the function of an anti-oxidant? Give examples of foods in which their use is important.
8. Describe two of the disadvantageous effects to health that are attributed to the consumption of food additives.
9. What are the two types of date marking found on food packages? Explain how each type is used.
10. List the other types of information that you would expect to find on a typical food package.

MULTIPLE-CHOICE QUESTIONS

Complete these questions *without* using the text and then refer back.

CHAPTER 1

1. The structure within a cell that is concerned with energy is: (a) the cytoplasm, (b) the cell membrane, (c) the nucleus, (d) the mitochondrion.
2. Which one of the following groups of chemicals is not a food nutrient?: (a) proteins, (b) enzymes, (c) carbohydrates, (d) vitamins.
3. The chemical reaction that takes place during digestion that involves breakdown with water is: (a) hydrolysis, (b) hydration, (c) oxidation, (d) regulation.
4. The teeth at the front of the mouth which are used for chopping are called: (a) incisors, (b) canines, (c) premolars, (d) molars.
5. When proteins are completely broken down the end products are: (a) glucose molecules, (b) glycerol molecules, (c) amino acids, (d) vitamins.
6. The part of the alimentary tract where churning of food occurs and where the acid gastric juice is secreted is: (a) the stomach, (b) the ileum, (c) the colon, (d) the duodenum.
7. Bile and pancreatic juice are secreted into: (a) the mouth, (b) the stomach, (c) the duodenum, (d) the colon.
8. Water reabsorption is the main function of: (a) the liver, (b) the pancreas, (c) the oesophagus, (d) the colon.
9. Movement of food along the alimentary tract is called: (a) secretion, (b) peristalsis, (c) absorption, (d) hydrolysis.
10. The surface area of the ileum is increased by the presence of: (a) villi, (b) enzymes, (c) blood capillaries, (d) chemicals.

CHAPTER 2

1. Which one of the following foods does not contain carbohydrate: (a) potato, (b) sugar, (c) meat, (d) rice.
2. Which one of the following is not a monosaccharide sugar: (a) glucose, (b) sucrose, (c) fructose, (d) galactose.
3. Which one of the following provides the greatest energy value per gram of nutrient: (a) carbohydrate, (b) fat, (c) protein, (d) water.
4. When starch is cooked in moist conditions it may: (a) caramelise, (b) coagulate, (c) gelatinise, (d) oxidise.
5. Which one of the following does not contain fat: (a) meat, (b) cheese, (c) butter, (d) sugar.
6. The point at which a blue haze is given off from the surface of fat or oil during heating is: (a) the smoke point, (b) the melting point, (c) the flash point, (d) the plastic point.
7. Proteins are made up of: (a) amino acids, (b) monosaccharides and disaccharides, (c) glycerol units, (d) vitamins and minerals.
8. Which of the following is not a function of amino acids (from protein digestion) in the body?: (a) energy production, (b) regulation of body processes, (c) growth of body tissues, (d) maintenance and repair of body tissues.
9. Which one of the following cooking processes does not rely on coagulation taking place: (a) frying chips, (b) making yoghurt, (c) whipping cream, (d) boiling an egg.
10. Approximately how much protein does an average adult male require each day?: (a) 24g, (b) 72g, (c) 120g, (d) 240g.

CHAPTER 3

1. Which one of the following vitamins dissolves in water? (a) D, (b) retinol, (c) thiamin, (d) K.
2. Rickets may arise in children that do not receive sufficient: (a) vitamin A, (b) B group vitamins, (c) vitamin C, (d) vitamin D.
3. Shortage of which vitamin may lead to an increase in dental decay because of its relationship with calcium, particularly in children?: (a) A, (b) B group, (c) C, (d) D.
4. A lack of vitamin B_1 – thiamin – may cause one of the following deficiency diseases: (a) beri-beri, (b) pellagra, (c) anaemia, (d) scurvy.
5. Which of the following symptoms does not occur in scurvy?: (a) night blindness, (b) bleeding in the skin, (c) inability to recover quickly from illness, (d) anaemia.

6. Which of the following foods is not a good source of iron?: (a) meat, (b) eggs, (c) milk, (d) liver.
7. The amount of calcium required per day in adults is: (a) 5 mg, (b) 50 mg, (c) 250 mg, (d) 500 mg.
8. Goitre of the neck may be caused if there is a lack of one of the following: (a) iodine, (b) iron, (c) fluorine, (d) phosphorus.
9. Which one of the following minerals is often added to the water supply in order to help reduce tooth decay?: (a) iodine, fluorine, (c) chlorine, (d) potassium.
10. Three of the following minerals and vitamins may be involved in anaemia of one type or another, which one is not?: (a) vitamin C, (b) calcium, (c) vitamin B_{12}, (d) iron.

CHAPTER 4

1. Excess energy from the diet is most likely to be stored in the body as: (a) fat, (b) fibre, (c) salt, (d) sugar.
2. The hormone which affects the metabolic rate of the body is: (a) thyroxin, (b) insulin, (c) glucagon, (d) none of these.
3. Which one of the following people is most likely to have the highest energy requirement from food, given that they are all of similar size, and so on: (a) a student, (b) a shop assistant, (c) an office worker, (d) a farmer.
4. Obesity is linked to several disorders of the body. Select one disorder from the following that may arise in a person who is significantly overweight: (a) cirrhosis of the liver, (b) heart disease, (c) lung cancer, (d) anaemia.
5. Following recent nutritional guidelines, which one of the following should be *increased* in the diet?: (a) fat, (b) fibre, (c) salt, (d) sugar.
6. Which vitamin deficiency disease may be found in severe alcoholism?: (a) beri-beri, (b) rickets, (c) pellagra, (d) xerophthalmia.
7. Constipation, haemorrhoids, diverticular disease and cancer of the bowel are associated with one of the following dietary faults: (a) excess fat, (b) too much sugar, (c) overconsumption of alcohol, (d) lack of fibre.
8. Which one of the following nutrients do adult women require in greater amounts than adult men?: (a) calcium, (b) protein, (c) iron, (d) vitamin D.
9. A vegan is: (a) a person who eats a diet consisting mainly of meat, (b) a person who does not eat vegetables, (c) a person

who eats no food of animal origin, (d) a person who eats no meat but may eat milk, cheese or eggs.

10. The following are examples of malnutrition that are common in Asia, Africa or Latin America. Which one is usually caused by children being weaned from their mother's milk too early?: (a) marasmus, (b) anaemia, (c) pellagra, (d) beri-beri.

CHAPTER 5

1. Which one of the following nutrients is not present in beef?:(a) fat, (b) carbohydrate, (c) protein, (d) iron.
2. Which one of the following does not contain elastin in its muscle structure?: (a) veal, (b) cod, (c) lamb, (d) duck.
3. What is collagen converted into if meat is cooked by a slow, moist method of cooking?: (a) fat, (b) myoglobin, (c) elastin, (d) gelatin.
4. Which of the following types of beef is likely to contain the least connective tissue?: (a) shank, (b) topside, (c) brisket, (d) neck.
5. Myoglobin, when combined with oxygen, as in a freshly-cut piece of red meat, will be: (a) pink, (b) brown, (c) bright red, (d) dark red.
6. The amount of protein per 100g of red meat is between: (a) 5–10g, (b) 15–20g, (c) 30–40g, (d) 50–60g.
7. Fat is a constituent of each of the following. Which one has a significant amount of *unsaturated* fat?: (a) chicken, (b) mackerel, (c) lamb, (d) beef.
8. Which of the following is likely to deteriorate in quality the quickest if not frozen or preserved in some other way?: (a) chicken, (b) kidney, (c) pork, (d) herring.
9. For a person who had received medical advice to cut down animal fats, which of the following protein foods would you recommend?: (a) pork, (b) salmon, (c) chicken, (d) minced beef.
10. Which of the following types of offal is made up mainly of muscle tissue?: (a) heart, (b) liver, (c) kidney, (d) sweetbread.

CHAPTER 6

1. The white fibrous proteins linking the yolk to white in an egg are called: (a) vitelline membranes, (b) yolk membranes, (c) chalazae, (d) the germ.
2. In many dishes that involve eggs, the property of coagulation is important. In which of the following dishes is one of the other

properties of eggs essential?: (a) mayonnaise, (b) meringue, (c) baked custard (d) scrambled eggs.

3. The dark layer that sometimes forms around the yolk of a hard-boiled egg is caused by: (a) lecithin, (b) cholesterol, (c) calcium carbonate, (d) iron sulphide.
4. Which of the following nutrients is not present in eggs?: (a) iron, (b) riboflavin (vitamin B_2), (c) vitamin C, (d) vitamin A.
5. Which of the following describes the process by which fat droplets are dispersed in milk to prevent a cream layer forming?: (a) homogenisation, (b) hydrogenation, (c) pasteurisation (d) Holder process.
6. Which of the following has a minimum fat content of 55 per cent?: (a) whipped cream, (b) single cream, (c) double cream, (d) clotted cream.
7. Which of the following types of cheese is characterised by mould growth on the surface?: (a) Brie, (b) Gruyère, (c) Stilton, (d) Cheddar.
8. Which of the following does not involve micro-organisms as an essential part of its production?: (a) butter, (b) margarine, (c) yoghurt, (d) camembert.
9. The following foods contain a high percentage of fat in their structure. Which contains the most?: (a) lard, (b) margarine, (c) cheddar cheese, (d) cream cheese.
10. In comparison to butter and margarine, low fat spreads contain more: (a) protein, (b) carbohydrate, (c) vitamin A, (d) water.

CHAPTER 7

1. Which one of the following is a true fruit in the biological sense?:(a) onion, (b) celery, (c) tomato, (d) rhubarb.
2. Which is the most important cereal crop grown in the UK and the USA?: (a) maize, (b) wheat, (c) barley, (d) rice.
3. The starch in a wheat grain is found mainly in the: (a) endosperm, (b) aleurone layer, (c) embryo, (d) bran.
4. White flour has an extraction rate of approximately: (a) 60–65%, (b) 70–75%, (c) 80–85%, (d) 90–95%.
5. Which nutrient is lost in large amounts from rice during the milling process and can lead to a deficiency disease in Asian countries for example?: (a) riboflavin (vitamin B_2), (b) iron, (c) thiamin (vitamin B_1), (d) vitamin C.
6. Pasta, such as spaghetti, is made from which type of flour?: (a) patent, (b) soft, (c) wheatmeal, (d) durum.

7. A suitable temperature for the storage of most vegetables is: (a) 0°C, (b) 5°C, (c) 15°C, (d) 20°C.
8. One of the following vegetables has a much higher protein content than the others: (a) potatoes, (b) spinach, (c) haricot beans, (d) turnips.
9. Which of the following procedures would *not* help to retain vitamin C in the preparation and cooking of potatoes?: (a) using a small amount of cooking liquid, (b) placing straight into boiling liquid, (c) cutting into small pieces, (d) cooking for the shortest possible time.
10. 50 per cent or more of almonds, brazil nuts and walnuts is: (a) fat, (b) protein, (c) carbohydrate, (d) water.

CHAPTER 8

1. The best conductor of heat amongst the following is: (a) iron, (b) stainless steel, (c) aluminium, (d) copper.
2. A method of cooking in which most of the heat transfer is by conduction is: (a) deep fat frying, (b) shallow frying, (c) grilling, (d) roasting.
3. The transfer of heat in a boiling liquid or hot air in an oven is by: (a) conduction, (b) convection, (c) infra-red radiation, (d) microwave radiation.
4. Which one of the following materials reflects microwave radiation and therefore should not be used in a microwave oven?: (a) glass, (b) china, (c) earthenware, (d) aluminium foil.
5. Which vitamin is most likely to be lost from stewing beef if it is boiled for a long time?: (a) vitamin A, (b) nicotinic acid, (c) vitamin C, (d) vitamin D.
6. In which one of the following methods of cooking is the highest cooking temperature reached?: (a) deep fat frying, (b) boiling, (c) roasting, (d) steaming.
7. Which one of the following methods of cooking is only really suitable for thin tender foods?: (a) grilling, (b) roasting, (c) steaming, (d) poaching.
8. The temperature at which fat is used for deep frying is likely to be approximately: (a) 150°C, (b) 185°C, (c) 210°C, (d) 225°C.
9. Which one of the following vitamins is *least* affected by cooking and preparation?: (a) vitamin A, (b) the B group, (c) vitamin C, (d) vitamin D.
10. Which one of the following methods of cooking may cause an *increase* in the nutritional value of the food being cooked?: (a) boiling, (b) steaming, (c) deep frying, (d) roasting.

CHAPTER 9

1. The smallest micro-organisms are: (a) the bacteria, (b) the fungi, (c) the viruses, (d) the protozoa.
2. *Salmonella* has a cell shape which is: (a) spherical, (b) rod-shaped, (c) comma-shaped, (d) spiral.
3. The part of the cell in bacteria which gives protection is: (a) the cell wall, (b) the cell membrane, (c) the flagella, (d) the cytoplasm.
4. Yeasts reproduce by: (a) binary fission, (b) production of hyphae, (c) budding, (d) spore formation.
5. Which one of the following factors for growth of micro-organisms cannot be exploited during food processing to prevent microbial browth on its own?: (a) control of temperature, (b) removal of water, (c) removal of oxygen, (d) control of pH conditions.
6. Most micro-organisms grow best when the pH is: (a) pH2–4, (b) pH4–6, (c) pH6–8, (d) pH8–10.
7. The temperature at which pathogens grow best is: (a) 5°–10°C, (b) 15°–20°C, (c) 25°–30°C, (d) 35°–40°C.
8. Which one of the following micro-organisms is used in the production of beer?: (a) *Streptococcus thermophilis*, (b) *Acetobacter*, (c) *Lactobacillus bulgaricus*, (d) *Saccharomyces cerevisiae*.
9. Which one of the following cheeses is ripened by mould growth as opposed to bacterial growth?: (a) Camembert, (b) Gruyère, (c) Cheddar, (d) Wensleydale.
10. In the growth pattern of a bacterial colony, which phase involves the rapid increase in numbers of bacterial cells?: (a) the stationary phase, (b) the log phase, (c) the decline phase, (d) the lag phase.

CHAPTER 10

1. Which one of the following factors does not affect *oxidative* rancidity?: (a) enzymes, (b) oxygen, (c) temperature, (d) ultra-violet light.
2. Most foods should be stored under cool, dry conditions. One of the following groups has a longer life if conditions are *not* too dry: (a) meat and poultry, (b) fruit and vegetables, (c) cereals, (d) dried fruits.
3. Which one of the following chemicals has been associated with chemical food poisoning?: (a) lead, (b) iron, (c) calcium, (d) phosphorus.

4. The time between consumption of contaminated food and the onset of the symptoms of food poisoning is: (a) duration of illness, (b) the infective period, (c) the incubation period, (d) the 'carrying' period.

5. Many food processing techniques are based on destroying one of the following bacteria and its spores in particular: (a) *Salmonella*, (b) *Clostridium botulinum*, (c) *Staphylococcus*, (d) *Bacillus cereus*.

6. Only one of the following bacteria produces a toxin (that is, an exotoxin): (a) *Staphylococcus*, (b) *Salmonella*, (c) *Campylobacter*, (d) *Vibrio parahaemolyticus*.

7. Which one of the following organisms causes food poisoning that is often fatal?: (a) *Bacillus cereus*, (b) *Staphylococcus*, (c) *Clostridium perfringens*, (d) *Clostridium botulinum*.

8. Which one of the following bacteria is associated with fish and shellfish?: (a) *Bacillus cereus*, (b) *Campylobacter*, (c) *Salmonella*, (d) *Vibrio parahaemolyticus*.

9. Which one of the following foods is not a 'high risk' food?: (a) sausage, (b) trifle, (c) quiche lorraine, (d) pickled onions.

10. *Shigella* causes which one of the following food-borne diseases?: (a) cholera, (b) brucellosis, (c) dysentery, (d) enteric fever.

CHAPTER 11

1. Which one of the following is not a suitable material for a food preparation surface?: (a) stainless steel, (b) compressed rubber, (c) hardwood, (d) plastic laminate.

2. Which method of fly control would you recommend in a restaurant kitchen?: (a) mesh screens, (b) sticky fly papers, (c) chemical aerosol sprays, (d) fly swatter.

3. Which one of the following is capable of destroying all bacteria and their spores?: (a) disinfectant, (b) detergent, (c) antiseptic, (d) sterilant.

4. The temperature of the water in the rinsing sink of a double sink method of washing-up should be: (a) 40°C, (b) 60°C, (c) 80°C, (d) 100°C.

5. Which one of the following items of the traditional chef's clothing do you consider to be the least effective in maintaining good hygiene?: (a) chef's hat, (b) the double-breasted jacket, (c) the loose fitting trousers, (d) the apron.

6. Which one of the following methods of hand drying do you think is most hygienic at a wash-handbasin in a kitchen?: (a)

disposable paper towels, (b) a hand towel, (c) a roller towel, (d) a hot air dryer.

7. Which one of the following groups of foods is most likely to contain some food-poisoning bacteria when purchased?: (a) breakfast cereals, (b) pasteurised milk, (c) fresh meat and poultry, (d) jams and marmalades.

8. Which one of the following food-poisoning bacteria is often found in the human nose, mouth and throat?: (a) *Salmonella*, (b) *Clostridium perfringens*, (c) *Bacillus cereus*, (d) *Staphylococcus*.

9. Grease smears on walls and skirting boards, shredded paper and cardboard and damaged plumbing pipes are signs that indicate an infestation of: (a) cockroaches, (b) flies, (c) rats, (d) fungi.

10. Which one of the following statements about detergents is not necessarily true?: (a) They should reduce the surface tension of the washing water, (b) They should emulsify grease particles, (c) They should destroy bacteria, (d) they should be easily rinsed away.

CHAPTER 12

1. The food hygiene regulations state that cooked food prior to service must be kept above or below certain temperatures: (a) below 0°C or above 100°C, (b) below 10°C or above 63°C, (c) below 37°C or above 60°C, (d) below 20°C or above 50°C.

2. In which one of the following canned foods can the heat treatment of the canning process be lowest?: (a) potatoes (pH6), (b) tomatoes (pH4), (c) corned beef (pH7), (d) salmon (pH7).

3. The HTST method of canning involves heat treatment at a temperature of approximately: (a) 60°C, (b) 80°C, (c) 100°C, (d) 120°C.

4. Most foods can be stored in a domestic freezer for approximately: (a) 6 weeks, (b) 12 weeks, (c) 12 months, (d) 3 years.

5. Which one of the following is not a chemical preservative found in food?: (a) sulphur dioxide, (b) sorbic acid, (c) sodium nitrate, (d) carbon dioxide.

6. Which one of the following statements is not true?: (a) Refrigerators extend the shelf life of some foods, (b) Refrigerators should be kept between 1°C and 5°C, (c) Refrigerators remove the risk of food poisoning, (d) Refrigerators should be defrosted regularly to function correctly.

7. Which one of the following canned foods is often only pasteurised as opposed to sterilised?: (a) salmon, (b) pear halves, (c) ham, (d) carrots.
8. Which one of the following processes for milk involves heating to 72°C for 15 seconds and rapid cooling?: (a) HTST pasteurisation, (b) the Holder Process of pasteurisation, (c) UHT sterilisation, (d) the in-bottle method of sterilisation.
9. Which one of the following frozen foods often produces 'drip' on thawing?: (a) chips, (b) peas, (c) fish fingers, (d) meat.
10. Which one of the following foods would be suitable for spray drying?: (a) French beans, (b) sultanas, (c) milk, (d) potato.

CHAPTER 13

1. Which one of the following is not given an E number?: (a) vitamin C, (b) salt, (c) sulphur dioxide, (d) tartrazine.
2. Which type of additive is required in foods containing fats and oils to prevent rancidity?: (a) preservatives, (b) emulsifiers, (c) solvents, (d) anti-oxidants.
3. Which type of additive is required to prevent separation in mayonnaise, salad cream, and so on?: (a) an emulsifier, (b) a solvent, (c) a humectant, (d) an anti-oxidant.
4. Three of the following are used in food as preservatives against micro-organisms. Identify the one that is not: (a) sulphur dioxide, (b) the antibiotic Nisin, (c) salt, (d) BHA.
5. One of the following groups of additives has not as yet been given E numbers: (a) flavourings, (b) colourings, (c) preservaives, (d) anti-oxidants.
6. In which one of the following foods are fortifying agents added by law: (a) white flour. (b) coffee, (c) sugar, (d) sausages.
7. Which one of the following additives is linked to hyperactivity in children?: (a) sulphur dioxide, (b) sorbitol, (c) monosodium glutamate (MSG), (d) tartrazine.
8. A 'sell by' date is used for foods that cannot be kept for more than: (a) 3 months, (b) 6 months, (c) 12 months, (d) 18 months.
9. Which one of the following pieces of information is not necessarily required on, for example, a yoghurt carton: (a) manufacturer's address, (b) the net weight, (c) nutritional information, (d) storage details.
10. You have read this book and completed the exercises, tasks and multiplechoice questions because: (a) your lecturer made you, (b) your mother made you, (c) you wanted to pass an examination, (d) you enjoyed it.

GLOSSARY

Acrolein A breakdown product formed when fats are heated to high temperatures.

Adipose tissue Tissue in which the cells contain large amounts of fat. Found mainly in the lower layers of the skin and also around some organs in the body.

Allergy An abnormal reaction of the body, such as a skin rash, asthma or headache, caused by coming into contact with a foreign protein to which body tissues are sensitive.

Amino acids Small organic units of which protein molecules are made.

Amylose and **Amylopectin** Straight chains and branched chains of glucose molecules which are the components of starch.

Anti-oxidant A substance that slows down or prevents the process of oxidation, for example, to prevent oxidative rancidity in fats and oils.

Ascorbic acid The chemical name for vitamin C.

Aseptic Adjective to describe conditions that are sterile, that is, contain no microbial contamination.

Atom The smallest unit of matter that can exist separately.

Autolysis The self-breakdown of plant or animal tissue that occurs naturally.

Basal Metabolic Rate The rate at which energy is used up in the body to maintain life.

BHA, BHT Butylated hydroxyanisole and butylated hydroxytoluene – chemicals which act as anti-oxidants in fats.

Binary fission To split into two parts – a term used to describe asexual reproduction in bacteria whose cells increase in size and divide into two new daughter cells.

Biological value A measure of the nutritional quality of a protein. It refers to the ratio of protein retained in the body to the amount in the diet.

Blanching The part-cooking of food for the main purpose of inactivating the autolytic enzymes prior to storage or further processing.

Botulism A type of food poisoning caused by consuming food contaminated with *Clostridium botulinum* which forms a highly poisonous, and often fatal, exotoxin.

Bromelin A protein-digesting enzyme found in pineapple. Used in the tenderisation of meat.

Calorie A unit of heat energy – used to show the energy value of foods. 1 calorie = the heat required to raise 1 g of water through 1°C.

Caramelisation The production of a brown polymer by heating sugar in a small amount of water.

Carbohydrate Organic compounds consisting of the elements carbon, hydrogen and oxygen, for example, sugars and starches.

Carcinogen A substance that is cancer forming.

Carrier A person who is contaminated with a disease-causing organism, such as food-poisoning bacteria, but who does not show the symptoms of the disease.

Catalyst A substance which changes the rate of a chemical reaction, usually speeding it up.

Cholesterol A type of lipid found in animals (particularly the cell membranes of animal cells).

Cirrhosis (of the liver) Irreversible damage to the structure of the liver causing weight loss, nausea, indigestion, and other symptoms. Often caused by excessive consumption of alcohol.

Collagen A protein found in connective tissue. It can be broken down into gelatin during moist cooking.

Deamination The breakdown of amino acids in the liver, involving the removal of the amino group which is then converted to urea.

Denaturation A change in the structure of proteins which affects their properties, e.g. solubility.

Detergent A chemical capable of cleaning.

Dextrins Soluble products formed when starch is broken down during cooking.

Disaccharide Carbohydrates which contain two sugar units, for example, sucrose, maltose.

Disinfectant A chemical capable of killing vegetative micro-organisms but not necessarily their spores.

Double bond A chemical linkage between two atoms, often two carbon atoms, which comprise two bonds.

E numbers These are the numbers that are assigned to permitted food additives by the EC, and are often displayed on food packages.

Elastin   A protein found in connective tissue which, unlike collagen, does not become soluble on heating.

Emulsifying agent   A substance which aids the dispersal of one liquid in another, and therefore stabilises an emulsion.

Emulsion   A mixture of two immiscible (unmixable) liquids in which one liquid is 'dispersed' throughout the other.

Endosperm   The portion of a cereal grain in which the food reserves are stored, mainly starch.

Energy density   Refers to the ratio of energy in a food or nutrient to its mass, for example, fat, 38 kJ/g (9 kcal/g) has a higher density than carbohydrate, 16 kJ/g (3.8 kcal/g).

Enzymes   Proteins produced by living organisms to catalyse biochemical reactions.

Epithelium   A group of cells forming a 'lining' tissue, for example, in the digestive and respiratory systems.

Excretion   The removal of the waste products from the body's metabolism.

Fatty acid   Organic chemical consisting of a carbon chain which ends in an acid group (COOH). A triglyceride fat is made up of three fatty acids joined to glycerol.

Fibre   Indigestible material present in food, such as the structural carbohydrates found in plants, for example, cellulose.

Flash point   The temperature at which a fat or an oil would ignite.

Fortifying agents   Substances such as vitamins and minerals added to food to replace those lost during processing.

Freezer burn   Dried and discoloured areas on frozen meat, fish, poultry, and so on, caused by incorrect storage, for example, food not wrapped properly in freezer.

Fructose   A type of sugar. Consists of a single sugar (saccharide) unit.

Galactose   A type of sugar. Found in milk, it consists of a single sugar (saccharide) unit.

Gel   A food gel consists of a liquid 'dispersed' in a solid, that gives a 'set' appearance, for example, table jelly contains water dispersed in a gelatin network.

Gelatinisation (of starch)   The thickening of a starch solution that occurs when heat is applied. The solution may or may not set to form a gel, depending on the ratio of starch to liquid.

Gelation   The formation of a gel.

Germ   The part of, for example, a cereal grain, that contains the embryo.

Glucagon   A hormone produced by the pancreas which causes glycogen to be converted into glucose, so raising the blood sugar level.

Glucose   A type of sugar. Consists of a single sugar (saccharide) unit.

Gluten   A mixture of the two proteins glutenin and gliadin, found in wheat.

Glycogen   A polysaccharide carbohydrate made up of glucose units. Important as an energy storage compound, referred to as animal starch.

Haemoglobin   The red pigment of the red blood cells which combines with oxygen.

Holder Process   A heat process used in the pasteurisation of milk.

Hormones   Chemical messengers produced in the body which travel in the blood bringing about specific actions, for example, insulin is produced by the pancreas, travels in the blood to the liver, and causes glucose to be stored as glycogen.

HTST (high temperature, short time)   A type of heat treatment used for the sterilisation of milk and other foods.

Humectant   A substance that absorbs water, often used to keep foods in a moist condition without causing mould growth.

Humidity   Refers to the amount of water vapour in the air.

Hydrogenation   In margarine manufacture hydrogen is added to unsaturated fats (reacting with the double bond) to saturate them and produce a more solid product. This is an example of hydrogenation.

Hydrolysis   Means literally to 'split with water'. In digestion large food molecules are broken down to smaller ones in this way.

Hydrophilic and **hydrophobic**   Terms used to describe the affinity of a molecule for water. Hydrophilic means 'water-liking', hydrophobic means 'water-hating' (see notes on detergency).

Inversion   The breakdown of sucrose into glucose and fructose by hydrolysis (see previous definition).

Iodophors   A type of chemical capable of disinfecting. They contain iodine.

Ionising radiation   Includes X-rays, gamma rays and high velocity electrons (see the electromagnetic spectrum). May be used to irradiate food to extend shelf life.

Joule   The SI (International System) unit of energy. (1000 joules = 1 kilojoule (kJ)).

Lactation   The production of breastmilk in women.

Lacteal   A small tube in each villus of the small intestine into which some fatty acids from digestion are absorbed. It is part of the lymphatic system.

Lactose   Milk sugar. Consists of two sugar (saccharide) units joined together.

Lactovegetarian   A person who does not eat meat but may eat eggs and dairy products.

Lecithin   A type of lipid, found in egg yolk (amongst other things) and having 'emulsifying' properties.

Legume   Vegetable which produces seeds in pods, such as peas and beans.

Lignin   A 'woody' type of chemical found in the cell walls of some plants.

Lipase   An enzyme which breaks down a fat or oil into glycerol and fatty acids, by hydrolysis.

Lipids   A group of compounds characterised by the presence of fatty acids. Main examples here are fats and oils.

Lymphatic system   A network of vessels throughout the body which carry a liquid (lymph) similar to blood plasma. Involved in fat absorption, transfer of substances at the tissues, and body defence.

Maillard reaction   A reaction between amino acids and sugars within food during heating or storage which leads to the formation of brown coloured compounds. This is non-enzymic browning and occurs during the baking of flour products and the cooking of meat (although other types of browning also occur at the same time).

Malnutrition   Any disease or disorder that arises from eating a diet having a deficiency or excess of one or more nutrients.

Maltose   A type of sugar. Consists of two sugar (saccharide) units joined together.

Mesophiles   Micro-organisms that grow best at temperatures between 20°C and 40°C.

Molecule   Two or more atoms, of the same type or different, joined together chemically.

Monosaccharide   A carbohydrate consisting of one sugar unit.

Monosodium glutamate   A chemical additive used in some foods to intensify the flavour that is present. Common in convenience foods and regularly used in Chinese cookery.

Mycelium   A network of fine threads or hyphae produced by a fungus.

Myoglobin   Red pigment found in muscle which is involved in the use of oxygen by the muscle.

Myosin   One of the fibrous proteins found in muscle.

Organic   A term describing chemical substances that contain the element carbon.

Osmosis   The movement of water from a dilute solution to a more concentrated solution through a semi-permeable membrane.

Osmotic pressure   The pressure that builds up in a solution when water enters it by osmosis.

Osteomalacia A deficiency disease in adults in which insufficient calcium is obtained from the diet, resulting in the decalcification of bone in the body, that is, calcium is taken from the bones for other essential purposes.

Oxidation A chemical reaction which involves the addition of oxygen or the removal of hydrogen (or the loss of electrons).

Papain A protein-digesting enzyme from the papaya (paw-paw) plant. Used in meat tenderising salts.

Pathogen A micro-organism capable of causing disease.

Peristalsis The process by which food is moved along the alimentary tract.

pH scale A measurement scale for showing how acid or alkaline a substance is.

Phenolic compounds Organic chemicals often used for their disinfectant properties.

Photosynthesis The process by which plants make complex organic compounds from simpler chemicals using sunlight for energy.

Plasticity The ability to be moulded. Fats used in various cooking processes are plastic at certain temperatures.

Polysaccharide A carbohydrate consisting of many single sugars joined together in a straight or branched chain, for example, starch, cellulose.

Polyunsaturated An unsaturated fatty acid is one which contains one or more double bonds in its carbon chain. Polyunsaturated means it possesses more than one double bond.

Protease An enzyme that breaks down protein molecules into smaller units by hydrolysis.

Psychrophiles Micro-organisms that grow best in cold conditions, for example, 10°C–15°C.

QAC Quaternary ammonium compound – a chemical used in disinfection.

Rancidity Chemical reactions that take place in fats and oils giving unpleasant odours and tastes. There are two types – oxidative and hydrolytic (see text).

RDA Recommended daily allowances – these are the guidelines issued by nutritionists that indicate the amounts of each of the important nutrients that should be eaten by different members of the population to remain healthy.

Reduction A chemical reaction which involves the removal of oxygen or the addition of hydrogen (or the gain of electrons).

Rigor mortis The stiffness found in the muscles of an animal shortly after death.

Saccharide A single sugar unit.

Sanitiser A term often used to describe a solution containing a detergent and a disinfectant.

Saprophyte An organism that obtains its food by living on dead and decomposing organic matter, for example, many fungi.

Saturated When used with reference to fats and oils this means that the carbon chains in the fat or oil contain no double bonds and are 'saturated' with hydrogen atoms.

Smoke point The temperature at which a fat or oil begins to breakdown and give off a blue hazy smoke.

Sol This consists of a solid 'dispersed' in a liquid, for example, hot table jelly and hot custard.

Spore In bacteria this is the hard, resistant resting stage which can survive until conditions improve; in fungi it is the reproductive body capable of germinating into a new fungus.

Sterilisation The process by which all living organisms, including spores, are destroyed. A chemical which can achieve this is a *sterilant*.

Sucrose Table sugar. Consists of two sugar (saccharide) units, joined together.

Surface tension The force between molecules at the surface of a liquid which creates a 'skin-like' film. A *surfactant* is a chemical which reduces surface tension and allows 'wetting' to take place.

Thermophiles Micro-organisms that grow best under warm or hot conditions, for example, 45°C–55°C.

Toxin A poisonous chemical produced by a micro-organism.

Trichinosis A disease caused by eating food, usually pork, contaminated with the parasitic worm *Trichinella spiralis*.

Triglycerides Lipids which consist of one glycerol molecule joined to three fatty acid molecules. Fats and oils are triglycerides.

TVP Textured vegetable protein – a protein food made from soya beans or a variety of seeds or nuts which is used as a meat extender or meat substitute.

UHT Ultra-high temperature – a method of sterilisation for milk.

Unsaturated With reference to fats and oils this means that the carbon chains in the fat or oil contain one or more double bonds in their structure and are *not* saturated with hydrogen atoms.

Urea A waste product formed when excess amino acids are broken down in the liver. It is excreted by the kidneys.

Vegan A person who does not eat *any* food of animal origin.

Villi The small finger-like projections found in the small intestine that increase the surface area for absorption of the products of digestion.

APPENDICES

APPENDICES

APPENDIX 1

UNITS OF MEASUREMENT

Although in the UK many people still use imperial measurements the International System (SI) of measurements is metric (SI = Système Internationale d'Unités).

1. **Units of length**
   The SI unit of length is the *metre* (m) (1 km (kilometre) = 1000 metres)

   1 m   = 100 centimetres (cm)
   1 cm = 10 millimetres (mm)
   1 mm = 1000 micrometres (μm)
   1 μm = 1000 nanometres (nm)
   (Conversion: 2.5 cm = approximately 1 inch)

2. **Units of mass**
   The SI unit of mass is the *kilogram* (kg)

   1 metric tonne = 1000 kilograms (kg)
   1 kg   = 1000 grams (g)
   1 g   = 1000 milligrams (mg)
   1 mg   = 1000 micrograms (μg)
   (Conversion: 1 kg = approximately 2.2 pounds)

3. **Units of volume**
   The metric unit of volume is the *litre* (l)

   1 litre = 1000 millilitres (ml) (1 ml = 1 cm^3 = 1 cc)
   (Conversion: 1 litre = approximately 1.75 pints)

254

4. **Units of energy**
   The metric unit of energy is the *joule* (J)

   1000 J = 1 kilojoule (kJ)
   (Conversion: 1 calorie = 4.2 joules or 1 Calorie (kilocalorie) = 4200 joules (4.2kJ))

5. **Units of temperature**
   The metric unit of temperature is the *degree Celsius* (°C)
   The traditional unit is the *degree Fahrenheit* (°F)

   Comparison: water freezes at 0°C which is equivalent to 32°F;
   water boils at 100°C which is equivalent to 212°F.

   To convert °C into °F: multipy by 9/5 and then add 32
   To convert °F into °C: subtract 32 and then multiply by 5/9

RECOMMENDED DAILY

AMOUNTS OF NUTRIENTS FOR

POPULATION GROUPS

Recommended daily amounts of nutrients for population groups

Age Ranges (years)	Energy (MJ)	Energy (kcal)	Protein (g)	Calcium (mg)	Iron (mg)	Vitamin A (retinol equivalent) (µg)	Thiamin (mg)	Riboflavin (mg)	Niacin equivalent (mg)	Vitamin C (mg)	Vitamin D (µg)
Boys											
Under 1	3.25	780	19	600	6	450	0.3	0.4	5	20	7.5
1	5.0	1200	30	600	7	300	0.5	0.6	7	20	10.0
2	5.75	1400	35	600	7	300	0.6	0.7	8	20	10.0
3–4	6.5	1560	39	600	8	300	0.6	0.8	9	20	10.0
5–6	7.5	1740	43	600	10	300	0.7	0.9	10	20	—
7–8	8.25	1980	49	600	10	400	0.8	1.0	11	20	—
9–11	9.5	2280	56	700	12	575	0.9	1.2	14	25	—
12–14	11.0	2640	66	700	12	725	1.1	1.4	16	25	—
15–17	12.0	2880	72	600	12	750	1.2	1.7	19	30	—
Girls											
Under 1	3.0	720	18	600	6	450	0.3	0.4	5	20	7.5
1	4.5	1100	27	600	7	300	0.4	0.6	7	20	10.0
2	5.5	1300	32	600	7	300	0.5	0.7	8	20	10.0
3–4	6.25	1500	37	600	8	300	0.6	0.8	9	20	10.0
5–6	7.0	1680	42	600	10	300	0.7	0.9	10	20	—
7–8	8.0	1900	48	600	10	400	0.8	1.0	11	20	—
9–11	8.5	2050	51	700	12[2]	575	0.8	1.2	14	25	—
12–14	9.0	2150	53	700	12[2]	725	0.9	1.4	16	25	—
15–17	9.0	2150	53	600	12[2]	750	0.9	1.7	19	30	—

Men											
18–34	Sedentary	10.5	2510	62	500	10	750	1.0	1.6	18	30	—
	Moderately active	12.0	2900	72	500	10	750	1.2	1.6	18	30	—
	Very active	14.0	3350	84	500	10	750	1.3	1.6	18	30	—
35–64	Sedentary	10.0	2400	60	500	10	750	1.0	1.6	18	30	—
	Moderately active	11.5	2750	69	500	10	750	1.1	1.6	18	30	—
	Very active	14.0	3350	84	500	10	750	1.3	1.6	18	30	—
65–74		10.0	2400	60	500	10	750	1.0	1.6	18	30	—
75 and over		9.0	2150	54	500	10	750	0.9	1.6	18	30	—
Women											
18–54	Most occupations	9.0	2150	54	500	12[2]	750	0.9	1.3	15	30	—
	Very active	10.5	2500	62	500	12[2]	750	1.0	1.3	15	30	—
55–74		8.0	1900	47	500	10	750	0.8	1.3	15	30	—
75 and over		7.0	1680	42	500	10	750	0.7	1.3	15	30	—
Pregnant		10.0	2400	60	1200	13	750	1.0	1.6	18	60	10.0
Lactating		11.5	2750	69	1200	15	1200	1.1	1.8	21	60	10.0

1. Most people who go in the sun need no dietary source of vitamin D, but children and adolescents in whinter, and housebound adults, are recommended to take 10 μg vitamin D daily.

2. These iron recommendations may not cover heavy menstrual losses.

Source: DHSS (1979).

COMPOSITION OF FOOD

PER 100g

(RAW EDIBLE WEIGHTS)

APPENDIX 2b

Composition per 100 g raw edible weight (except where stated)

No.	Food	Inedible waste (%)	Energy (kcal)	Energy (kJ)	Protein (g)	Fat (g)	Carbohydrate (as mono-saccharide) (g)	Water (g)	Calcium (mg)	Iron (mg)	Sodium (mg)	Vitamin A (retinol equivalent) (µg)	Thiamin (mg)	Riboflavin (mg)	Niacin equivalent (mg)	Vitamin C (mg)	No.
Milk																	
1	Cream-double	0	447	1841	1.5	48.2	2.0	49	50	0.2	30	500	0.02	0.08	0.4	1	1
2	Cream-singe	0	195	806	2.4	19.3	3.2	72	79	0.3	40	155	0.03	0.12	0.8	1	2
3	Milk, liquid, whole	0	65	272	3.2	3.9	4.6	88	103	0.1	50	56	0.05	0.17	0.9	1.5	3
4	Milk, liquid, skimmed	0	32	137	3.4	0.1	4.7	91	108	0.1	50	1	0.05	0.18	0.9	1.5	4
5	Milk, condensed whole, sweetened	0	170	709	8.5	10.2	11.7	30	207	0.2	140	123	0.09	0.46	2.3	4.1	5
6	Milk, whole, evaporated	0	149	620	8.4	9.4	8.1	69	260	0.3	170	125	0.07	0.42	2.1	1.5	6
7	Milk, dried, skimmed	0	339	1442	36.1	0.6	50.4	3	1230	0.3	510	550	0.38	0.16	9.5	13.2	7
8	Yoghurt, low fat, natural	0	65	276	5.1	0.8	10.0	86	200	0.1	80	12	0.06	0.25	1.2	0.8	8
9	Yoghurt, low fat, fruit	0	89	382	4.1	0.7	17.9	77	150	0.1	70	12	0.05	0.21	1.2	0.7	9
Cheese																	
10	Cheddar	0	406	1682	26.0	33.5	0	37	800	0.4	610	363	0.04	0.50	6.2	0	10
11	Cottage	0	96	402	13.6	4.0	1.4	79	60	0.1	450	41	0.02	0.19	3.3	0	11
12	Cheese spread	0	283	1173	18.3	22.9	0.9	51	510	0.7	1170	198	0.02	0.24	0.1	0	12
13	Feta	0	245	1017	16.5	19.9	0	56	384	0.2	1260	270	0.03	0.11	4.2	0	13
14	Brie	0	300	1246	22.8	23.2	0	48	380	0.8	1410	238	0.09	0.60	6.2	0	14
Meat																	
15	Bacon, rashers, raw	11	339	1402	13.9	31.5	0	51	7	0.6	1340	0	0.45	0.14	6.5	0	15
16	Bacon, rashers, grilled	0	393	1632	28.1	31.2	0	34	14	1.3	2404	0	0.57	0.27	12.5	0	16
17	Beef, average, raw	17	313	1296	16.6	27.4	0	55	7	1.9	70	10	0.05	0.23	6.9	0	17
18	Beef, mince, stewed	0	229	955	23.1	15.2	0	59	18	3.1	320	0	0.05	0.33	9.3	0	18
19	Beef, stewing steak, raw	4	176	736	20.2	10.6	0	69	8	2.1	72	0	0.06	0.23	8.5	0	19
20	Beef, stewing steak, cooked	0	223	932	30.9	11.0	0	57	15	3.0	360	0	0.03	0.33	10.2	0	20
21	Black pudding, fried	0	305	1270	12.9	21.9	15.0	44	35	20.0	1210	0	0.09	0.07	3.2	0	21
22	Chicken raw	41	194	809	19.7	12.8	0	67	9	0.7	75	0	0.11	0.13	9.6	0	22
23	Chicken, roast, meat and skin	0	213	888	24.4	12.8	0	62	13	0.5	90	0	0.05	0.19	13.6	0	23
24	Chicken, roast, meat only	0	148	621	24.8	5.4	0	68	9	0.8	81	0	0.08	0.19	12.8	0	24
25	Corned beef	0	202	844	25.9	10.9	0	59	27	2.4	854	0	0	0.20	9.1	0	25
26	Ham	0	166	690	16.4	11.1	0	67	4	0.6	1405	0	0.54	0.20	6.3	0	26
27	Kidney, pigs, raw	6	86	363	15.5	2.7	0	80	10	6.4	200	160	0.56	2.58	11.1	6.5	27

APPENDIX 2b

Composition per 100 g raw edible weight (except where stated)

No.	Food	Inedible waste (%)	Energy (kcal)	Energy (kJ)	Protein (g)	Fat (g)	Carbohydrate (as monosaccharide) (g)	Water (g)	Calcium (mg)	Iron (mg)	Sodium (mg)	Vitamin A (retinol equivalent) (µg)	Thiamin (mg)	Riboflavin (mg)	Niacin equivalent (mg)	Vitamin C (mg)	No.
28	Kidney, pigs, fried	0	202	848	29.2	9.5	0	58	12	9.1	220	220	0.41	3.70	20.1	11.9	28
29	Lamb, average, raw	23	295	1223	16.2	25.6	0	56	7	1.4	71	0	0.09	0.21	7.1	0	29
30	Lamb, roast	0	266	1106	26.1	17.9	0	55	8	2.5	65	0	0.12	0.31	11.0	0	30
31	Liver, lambs, raw	0	140	587	20.3	6.2	0.8	70	6	7.5	73	19900	0.39	4.64	20.7	19.2	31
32	Liver, lambs, fried	0	237	989	30.1	12.9	0	54	8	10.9	83	30500	0.38	5.65	24.7	18.6	32
33	Luncheon meat	0	266	1153	12.9	23.8	3.3	54	39	1.0	913	0	0.06	0.15	3.9	0	33
34	Paté, average	26	347	1436	13.7	31.9	1.4	47	14	8.2	762	8300	0.14	1.32	4.3	0	34
35	Pork, average, raw	26	297	1231	16.9	25.5	0	57	8	0.9	65	0	0.49	0.20	8.9	0	35
36	Pork chop, cooked	0	332	1380	28.5	24.2	0	57	11	1.2	84	0	0.66	0.20	11.0	0	36
37	Sausage, beef, cooked	0	267	1114	12.9	17.7	15.0	48	68	1.6	1095	0	0.01	0.14	9.0	0	37
38	Sausage, pork, cooked	0	317	1318	13.6	24.5	11.2	45	54	1.5	1075	0	0.12	0.16	7.2	0	38
39	Steak & kidney pie	0	274	1146	9.3	17.1	22.2	51	47	1.8	402	0	0.09	0.25	4.9	0	39
40	Turkey, roast, meat & skin	0	189	793	26.2	9.4	0	63	7	0.9	70	0	0.09	0.16	12.2	0	40
Fish																	
41	White fish, filleted	3	77	324	17.1	0.9	0	82	22	0.5	99	1	0.07	0.09	6.0	0	41
42	Cod, fried	0	235	982	19.6	14.3	7.5	57	80	0.5	100		0.06	0.07	4.9	0	42
43	Fish fingers, raw	0	178	749	12.6	7.5	16.1	64	43	0.7	320	0.2	0.09	0.06	3.5	0	43
44	Herrings, whole	46	251	1040	16.8	20.4	0	64	33	0.8	67	46	0.09	0.18	7.2	0	44
45	Mackerel	40	282	1170	19.0	22.9	0	57	24	1.0	130	45		0.35	11.6	0	45
46	Pilchards, canned in tomato sauce	0	126	531	18.8	5.4	0.7	74	300	2.7	370	8	0.02	0.29	11.1	0	46
47	Sardines, canned in oil, fish only	0	217	906	23.7	18.6	0	58	550	2.9	650	7	0.04	0.36	12.6	0	47
48	Tuna in oil	0	289	1202	22.8	22.0	0	55	7	1.1	420	0	0.04	0.11	17.2	0	48
49	Prawns boiled	0	107	451	22.6	1.8	0	70	150	1.1	1590	0	0.03	0.03	7.4	0	49
Eggs																	
50	Eggs, boiled	12	147	612	12.3	10.9	0	75	52	2.0	140	190	0.09	0.47	3.7	0	50
51	Eggs, fried	0	232	961	14.1	19.5	0	63	64	2.5	220	140	0.07	0.42	4.2	0	51
Fats																	
52	Butter	0	740	3041	0.4	82.0	0	15	15	0.2	870	985	0	0	0.1	0	52
53	Lard, cooking fat, dripping	0	892	3667	0	99.1	0	1	1	0.1	2	0	0	0	0	0	53

No.	Food	(1)	(2)	(3)	(4)	(5)	(6)	(7)	(8)	(9)	(10)	(11)	(12)	(13)	(14)	(15)	No.
54	Low fat spread	0	366	1506	0	40.7	0	51	0	0	690	900	0	0	0	0	54
55	Margarine, average	0	730	3000	0.1	81.0	0	16	4	0.3	800	860	0	0	0.1	0	55
56	Cooking and salad oil	0	899	3696	0	99.9	0	0	0	0	0	0	0	0	0	0	56
	Preserves, etc.																
57	Chocolate, milk	0	529	2214	8.4	30.3	59.4	2	220	1.6	120	6.6	0.10	0.23	1.6	5	57
58	Honey	0	288	1229	0.4	0	76.4	23	5	0.4	11	0	0	0.05	0.2	0	58
59	Jam	0	262	1116	0.5	0	69.2	30	18	1.2	14	2	0	0	0	10	59
60	Marmalade	0	262	1114	0.1	0	69.5	28	35	0.6	18	8	0	0	0	10	60
61	Sugar, white	0	394	1680	0	0	105.3	0	2	0	0	0	0	0	0	0	61
62	Syrup	0	298	1269	0.3	0	79.0	28	26	1.5	270	0	0	0	0	0	62
63	Peppermints	0	392	1670	0.5	0.7	102.2	0	7	0.2	9	0	0	0	0	0	63
	Vegetables																
64	Aubergines	23	14	62	0.7	0	3.1	93	10	0.4	3	0	0.05	0.03	1.0	5	64
65	Baked beans	0	81	345	4.8	0.6	15.1	74	48	1.4	550	12	0.08	0.06	1.3	0	65
66	Beans, runner, boiled	1	19	83	1.9	0.2	2.7	91	22	0.7	1	67	0.03	0.07	0.8	5	66
67	Beans, red kidney, raw	0	272	1159	22.1	1.7	45.0	11	140	6.7	40	0	0.54	0.18	5.5	0	67
68	Beans, soya, boiled	0	141	592	12.4	6.4	9.0	67	145	2.5	15	0	0.26	0.16	3.4	0	68
69	Beetroot, boiled	0	44	189	1.8	0	9.9	83	30	0.4	64	0	0.02	0.04	0.4	5	69
70	Brussels sprouts, boiled	43	18	75	2.8	0	1.7	92	25	0.5	2	67	0.06	0.10	0.9	40	70
71	Cabbage, raw	0	22	92	2.8	0	2.8	88	57	0.6	7	50	0.06	0.05	0.8	55	71
72	Cabbage boiled	4	15	66	1.7	0	2.3	93	38	0.4	4	50	0.03	0.03	0.5	20	72
73	Carrots, old	0	23	98	0.7	0	5.4	90	48	0.6	95	2000	0.06	0.05	0.7	6	73
74	Cauliflour, cooked	0	9	40	1.6	0	0.8	95	18	0.4	4	5	0.06	0.06	0.8	20	74
75	Celery	27	8	36	0.9	0	1.3	94	52	0.6	140	0	0.03	0.03	0.5	7	75
76	Courgettes. raw	13	29	122	1.6	0.4	5.0	92	30	1.5	1	58	0.05	0.09	0.6	16	76
77	Cucumber	23	10	43	0.6	0.1	1.8	96	23	0.3	13	0	0.04	0.04	0.3	8	77
78	Lentils, cooked	0	99	420	7.6	0.5	17.0	72	13	2.4	12	3	0.11	0.04	1.6	0	78
79	Lettuce	30	12	51	1.0	0.4	1.2	96	23	0.9	9	167	0.07	0.08	0.4	15	79
80	Mushrooms	25	13	53	1.8	0.6	0	92	3	1.0	9	0	0.10	0.40	4.6	3	80
81	Onion	3	23	99	0.9	0	5.2	93	31	0.3	10	0	0.03	0.05	0.4	10	81
82	Parsnips, cooked	0	56	238	1.3	0	13.5	83	36	0.5	4	0	0.07	0.06	0.9	10	82
83	Peas, frozen, boiled	0	72	307	6.0	0.9	10.7	78	35	1.6	2	50	0.30	0.09	1.6	12	83
84	Peas, canned processed	0	86	366	6.9	0.7	18.9	70	33	1.8	380	10	0.10	0.04	1.4	0	84
85	Peppers, green	14	12	51	0.9	0	2.2	94	9	0.4	2	33	0.08	0.03	0.9	100	85
86	Potatoes	10[1] 20[2]	74	315	2.0	0.2	17.1	79	8	0.4	8	0	0.20	0.02	1.5	8–19	86

APPENDIX 2b

Composition per 100 g raw edible weight (except where stated)

No.	Food	Inedible waste (%)	Energy (kcal)	Energy (kJ)	Protein (g)	Fat (g)	Carbohydrate (as monosaccharide) (g)	Water (g)	Calcium (mg)	Iron (mg)	Sodium (mg)	Vitamin A (retinol equivalent) (µg)	Thiamin (mg)	Riboflavin (mg)	Niacin equivalent (mg)	Vitamin C (mg)	No.
87	Potatoes, boiled	0	76	322	1.8	0.1	18.0	80	4	0.4	7	0	0.20	0.02	1.2	5–9	87
88	Potato crisps	0	533	2224	6.3	35.9	49.3	3	37	2.1	550	0	0.19	0.07	6.1	17	88
89	Potatoes, fried (chips)	0	234	983	3.6	10.2	34.0	44	14	0.84	41	0	0.2	0.02	1.5	6–14	89
90	Potatoes, oven chips	0	162	687	3.2	4.2	29.8	59	1	0.8	53	0	0.1	0.04	3.1	12	90
91	Potatoes, roast	0	150	632	3.0	4.5	25.9	65	10	0.62	9	0	0.2	0.02	1.3	5–12	91
92	Spinach, boiled	0	30	128	5.1	0.5	1.4	85	136	4.0	120	1000	0.07	0.15	1.8	25	92
93	Sweetcorn, canned	0	85	379	2.9	1.2	16.8	72	4	0.5	270	4	0.04	0.06	1.8	0	93
94	Sweet potato	14	91	387	1.2	0.6	21.5	70	22	0.7	19	4000³	0.10	0.06	1.2	25	94
95	Tomatoes, fresh	0	14	60	0.9	0	2.8	93	13	0.4	3	100	0.06	0.04	0.8	20	95
96	Turnips, cooked	0	14	61	0.7	0.3	2.3	95	55	0.4	28	0	0.03	0.04	0.6	17	96
97	Watercress	23	14	61	2.9	0	0.7	91	220	1.6	60	500	0.10	0.10	1.1	60	97
98	Yam, boiled	0	119	508	1.6	0.1	29.8	66	9	0.3	17	2	0.05	0.01	0.8	2	98
	Fruit																
99	Apples	20	46	196	0.3	0	11.9	84	4	0.3	2	5	0.04	0.02	0.1	5	99
100	Apricots, canned in syrup	0	106	452	0.5	0	27.7	68	12	0.7	1	166	0.02	0.01	0.4	2	100
101	Apricots, dried	0	182	772	4.8	0	43.4	15	92	4.1	56	600	0.10	0.2	3.8	0	101
102	Avocado pear	29	223	922	4.2	22.2	1.8	69	15	1.5	2	17	0.04	0.10	1.8	15	102
103	Bananas	40	76	326	1.1	0	19.2	71	7	0.4	1	33	0.04	0.07	0.8	10	103
104	Blackcurrants	2	28	121	0.9	0	6.6	77	60	1.3	3	33	0.03	0.06	0.4	200	104
105	Cherries	13	47	201	0.6	0	11.9	82	16	0.4	3	20	0.05	0.07	0.4	5	105
106	Dates, dried	14	248	1056	2.0	0	63.9	15	68	1.6	5	10	0.07	0.04	2.9	0	106
107	Figs, dried	0	213	908	3.6	0	52.9	17	280	4.2	87	8	0.10	0.08	2.2	0	107
108	Gooseberries, cooked unsweetened	0	14	62	0.9	0	2.9	90	24	0.3	2	25	0.03	0.03	0.5	31	108
109	Grapes	5	63	268	0.6	0	16.1	79	19	0.3	2	0	0.04	0.02	0.3	4	109
110	Grapefruit	50	22	95	0.6	0	5.3	91	17	0.3	1	0	0.05	0.02	0.3	40	110
111	Lemon juice	64	7	31	0.3	0	1.6	91	8	0.1	2	0	0.02	0.01	0.1	50	111
112	Mango	34	59	253	0.5	0	15.3	83	10	0.5	7	200	0.03	0.04	0.4	30	112
113	Melon	40	23	97	0.8	0	5.2	94	16	0.4	17	175	0.05	0.03	0.3	50	113
114	Oranges	25	35	150	0.8	0	8.5	86	41	0.3	3	8	0.10	0.03	0.3	50	114
115	Orange juice	0	38	161	0.6	0	9.4	88	12	0.3	2	8	0.08	0.02	0.3	25–45	115

No.	Food														
116	Peaches	13	37	156	0.6	9.1	86	5	0.4	3	83	0.02	0.05	1.1	8
117	Peaches, canned in syrup	0	87	373	0.4	22.9	74	4	0.4	1	41	0.01	0.02	0.6	4
118	Pears	28	41	175	0.3	10.6	83	8	0.2	2	2	0.03	0.03	0.3	3
119	Pineapple	8	46	194	0.5	11.6	77	12	0.4	1	7	0.08	0.02	0.3	20-40
120	Plums	17	32	137	0.6	7.9	85	12	0.3	2	37	0.05	0.03	0.6	3
121	Prunes, dried	0	161	686	2.4	40.3	23	38	2.9	12	160	0.10	0.20	1.9	
122	Raspberries	0	25	105	0.9	5.6	83	41	1.2	3	13	0.02	0.03	0.5	25
123	Rhubarb, cooked with sugar	3	45	191	0.5	11.4	85	84	0.3	2	8	0	0.03	0.4	7
124	Strawberries	0	26	109	0.6	6.2	89	22	0.7	2	5	0.02	0.03	0.5	60
125	Sultanas		250	1066	1.8	64.7	18	52	1.8	53	5	0.10	0.08	0.6	0
	Nuts														
126	Almonds	63	565	2336	16.9	4.3	5	250	4.2	6	0	0.24	0.92	4.7	0
127	Coconut, desiccated	0	604	2492	5.6	6.4	2	22	3.6	28	0	0.06	0.04	1.8	0
128	Peanuts, roasted & salted	0	570	2364	24.3	8.6	5	61	2.0	440	0	0.23	0.10	21.3	
	Cereals														
129	Biscuits, chocolate	0	524	2197	5.7	67.4	2.2	110	1.7	160	0	0.03	0.13	2.7	0
130	Biscuits, plain, digestive	0	471	1978	6.3	68.6	2.5	92	3.2	600	0	0.14	0.11	2.4	0
131	Biscuits, semi-sweet	0	457	1925	6.7	74.8	2.5	120	2.1	410	0	0.13	0.08	2.9	0
132	Bread, brown	0	217	924	8.4	44.2	40	99	2.2	540	0	0.27	0.10	2.3	0
133	Bread, white	0	230	980	8.2	48.6	38	105	1.6	525	0	0.21	0.06	2.3	0
134	Bread, wholemeal	0	215	911	9.0	41.6	38	54	2.7	560	0	0.34	0.09	1.8	0
	Breakfast cereals														
135	Cornflakes	0	368	1567	8.6	85.1	3.0	3	6.7	1160	0	1.8	1.6	21.9	0
136	Weetabix	0	340	1444	11.4	70.3	1.8	33	7.6	360	0	1.0	1.5	14.3	0
137	Muesli	0	368	1556	12.9	66.2	5.8	200	4.6	180	0	0.33	0.27	5.7	0
138	Cream crackers	0	440	1857	9.5	68.3	4.3	110	1.7	610	0	0.13	0.08	3.4	0
139	Crispbread, rye	0	321	1367	9.4	70.6	6.4	50	3.7	220	0	0.28	0.14	2.9	0
140	Flour, white	0	337	1435	9.4	76.7	14.0	140	2.0	2	0	0.31	0.04	3.5	0
141	Flour, wholemeal	0	306	1302	12.7	62.8	14.0	38	3.9	2	0	0.47	0.09	8.3	0
142	Oats, porridge	0	374	1582	10.9	66.0	8.2	52	3.8	9	0	0.90	0.09	3.3	0
143	Rice, raw	0	359	1529	7.0	85.8	11.4	4	0.5	4	0	0.41	0.02	5.8	0
144	Spaghetti, raw	0	342	1456	12.0	74.1	9.8	25	2.1	3	0	0.22	0.03	3.1	0
	Cakes, etc.														
145	Chocolate cake with butter icing	0	500	2092	5.8	53.1	8.4	130	1.6	440	298	0.07	0.09	2.0	0
146	Currant buns	0	296	1250	7.6	52.7	27.7	110	1.9	230	0	0.37	0.16	3.1	0
147	Fruit cake, rich	0	322	1357	4.9	50.7	20.6	84	3.2	220	0	0.07	0.09	1.3	0
148	Jam tarts	0	368	1552	3.3	63.4	14.4	72	1.7	130	0	0.06	0.02	1.2	0
149	Plain cake, Madeira	0	393	1652	5.4	58.4	20.2	42	1.1	380	0	0.06	0.11	1.6	0

APPENDIX 2b

Composition per 100 g raw edible weight (except where stated)

No.	Food	Inedible waste (%)	Energy (kcal)	Energy (kJ)	Protein (g)	Fat (g)	Carbohydrate (as monosaccharide) (g)	Water (g)	Calcium (mg)	Iron (mg)	Sodium (mg)	Vitamin A (retinol equivalent) (µg)	Thiamin (mg)	Riboflavin (mg)	Niacin equivalent (mg)	Vitamin C (mg)	No.
	Puddings																
150	Apple pie	0	369	1554	4.3	15.5	56.7	22.9	51	1.2	210	0	0.05	0.02	0.4	0	150
151	Bread and butter pudding	0	157	661	6.1	7.7	16.9	67.5	130	0.6	150	78	0.07	0.23	1.8	0	151
152	Cheesecake, frozen, fruit topping	0	239	1005	5.2	10.6	32.8	44.0	68	0.5	160	0	0.04	0.16	1.7	0	152
153	Custard	0	118	496	3.8	4.4	16.7	74.9	140	0.1	76	38	0.05	0.20	1.0	0	153
154	Ice cream, dairy	0	165	691	3.3	8.2	20.7	65.7	120	0.3	70	0	0.04	0.15	0.9	0	154
155	Rice pudding	0	131	552	4.1	4.2	20.4	71.8	30	0.1	55	33	0.04	0.14	1.1	0	155
156	Trifle	0	165	690	2.2	9.2	19.5	68.1	68	0.3	63	50	0.06	0.10	0.6	0	156
	Beverages																
157	Chocolate, drinking	0	366	1554	5.5	6.0	77.4	2	33	2.4	2	2	0.06	0.04	2.1	0	157
158	Cocoa powder	0	312	1301	18.5	21.7	11.5	3	130	10.5	7	7	0.16	0.06	7.3	0	158
159	Coffee, ground, infusion	0	3	12	0.3	0	0.4	98	3	0.1	1	0	0	0.01	0.6	0	159
160	Coffee, instant powder	0	100	424	14.6	0	11.0	3	140	4.6	81	0	0.04	0.21	27.9	0	160
161	Coca Cola	0	38	166	0	0	10.0	91	4	0.1	8	0	0	0	0	0	161
162	Tea, dry	0	0	0	0	0	0	0	0	0.1	0	0	0	0.09	6.0	0	162
163	Squash, fruit undiluted	0	98	418	0	0	26.1	72	11	0.1	35	0	0	0.01	0.1	0	163
	Alcoholic beverages																
164	Beer, keg bitter	0	37	156	0	0	2.3	93	8	0	6	0	0	0.03	0.17	0	164
165	Spirits	0	222	919	0	0	0	68	0	0	0	0	0	0	0	0	165
166	Wine, medium white	0	89	371	0	0	2.5	85	10	0.4	1	0	0	0	0.1	0	166
167	Cider, average	0	43	180	0	0	2.9	92	5	0.2	7	0	0	0	0	0	167
	Miscellaneous																
168	Curry powder	0	325	1395	12.7	13.8	41.8	9	478	29.6	52	99	0.25	0.28	3.5	11	168
169	Marmite	0	179	759	41.4	0.7	1.8	25	95	3.7	4500	0	3.10	11.0	67	0	169
170	Peanut butter	0	623	2581	22.6	53.7	13.1	1	37	2.1	350	0	0.17	0.10	15	0	170
171	Soy sauce	0	56	240	5.2	0.5	8.3	71	65	4.8	5720	0	0.04	0.17	1.8	0	171

BIBLIOGRAPHY

172	Tomato sauce	55	230	0.8	3.3	5.9	84	17	0.4	460	35	0.03	0.02	0.6	0	0
173	Tomato ketchup	98	420	2.1	0	24.0	65	25	1.2	1120	0	0.06	0.05	0.3	0	0
174	Pickle, sweet	134	572	0.6	0.3	34.4	59	19	2.0	1700	0	0.03	0.01	0.2	0	0
175	Salad cream	311	1288	1.9	27.4	15.1	52.7	34	0.8	840	0	0	0	0	0	0

1. Old potatoes
2. New potatoes
3. The vitamin A content of white and yellow varieties may vary between 0 and 12000 µg.

Source: *Manual of Nutrition* (HMSO Crown copyright, 9th edn).

BIBLIOGRAPHY

Barnett, A. and M. Palmer, *Eat for Health* (Blackwell, 1984).

Bender, A. E., *Dictionary of Nutrition and Food Technology*, 4th edn (Butterworths, 1975).

Board, R. G., *A Modern Introduction to Food Microbiology* (Blackwell Scientific Publications, 1983).

Brown, M. A. and A. G. Cameron, *Experimental Cooking* (Edward Arnold, 1977).

Brownsell, V. L., C. J. Griffith and Eleri Jones, *Basic Science for Food Studies* (Longman, 1985).

Cameron, A., *The Science of Food and Cooking*, 2nd edn (Edward Arnold, 1978).

Campbell, A. M., M. P. Penfield and R. M. Griswold, *The Experimental Study of Food*, 2nd edn (Constable, 1980).

Crockett, R. G. and F. A. Adams, *Experimental Catering Science Workbook* (Edward Arnold, 1975).

Davis, B., *Food Commodities* (Heinemann, 1978).

Food and Drink Industries Council, *Food Additives*, (FDIC, 1983).

Foulger, R. and E. Routledge, *The Food Poisoning Handbook*, (Chartwell-Bratt, 1981).

Fox, B. A. and A. G. Cameron, *Food Science a Chemical Approach*, 3rd edn (Hodder & Stoughton Education, 1977).

Gaman, P. M. and K. B. Sherrington, *The Science of Food*, 2nd edn (Pergamon Press, 1981).

Garrow, J. S., *Treat Obesity Seriously* (Churchill Livingstone Medical Publishers, 1981).

Hanssen, M., *E for Additives* (Thorsons Publishing Group, 1984).

Health Education Council, *Beating Heart Disease* (HEC).

Health Education Council, *Food for Thought* (HEC 1984).

Hobbs, B. C. and R. J. Gilbert, *Food Poisoning and Food Hygiene*, 4th edn (Edward Arnold, 1978).

Kilgour, O. F. G., *Mastering Nutrition* (Macmillan Education Ltd, 1985).

Madden, D., *Food and Nutrition* (Gill and Macmillan Ltd, 1980).

Ministry of Agriculture, Fisheries and Food, *The Manual of Nutrition* (HMSO, 1976, 1986) 8th and 9 th edns.

Ministry of Agriculture, Fisheries and Food, *Look at the Label*, 8th edn (HMSO, 1985).

Paul, A. A. and D. A. Southgate, *The Composition of Foods* (HMSO, 1979).

Pyke, M., *Success in Nutrition* (John Murray, 1975).

Robins, G. V., *Food Science in Catering* (Heinemann, 1980).

Stretch, J. A. and H. A. Southgate, *The Science of Catering* (Edward Arnold, 1986).

Taylor, T. Geoffrey, *Principles of Human Nutrition* (Edward Arnold, 1978).

Taylor, T. Geoffrey, *Nutrition and Health* (Edward Arnold, 1982).

Trickett, J., *The Prevention of Food Poisoning* (Stanley Thornes, 1978).

Walker, C. and G. Cannon *The Food Scandal* (Century Publications, 1984).

MULTIPLE-CHOICE
ANSWERS

CHAPTER 1		**CHAPTER 2**	
	1 – d		1 – c
	2 – b		2 – b
	3 – a		3 – b
	4 – a		4 – d
	5 – c		5 – d
	6 – a		6 – a
	7 – c		7 – a
	8 – d		8 – b
	9 – b		9 – a
	10 – a		10 – b
CHAPTER 3		**CHAPTER 4**	
	1 – c		1 – a
	2 – d		2 – a
	3 – d		3 – d
	4 – a		4 – b
	5 – a		5 – b
	6 – c		6 – a
	7 – d		7 – d
	8 – a		8 – c
	9 – b		9 – c
	10 – b		10 – a
CHAPTER 5		**CHAPTER 6**	
	1 – b		1 – c
	2 – b		2 – a
	3 – d		3 – d
	4 – b		4 – c
	5 – c		5 – a
	6 – b		6 – d
	7 – b		7 – a
	8 – d		8 – b
	9 – c		9 – a
	10 – a		10 – d

CHAPTER 7		**CHAPTER 8**	
1 – c		1 – d	
2 – b		2 – b	
3 – a		3 – b	
4 – b		4 – d	
5 – c		5 – b	
6 – d		6 – c	
7 – b		7 – a	
8 – c		8 – b	
9 – c		9 – d	
10 – a		10 – c	

CHAPTER 9		**CHAPTER 10**	
1 – c		1 – a	
2 – b		2 – b	
3 – a		3 – a	
4 – c		4 – c	
5 – c		5 – b	
6 – c		6 – a	
7 – d		7 – d	
8 – d		8 – d	
9 – a		9 – d	
10 – b		10 – c	

CHAPTER 11		**CHAPTER 12**	
1 – c		1 – b	
2 – a		2 – b	
3 – d		3 – d	
4 – c		4 – b	
5 – a		5 – d	
6 – a		6 – c	
7 – c		7 – c	
8 – d		8 – a	
9 – c		9 – d	
10 – c		10 – c	

CHAPTER 13	
1 – b	
2 – d	
3 – a	
4 – d	
5 – a	
6 – a	
7 – d	
8 – a	
9 – c	
10 – b	

INDEX

This book has extensive contents pages (pp. vii–xii), together with a glossary (pp. 243–9). These should be referred to *before* the index.